ROUTLEDGE
ACCOU:

Volume 30

HISTORY OF THE SOCIETY OF INCORPORATED ACCOUNTANTS 1885–1957

HISTORY OF THE SOCIETY OF INCORPORATED ACCOUNTANTS 1885–1957

A.A. GARRETT

Routledge
Taylor & Francis Group

LONDON AND NEW YORK

First published in 1984 by Garland Publishing, Inc.

This edition first published in 2021
by Routledge
2 Park Square, Milton Park, Abingdon, Oxon OX14 4RN

and by Routledge
52 Vanderbilt Avenue, New York, NY 10017

Routledge is an imprint of the Taylor & Francis Group, an informa business

© 1961 A.A. Garrett

British Library Cataloguing in Publication Data
A catalogue record for this book is available from the British Library

ISBN: 978-0-367-33564-9 (Set)
ISBN: 978-1-00-304636-3 (Set) (ebk)
ISBN: 978-0-367-53528-5 (Volume 30) (hbk)
ISBN: 978-0-367-53532-2 (Volume 30) (pbk)
ISBN: 978-1-00-308235-4 (Volume 30) (ebk)

Publisher's Note
The publisher has gone to great lengths to ensure the quality of this reprint but points out that some imperfections in the original copies may be apparent.

Disclaimer
The publisher has made every effort to trace copyright holders and would welcome correspondence from those they have been unable to trace.

HISTORY OF THE
SOCIETY OF INCORPORATED ACCOUNTANTS
1885-1957

BY

A. A. GARRETT, M.A.
SECRETARY 1919-1949

PRINTED AT THE
UNIVERSITY PRESS, OXFORD
1961

PRINTED IN GREAT BRITAIN
AT THE UNIVERSITY PRESS, OXFORD
BY VIVIAN RIDLER
PRINTER TO THE UNIVERSITY

INCORPORATED ACCOUNTANTS' HALL
Sketch by Hanslip Fletcher

HISTORY OF THE
SOCIETY OF
INCORPORATED
ACCOUNTANTS
1885-1957

To all who contributed
to the work of
THE SOCIETY OF
INCORPORATED ACCOUNTANTS
at home and overseas

FOREWORD

by s. JOHN PEARS, F.C.A.

*President of the Institute of Chartered Accountants
in England and Wales*

THIS book marks the closing of a long and important chapter in the history of the accountancy profession. The Society of Incorporated Accountants came into existence a few years after the establishment of the Institute by Royal Charter. Thereafter the Society grew alongside the Institute, first in opposition and later in a paradox of friendly rivalry and co-operation until finally the schemes of integration brought the Society's history to a close on 2 November 1957. The great majority of its members have now become members of my Institute and most of the remainder have become members of The Institute of Chartered Accountants of Scotland or The Institute of Chartered Accountants in Ireland.

It is always a sad affair when an old and respected institution goes out of existence. Few of those who open this book will do so without a sense of sorrow. Integration is, however, an accomplished fact and as they turn the pages the readers of this book will find that such feelings disappear and give place to a sense of pride in what the Society was able to achieve and the strength which it has thereby brought to the Institute.

Mr. Garrett has undertaken a monumental task and after his long period as Secretary of the Society it must often have been heartbreaking work. He can, however, rightly feel that he has now made one further great contribution to the Society in putting its history on record. He has come out of retirement to perform a service which I am sure he could never have contemplated at the time when he ceased to be Secretary of the Society. He has done it well.

31 October 1960

ACKNOWLEDGEMENTS

Iᴛ is in no formal sense that I make warm acknowledgements of the help I have had from many people in the preparation of this history of the Society of Incorporated Accountants.

Mr. Edward Baldry and Mr. Bertram Nelson perused the typescript, and I have to thank Mr. Ian Craig and Mr. C. Evan-Jones, the last Secretary and Deputy Secretary of the Society, for their assistance in many ways. The secretaries of the other accountancy bodies, friends overseas, and several of my former colleagues assisted me with information and verification of facts, particularly Miss A. H. Page and Mrs. Irene Duncalf. And I am greatly indebted to Miss Page for her skilful work in reading proofs and for many suggestions.

Accountancy (formerly the Society's periodical) and *The Accountant* have been invaluable sources of information. I pay my tribute to Leo T. Little, the able Editor of *Accountancy*, whose recent death caused much sorrow among his friends. The publication of this book enables me to acknowledge many courtesies from successive Editors of *The Accountant* during my active work for the Society, particularly Miss Vera Snelling and Mr. Derek du Pré. For events in the country, I have had recourse to the *Annual Register* and to Carter and Mears's *History of Britain*. But I must make it clear that the responsibility for what has been written rests upon myself.

Helpful reference facilities and advice have been afforded by the Librarian of each library at: the Society; the Institute of Chartered Accountants in England and Wales; the Guildhall, London; the Hon. Society of the Inner Temple; H.M. Stationery Office; the Board of Trade; Somerset House; the London School of Economics.

I have had the benefit of the great experience of the Printer to the University of Oxford, and I thank him for his advice in regard to the text and format.

My gratitude is extended to the ladies who, at considerable trouble, prepared the typescript from my manuscript.

And, finally, I have enjoyed the forbearance and unfailing encouragement of my wife.

A. A. G.

December 1960

CONTENTS

1914-1918

1919-1930

LIST OF ILLUSTRATIONS

INTRODUCTION

THE life and vitality of an institution find their inspiration both in its past history and its present hopes. A history of an institution is not simply a narrative of events, still less a catalogue: its purpose is also to trace the continuous trend of its policy and internal activities and the effect of external events; to discover its ethos and perhaps to find a pattern—a changing and expanding pattern—formed by the reaction of these influences upon one another; and throughout to indicate, and in some degree to assess, the influence of its leading personalities and groups of individuals. This book represents an attempt to implement those purposes relative to the Society of Incorporated Accountants, and is a tribute of gratitude and affection.

The stuff of history is stubborn facts and controversies; personalities contending with difficulties, resolving differences by negotiation, suffering disappointment and delighting in achievement; more rarely in triumph. The Society knew all. It is almost trite to say that its record over seventy-two years represented attainment beyond the highest hopes of its early years; yet, as might be expected, progress was attended by some discomfiture and unavoidable disappointments. But who can say that vigour, resolution, and wisdom did not grow from that variety of experience?

It is tempting to speculate with after-acquired wisdom that this course or that ought to have been taken by the Society—or in some other quarter. Without complacency, but with thankfulness, the Society in 1957 could contemplate its achievements and strength and reflect that, at any particular juncture, another course of events, however seemingly favourable, might have curbed its own volition and service. The Society indeed enjoyed 'the first of earthly blessings, independence'.[1]

The material for these chapters has been taken from the printed and written records of the first twenty-five years of the Society's activities, read in the light of a sustained tradition; and, in the subsequent period, drawn from personal recollection,

[1] Gibbon, *Autobiography*.

refreshed by valuable records and perhaps biased by affection. The time is yet too soon to pass historical judgement.

More particularly, this narrative is concerned with the main policy of the Society, its leading personalities, its organization, and the general will of the whole body of members. And scarcely less with relevant economic and business affairs, legislation, and constitutional development, particularly in the British Empire and Commonwealth. To these elements must be added the relationship of different sections of the profession *inter se* and developments in other countries.

It is hoped that past events are related, if with some embellishment, without distortion. Some were the subject of deeply felt convictions, and like many convictions they were at times held and pursued in an atmosphere of vigorous controversy. These circumstances applied mainly to the distant past relationship of the accountancy bodies and their individual claims. May the facts be recorded without reviving the controversies of the past, and with the happier experience that the profession has long since substituted helpful co-operation for unfruitful controversy and mutual regard for asperities.

And so we turn to facts and events in the belief that 'the sum of things is ever being replenished and mortals live one and all by give and take'.[1]

*　　　*　　　*

It may be convenient to consider the work of the Society in nine successive periods—not necessarily of equal length: at the end of each period there occurred a major event which influenced the course of policy and events in the following years. Events and developments of policy cannot be contained precisely within each period, but the dates selected offer convenient divisions for the purpose of this review. The final section deals with events subsequent to Integration.

[1] Lucretius, *De Rerum Natura.*

1885—1897

I. FOUNDATIONS

The Incorporation of the Society

DURING the year 1885 a number of accountants, mainly in England and Wales, joined later by a few in Scotland and Ireland, came together, and after a meeting in London resolved to form themselves into 'The Society of Accountants'. After the Society was founded, steps were taken to obtain formal incorporation under the Companies Act, 1867, and the grant of a licence by the Board of Trade to omit the use of the word 'Limited' from the title.

This was (and is) a privilege which in the discretion of the Board of Trade could be granted upon certain conditions to a body, the main object of which was to promote a public, professional, or benevolent purpose. Among the essential conditions were that the body was excluded from making profits as such, or from distributing any funds or surplus to its members. The body required to be fortified by a financial guarantee of its liabilities from each member and by the approval of the Board of Trade to its objects, comprised in the memorandum of association, and to its powers in regard to membership, administration, and finance set forth in the articles of association. The conditions were fulfilled, and after some opposition incorporation was effected and a licence was granted by the Board of Trade in December 1885 under the title of 'The Society of Accountants and Auditors'—described in the first report of the Society in 1886 as 'The Society of Accountants and Auditors (Incorporated)'. This was changed to 'The Society of Incorporated Accountants and Auditors', in 1908 in circumstances to which subsequent reference will be made. And in

1954 this title commendably took a more concise yet comprehensive form, 'The Society of Incorporated Accountants'.

*   *   *

It appears that the early efforts of the original body (the Society) were faced with some internal dissension and external opposition which were soon overcome. The licence of the Board of Trade in December 1885 was followed by the first annual general meeting in May 1886, when a new Council consisting of thirty members was elected; and Joseph Shaw Green, Warrington, was appointed President and James Martin, London, Vice-President. In the reorganization of 1886 his colleagues became impressed with the personality and character of James Martin, who was the senior partner of Messrs. Martin & Farlow, London. While Vice-President he acted as temporary Secretary; in November 1886 he resigned from the position of Vice-President and was appointed Secretary, an office he continued to hold, with incalculable advantage to the Society, until May 1919. To a fine presence and a courageous and strong temperament he brought an uncommon flair for the needs of a situation, high ability in diplomatic negotiation, and sound judgement. These qualities he placed at the disposal of the Society during the whole of his lifetime. The Society was led by a succession of able Presidents of robust character and energy. Martin continued a partner in his firm, and the Society's business was carried on from his office in Newgate Street, London —within sight of his old school, Christ's Hospital—and later in King Street, Cheapside. Reginald E. Emson, London, was elected Vice-President, and thus there was started a convention—occasionally varied—that one of the principal offices should be held by a London member and the other by a provincial member. Emson was a man of calm and somewhat massive personality, possessed of *bonhomie* which was complementary to the more austere characteristics of his President, J. Shaw Green, Warrington. It is from May 1886 that the essential nucleus of the Society's organization was formed and its continuous progress commenced.

The reference to Christ's Hospital, which until its removal to Horsham in 1902 was in Newgate Street, recalls James Martin's reminiscence of that ancient and eminent Foundation.

According to him, its piety and learning were inculcated from highest principles, but with a considerable degree of corporal punishment. His acknowledgement of the place which the classics held in his time at Christ's Hospital was reflected in Martin's clear and succinct expression in writing and speech. In later years his firm became auditors of the Foundation; and the school contributed no less than three Presidents of the Society.

The impetus to the formation of the Society came generally from the development of accounting as a necessary service in business and public affairs, and probably from a belief in its future as a profession. Those who might claim to be members of what was then almost a nascent profession were not wholly covered by the membership or facilities provided by existing bodies of accountants. There were three well-established bodies of chartered accountants in Scotland of some thirty years' standing—although at that time they were probably less well known south of the border than they were later. They had built up a high reputation in Scotland and if, after they had become firmly established, their conditions of admission were conservative, elasticity was secured by a lack of restriction upon the number of apprentices which each practising Scottish chartered accountant could take. To repute were added the characteristics of hard work, study, and thoroughness on the part of individual members. The Institute of Chartered Accountants in England and Wales had been incorporated by royal charter in 1880. It was formed by the amalgamation of five smaller bodies in London and the provinces—effected not without preliminary difficulty—and by the admission of practising accountants who by 1880 had been in practice for at least three years, and of clerks in practising accountants' offices with five years' service or persons with five years' service and practice combined. A small body, the Scottish Institute of Accountants, which nineteen years later merged with the Society, had been established in Scotland in the same year.

In the unquestionable desire to secure a high professional standard, the English Institute's charter and by-laws had provided rigid conditions for admission, subsequent to the constitution of the original membership. Apart from some temporary and transitional initial provisions requiring long pre-charter practice or service in a public accountant's office—in a number of cases with the passing of the final or equivalent to final examination—the admission of a candidate to the English Institute was subject to service under articles of clerkship for five years (university graduates three years) and the passing of the prescribed examinations. Thus the Institute's policy had the characteristics of a closed profession, but that policy was unsupported by legislative enactment restricting public practice in accountancy to its members or regulating the conditions of admission. Still, together with the Scottish Chartered Accountants, its members enjoyed the privilege of practising as chartered accountants, and among them were partners of old-established firms having high reputations. Here it may be mentioned that not at any time did the Society or its members attempt piratical and illegal use of the designation 'Chartered Accountant'. No virtue need be claimed for the Society by this abstention, as for one thing it devised a designation of its own and for another the use of the term by other than members of the existing chartered bodies was probably illegal, although it is believed it was not until 1896 that the legal implications were decided by the courts.

*   *   *

Between 1880 and 1885 there were others in public practice as accountants who were not members of the Institute. Some had practised before or about 1880, while others probably were stimulated to do so by their practical experience in accountancy and by personal opportunities, and it may be by the formation of the Institute of Chartered Accountants. No doubt some of them carried on as well other classes of business, possibly estate agency and auctioneering. Further there was a moderate number of the more ambitious among clerks to practising accountants, whose service was substantial but who were unable to comply with the Institute's original conditions. For them service under articles of clerkship for one reason or another was out of the question. In addition to those engaged in the practising side of accountancy, there were some municipal and county treasurers and accountants who sought professional status. They were men with a high degree of accounting knowledge and exercised considerable responsibility; the importance of their work had become enhanced by the Municipal Corporations Act, 1882 (cities and boroughs), and by the Local Government Act, 1888 (county councils). And there were in smaller numbers accountants occupying responsible positions in business and the Government. It was men in the several capacities described who formed, and became the first or early members of, the Society.

This was the beginning of the Society: if the area of its *first membership* was wider than subsequently approved *fields of training* for admission to the Society's examinations, in a small dimension it foreshadowed the wide ramifications of the Society's membership in future years—indeed of the membership of the whole profession.

Municipal treasurers and accountants and accountants of other local authorities and public bodies have always formed an integral part of the Society's membership. But in the light of the situation outlined, it may be well to bring into focus a statement in a book[1] on the professions, to the effect that 'many accountants were being trained in local government, and a further society was created to regulate their professional qualifications—the Incorporated Society of Accountants and Auditors—in 1890'. Clearly this statement is deficient.

* * *

In the first year book of the Society, published in 1885, the number of members of the Society whose names were recorded therein was 350. The book was issued from its first office at 37 Moorgate Street, London, E.C.

Development of Policy

What were the main lines of policy determined by the Council? First the Council adopted a broadly defined standard for admission to the Society and desired to include in its membership all reputable persons who complied with that standard. In a revised set of articles approved by the members and new by-laws prepared by the Council, which came into force on 1 January 1889, the following persons were stated to be eligible for membership: 'Public accountants, public accountants' clerks, accountants in the service of corporations and public bodies.'

[1] Roy Lewis and Angus Maude, *Professional People* (1952).

This is not the place to attempt a definition of what the combined wisdom of the profession has been unable to reach with certainty: but, in general terms, without any claim to precision, a public accountant (or his firm) maintains his own office and staff for the purpose of professional practice in accountancy (either on his own account or as a partner in a firm): he represents himself to the public with whom he is likely to come into contact and to his clients as offering a skilled service in accountancy matters with the implication of high personal probity and the observance of commonly recognized professional standards and conduct.

★   ★   ★

Examinations were established and first held in 1887. The number of candidates was small and, for a few years, admission to the Society was mainly upon election by the Council, after due inquiry and appropriate independent testimony. The records of the Society disclose that the powers of the Council were exercised with care, as those who knew its leading figures would expect: but inevitably a few mistakes were made. At no time was there any solicitation for members, and the Society relied on its own momentum. The by-laws of 1889 covered admission to the examinations of articled clerks (to members of the Society) and students with experience and training in accountancy. The establishment of examinations in 1887 marked the beginning of what became an essential and vital part of the Society's policy. By 1893 there were 124 candidates in the year for the preliminary, intermediate, and final examinations, of whom 94 passed and 30 failed. But at that stage it was not possible for the examinations to provide the only candidates for membership: and in the same year 155 new members (including some of those who had passed the final examination) were elected, and the total membership was 735.

To avoid hardship, which experience of the limited transitional regulations, without articled service, had disclosed, the English Institute approved new by-laws in 1891 and 1893. These by-laws gave examination facilities to accountants' clerks of substantial experience, and opportunities for election to practising accountants having had ten years' practice. Naturally the Society's Council was concerned at what seemed to it an appropriation of part of the Society's policy and a temptation to those of its members who could comply. Some accepted the facilities, but others, among them leading incorporated accountants, declined and stood by the Society. A similar facility was offered in Scotland about 1890 by one of the bodies of Scottish Chartered Accountants.

*   *   *

About three years after incorporation, a somewhat startled Council was invited to open membership of the Society to women, and at the annual meeting in 1889 a resolution to that effect was submitted by Arthur E. Piggott, and was seconded by W. O. Clough. In order to test feeling in the Society the Council, in advance of the meeting, had taken a plebiscite by postcard: 319 opinions were recorded of which 88 were favourable, 229 against, and 2 neutral. At the meeting the resolution was lost by a considerable majority. The question was again brought forward at the annual meeting in May 1891. W. O. Clough, M.P., referred to the achievements of women in education and public life and expressed the view that the parliamentary franchise for women was then a matter of practical politics, based upon his interpretation of a recent division in the House of Commons: but he was twenty-seven years too soon. There were other speeches at the meeting, at which the most hardened anti-feminist of 1960—if such there be—could scarce forbear to blush. A leading member of the Society averred that women could not be 'duly qualified'. He held that 'accountancy was amongst those professions which required for their proper fulfilment those masculine qualities and experience of the world and intellectual capacity and courage which were very rarely to be found in members of the weaker sex'. Tradition does not say whether he took home a copy of the *Journal* and showed the report of his gallant effort to his wife! In line, however, with the general opinion of that time the members would not accept so progressive a proposal.

*   *   *

An early and salutary recommendation of the Council was that members should use the designation 'Incorporated Accountant'—a decision which in later years was fraught with most favourable consequences to the Society. Initial letters were also used, namely F.S.A.A., A.S.A.A., Fellow or Associate of the Society of Accountants and Auditors; but the Council stressed the use of the designation. By a curious anomaly the articles of the Society were silent upon this important matter of the designation and letters used by members.

*   *   *

By modern standards the technique of the profession was comparatively simple, and then known methods necessarily involved laborious detailed work. But many practitioners have testified to the considerable benefits—both moral and as a means of acquiring knowledge—they derived from the detailed work which as juniors they undertook, whether in regard to audits or otherwise. Early awareness of the need to promote professional knowledge among members and students and interest in accountancy on the part of the public was categorically expressed in the Society's memorandum. The annual report for 1887 indicates that a first series of lectures was held in London and that among those who gave lectures was T. E. Scrutton, M.A., LL.B., barrister-at-law, who eventually became Lord Justice Scrutton. One of the earliest publications of the Society seems to have been lectures on 'The legal duties of accountants as official liquidators' given by Arnold Statham, barrister-at-law, in 1888. Contents of early issues of accountancy periodicals are an indication of the importance of bankruptcy as a branch of professional work at that time and of the functions of practising accountants as trustees in bankruptcy. In fact it was said that an impelling influence in the early development of accountancy as a profession was that commercial people needed skilled professional persons of integrity to be appointed as trustees in bankruptcy under the 1869 Act and to deal with commercial failures. There was a good deal of evidence that there had been too many adventurers—not always scrupulous—who thrust their services upon both debtors and creditors during the period when the 1869 Bankruptcy Act was operative. There were a Bankruptcy Act of 1883 and a Deeds of Arrangement Act, 1887, which demanded attention from practising accountants.

The *ad hoc* arrangements for lectures soon took a more promising form, for in 1890 some younger members of the Society and students petitioned the Council to form the

The Incorporated Accountants' Journal.

THE OFFICIAL ORGAN OF

THE INCORPORATED ACCOUNTANTS' JOURNAL *is published monthly, on the first day of each month, at an Annual Subscription of 7/6, which includes postage to all parts of the world. The price of a single copy is 6d., postage extra.*

Communications respecting the general business of the paper to be addressed to the Secretary of the Society of Accountants and Auditors, 4, King Street, Cheapside, London, E.C. Cheques and postal orders should be made payable to "James Martin," and crossed "Bank of England."

Letters for the Editors to be forwarded to them, care of the Secretary, as above. Correspondence, copies of reports and accounts, &c., will be welcomed from the profession.

Contents.

Professional Notes.

AFTER appearing before our readers for over six years, with marked success as a quarterly publication, *The Incorporated Accountants' Journal* will from to-day be issued monthly. Sufficient support has already been obtained before going to press to justify the departure and to ensure a new era of prosperity.

Although *The Incorporated Accountants' Journal* is published to advance the interests of the Society of Accountants and Auditors, we wish it to be distinctly understood that our columns are open to all sections of the Profession, and communications addressed to the Editors will meet with fair and impartial consideration.

Pressure on our space compels us to hold over until next month a general review of the report of the Inspector-General in Bankruptcy for the year 1894. It contains, however, a remarkable and novel feature, inasmuch as the Inspector-General tardily recognises the fact that the costs of Accountant-Trustees in Bankruptcy and Deeds of Arrangement, are in the great majority of cases of a reasonable character.

The Incorporated Law Society has long contended that all administration, interim or otherwise, both in the case of individuals and companies, should be left to the creditors, to whom in justice the estate belongs, the official control of the Board of Trade being confined to audit, inspection, and discipline. Seeing that creditors have at their disposal, to quote the Inspector-General, "the highly experienced body of Accountants, who are mainly trustees outside the ranks of officialism," there is no doubt of the soundness of this contention.

In the report of the Registrar of Building Societies reference is made to Section 8 of the Buildings Societies Act, 1894, and as to what constitutes publicly carrying on the business of an Accountant. The Registrar says "that the turning-point of the definition in the Act lies in the word 'publicly,' and therefore that many men who possess excellent credentials as Accountants in private employ, or in positions where the public cannot come to them and give them accountancy work to do, are not within it. To put the matter in familiar terms, the essential part of the qualification is a brass plate or other public notification that the business of an Accountant is carried on."

This goes much beyond the opinion of Mr. Cozens Hardy, Q.C., and other counsel, before referred to in these columns. The learned counsel say "that a person does not bring himself within the meaning of the 8rd Section of the Act simply by describing himself as a Public Accountant," but to satisfy the requirements of the Section he must "prior to and at the time of his proposed appointment as Auditor, have been holding himself out as bona fide practising as an Accountant, and have been and is in fact so practising."

Respecting the appointment of Public Auditors of Friendly Societies, the Chief Registrar states in his report that only seven Friendly Societies out of every 1,000 employ them. For the year ending June 30th, 1894, 866 Public Auditors were appointed.

Incorporated Accountants' Students' Society of London, a request granted with a considerable degree of pleasure. Among the members of the first committee was William Strachan, who continuously maintained an active interest in the Students' Society, and was finally in office as Hon. Treasurer in 1950 when he was over eighty years of age. The Hon. Secretary for a short period was H. Mead Taylor; he was succeeded by Walter Southwood Smith, who sustained the duties from 1892 to 1910. Reports of lectures were published annually in a bound volume of *Transactions*, a copy of which was sent to each member of the Students' Society. The committee elected as the first President Ebenezer Carr, at that time President of the parent society and subsequently for a long period chairman of its Finance Committee. An early issue of the *Incorporated Accountants' Journal* contains a letter from Ebenezer Carr setting forth his views as to how the time and efforts of an articled clerk should be organized. It reflected his own methodical mind and regard for the interest a principal should take in the training and progress of his pupils: but whether even the most careful articled clerk lived up to Carr's practical proposals and ideals—which included the cultivation of good handwriting—is perhaps another matter. Pupils from his office from time to time secured honours in the Society's examinations and evidently received advantage from their principal's interest and supervision. Carr, a tall, bearded man of fine bearing, was quiet in demeanour, firm in character, essentially methodical and clear-minded; he carried out his duties to the Society without any pretensions to *réclame* and contributed to the formation of its early policy.

*   *   *

Two valuable components were introduced at an early date into the Society's organization—a professional periodical and a library. It was soon found that the Society must have an organ of its own for members, recognized as a regular professional periodical. In June 1889 the *Incorporated Accountants' Journal* was first published on a subscription basis: it appeared quarterly until 1895, when it was changed to a monthly publication. It was issued on the responsibility of the Society, and while offering information on the activities of the Society and editorial comment on policy, it became in time a medium of critical review of the affairs of the profession generally and of information relative to the actual work of accountancy. It continued in this form with increasing circulation under the editorship of James Martin and William Strachan until 1935 and of William Strachan to 1937. The *Journal* was printed on light buff paper, and at the end of the year the twelve numbers were bound solidly in a dark brown cloth binding. It was carefully edited, contained good reading matter, and was published punctually; but its appearance suggested utility and reliability rather than artistic inspiration. Another periodical, into the hands of whose editor a later copy of the *Journal* had come, remarked with unchallengeable propriety, 'The *Incorporated Accountants' Journal* is a publication which can safely be left on the drawing room table!' For many years the subscription was 7s. 6d. per annum. The issues of the *Journal* and of *The Accountant* (a proprietary periodical owned by Messrs. Gee & Co.) in the 1890's and early 1900's provided plenty of provocative reading for subscribers; and there was no lack of mutual asperities and polemics. Read in 1960, they are certainly amusing, even a little startling, but at the time they were treated seriously. It is hoped this can be said with charity and without detracting from regard of those who through the *Journal* and in many other ways promoted and defended the Society's interests with zeal and great ability.

The beginning of a library was the subject of comment in early speeches of Presidents and in annual reports. A library was formed about 1887–8 by gifts of books and by voluntary subscriptions from members. Later gifts included a valuable collection of old works on accountancy and book-keeping.

The Benevolent Fund was established and commenced its humane work in 1892: it was constituted as a charitable trust and managed by trustees elected by subscribers. At one time proposals were considered for formal incorporation; but they presented too many legal difficulties and incorporation might have impeded the management of the fund: accordingly the proposals were abandoned.

*   *   *

The membership of the Society was to be found throughout

the country and clearly could not be entirely dependent upon the Council and the administration in London. Practical considerations apart, the members away from London have always felt they should have the opportunity to make their views known and facilities for meeting together. Thus between 1886 and 1896 seven District Societies away from London were formed. The senior was the Manchester District Society, founded in 1886, of which Arthur E. Piggott was Secretary for over fifty years, followed by the Sheffield District Society in 1887.

By 1890 the work of the Council had so expanded that there were four committees, the minutes of which were read at each Council meeting. But 'after considerable discussion' this laborious procedure was brought to an end in 1901; and 'until further notice' summaries were ordered to be circulated with the Council agenda. Evidently this reform was effected initially with considerable doubt; yet the loosening of the strings of privacy, if not of secrecy, was wisely beginning—and so was the modern colossus of paper work! No question of reversing the reform once made ever seems to have arisen; and it is a wholesome fact that there is no record of the confidence enjoyed by the Council and administrative staff of the Society having been marred by the improper leakage of information. To provide for the proper discharge of administrative work, in April 1902 William Strachan, James Martin's partner, was appointed Assistant Secretary, assisted by Richard A. Witty, then on the firm's staff.

*   *   *

As well as the cares of promoting the status of members, the Council turned its eyes outwards over the field—official, commercial, legislative—of services of accountants. Further there was the continuous juxtaposition *vis-à-vis* the Institute. The Council had the invaluable services of its solicitors, who at the date of the liquidation of the Society practised under the style of Messrs. Norton, Rose & Co.; no less than four of the Norton family, partners in the firm, have advised the Society.

The Companies (Winding-up) Act, 1890, and the Bankruptcy Act, 1890, lent themselves to more official control. The situation was viewed by the Society and by commercial people with much disfavour. Evidently there was a good deal of uneasiness about officialism, a theme recurring in the Council minutes and the subject of a report by the Law Society in 1892.

Conjoined with steps taken in regard to membership, examinations, and organization, was the necessity of presenting the Society to the public and of impressing the qualifications of its members upon Government, local, and other public authorities and the commercial and industrial public. It was essential that incorporated accountants should be eligible for all public appointments of an accountancy character: but in the absence of specific legislation this became the more important, since it was through eligibility for public appointments that the Society's standards became publicly recognized.

Arising from the report of the Select Committee on Friendly Societies in 1889, the Secretary of the Society discussed with Turton Norton (the solicitor) the possibility of an attempt to limit public appointments of auditors to chartered accountants. Norton assured him the position was that the Institute was incorporated in one way and the Society in another and he was convinced Parliament, by statute, would not concur in such exclusiveness. This general advice guided the Council in its parliamentary activities with favourable effect. For example, the provisions for auditors in the Building Societies Act, 1894, and the Savings Bank Act, 1904, although not entirely satisfactory precedents, met the point by non-restriction rather than positive prescription.

In cases in which qualifications for appointments were restricted to the exclusion of members of the Society action was taken by the Council, and with impressive effectiveness. Instances recorded, among others, are in regard to the appointment of an accountant official of the City of London and of professional auditors of the Manchester Corporation and of Salford. Under the Municipal Corporations Act, 1882, provision was made for a system of borough auditors. The borough auditors were the mayor's auditor (a member of the borough council appointed by the mayor) and two elective auditors, elected by the burgesses. No qualification was prescribed. Some of the borough auditors so appointed or elected were professional accountants, but others comprised people in a variety of occupations. The system was quite inadequate and not satisfactory; but it did preserve to the municipal corporations a measure of independence as regards the appointment of auditors, which many of the corporations valued, especially as in the background was the District Audit Department of the Local Government Board. The course of events in succeeding years indicated clearly that for the most part the corporations wished to keep themselves free from the activities of that department. Accordingly, a few years later cities and boroughs as they sought more extended powers from Parliament by local Acts commenced to include a clause to cover the appointment of professional auditors. A lesser number of boroughs included alternatively power for the appointment of district auditors— sometimes under parliamentary pressure and sometimes with official stimulation, but not entirely. The appointment of professional auditors under these local Acts was in some cases additional to, and sometimes in lieu of, the borough auditors. An interesting point is that this power was obtained from Parliament in face of the provisions of the (general) Municipal Corporations Act, 1882. It is also believed that in a few cases corporations appointed professional auditors under a general power 'to appoint officers'. The earliest recorded instance of a borough (England and Wales) which obtained *powers from Parliament* to appoint professional auditors was contained in the West Bromwich Corporation Act of 1889. (Some corporations had professional auditors prior to 1889.) This Act provided that the appointment was limited to persons who were members of the Institute of Chartered Accountants in England and Wales or members of the Society of Accountants and Auditors. It is noteworthy that recognition was thus given by Parliament to the Society's qualification concurrently with that of the Institute within five years of the foundation of the Society. This precedent was followed in a long series of local Acts of Parliament promoted by municipal corporations—about 74—and subsisted for about forty years. Some important phases of the history of the Society and indeed of the profession were connected with the qualifications for appointment as professional auditors of municipal corporations in England and Wales, as later pages will indicate.

*   *   *

At an early stage the Society claimed for itself a 'British Empire' policy. In 1886 a Commissioner for Australia was appointed: he established a committee in Victoria and endeavoured, but without success, to make the Society the nucleus of the then unformed profession in Australia. The Australians in Victoria decided to form their own organization, a move preceded in South Australia and followed in other States by the formation of separate incorporated institutes. However, the Society's qualification became recognized in statutes and later a committee was formed in New South Wales.

A voyage of recuperation to South Africa in 1894 by James Martin enabled him with the co-operation of Harry Gibson, Cape Town, to form a South African Committee. The first members of the committee were F. W. Diamond, Johannesburg, Harry Gibson, Cape Town, J. G. Hamilton, Johannesburg, William Palmer, Durban, G. W. Steytler, Cape Town, C. E. Taunton, Pietermaritzburg, with Harry Gibson as Hon. Secretary; not long afterwards the Hon. William J. O'Brien, Pietermaritzburg, joined the committee and was a member of the Natal Committee up to the date of Integration. Fortified by a power of attorney from the Council, Martin enabled many of the leading practising accountants in South Africa to become members of the Society. This was the beginning of a strong feature of the Society's organization which subsisted until 1957.

Attempted Statutory Registration

The mind of the Council soon turned towards obtaining statutory registration and control of the profession. The first minutes of the Council on the subject occur in 1892. The idea was to set up a first register of all practising accountants and to limit future additions to persons with prescribed qualifications. Accountancy would become a definite profession recognized by statute, so relieving the Institute and the Society of continually recurring problems. The Institute entertained similar ideas, it may be with rather less conviction and on a more restricted basis than the Society considered necessary to deal with the situation. At the inaugural dinner of the Birmingham District Society in March 1892 James Martin declared that:

Their policy was to make in reality what they, as a body, were now only termed by courtesy, a profession; and that could be done only by inducing Parliament to incorporate by Act into a profession all persons legitimately entitled to be styled professional accountants. . . . He was convinced a solution would not be found in anything short of parliamentary powers.

Pursuant to its declared policy, in 1893 the Society promoted a private member's Bill in Parliament, the Public Accountants Bill No. 1. The Institute put forward another Bill, the Public Accountants Bill No. 2. Negotiations resulted in deadlock and both Bills were discharged. The Scottish Chartered Accountants promoted Bills to protect the designation 'Chartered Accountant' in Scotland; but they made no progress.

At a special meeting of the Institute on 25 May 1893 resolutions on the question were adopted, although there was considerable criticism. The resolutions affirmed the desirability of legislation to restrict public accountancy to existing and future chartered accountants, and, with that purpose, of making arrangements with other existing bodies. But in the absence of such restriction, the title 'Chartered Accountant' should be protected by legislation. There was some apprehension, undoubtedly shared by the Society, at the encroachment of 'officialism', particularly (a) by district auditors in the audit of local authorities' accounts, and (b) in regard to insolvencies. The policy expressed in the resolutions would have tended to arrest that encroachment. Two observations on the resolutions are illuminating. At the meeting Frederick Whinney said 'they wanted all practitioners who upheld the calling of public accountant to be Chartered Accountants', and *The Accountant* in an editorial commented:

Were it not that a narrow policy as to admissions of members obtained in past years, the Institute would not now be in a position of having to reckon with another society of accountants. We may, however, take it that but a very small minority of members were in favour of the ultra-conservative policy that obtained heretofore.

*   *   *

Subsequent to an abortive attempt at discussions, subcommittees of each body met and produced an agreed draft Bill, which, had it passed, would have been cited as the Chartered

Accountants Act, 1897. The fact that a Bill was agreed reflected much credit on the immediate negotiators, notably G. Walter Knox, President of the Institute, Frederick Whinney, chairman of the Institute's Law and Parliamentary Committee, Reginald E. Emson, chairman of the Society's Parliamentary Committee, and James Martin, Secretary. The scheme was somewhat elaborate and attempted to combine the rigid views of the Institute on qualification with the more flexible ideas of the Society; and to make provision for bona fide practising accountants who were not members of either body. The bases of the proposed Bill were:

> The registration of all practising accountants: they were either members of the Institute or thereby became members.
> In effect the fusion of the Society with the Institute, through the election to the Institute of members of the Society by defined categories.
> A register for England and Wales and a register for Ireland.
> A definition of public accountant (not very satisfying).

(The Scottish Chartered Accountants were not mentioned at all: nor was the Irish Institute (founded 1887).)

All existing and future members of the Institute in practice, all members of the Society in practice on the appointed day (1 January 1897), and other persons who had been in practice for three years on the appointed day were entitled to be registered. There were provisions, subject mainly to their passing one or more examinations, enabling various categories of clerks to practising accountants—including associates of the Society who were so employed, and accepted candidates for the Society—to become members of the Institute: the provisions varied according to the length of their professional service, and whether the candidates had passed any of the Society's examinations. Fellows of the Society not in practice and Associates not employed by practising accountants could be elected Honorary Fellows and Honorary Associates. Up to 1 January 1908 the Institute could elect to membership, by the votes of seven-eighths of the members of Council, persons who had been continuously in practice for at least ten years. This was important from the point of view of public policy, since persons in practice on the appointed day who were not eligible for the first registration were given an opportunity to obtain subsequent registration; and the provision met any potential criticism that the Bill deprived persons of their livelihood. For the rest, there were disciplinary arrangements; no body of accountants not incorporated by royal charter should take or use the description 'Chartered'; and of fifty members of the Council of the Institute, five should be former Fellows of the Society.

*   *   *

In order to expedite consideration, it was arranged that the special meetings of the Institute and Society to discuss the Bill should be held simultaneously on 13 January 1897.

In the chair at the Institute's meeting was G. Walter Knox, London, and the enabling resolution was submitted by Frederick Whinney, London, in a statesmanlike speech. He said it was useless to endeavour to get provisions in public Bills stipulating that chartered accountants should be auditors: he stressed the benefits which would accrue from the consolidation of the profession, and, while recognizing that sacrifices were to be made, particularly by junior members who had served articles and passed examinations, he asked consideration not entirely from a personal point of view, but from a higher standpoint, and in the belief that the greatest benefits would be to the younger men. He added that he himself was not in very great love with the Bill, but they might get legislation at other hands and they did not want to be driven by others. The resolution was seconded by T. G. Shuttleworth, Sheffield, who said they were determined not to admit to the Institute persons not at present eligible, unless they got restrictive legislation. If they did not accept the Bill now, they would wish some years hence they had done so. Ernest Cooper, London, a man of strong character and highly regarded, led the opposition. They had only the interests of the Institute and of the public to consider and he had no hostile feelings towards the Society. As an Institute they were content to remain as they were, and he protested against the inclusion of 'outside accountants' to the detriment of younger members and to the consequent watering down of the term 'Chartered Accountant', which would not carry the same degree of competency as hitherto. Strong support to the resolution was given by C. Fitch Kemp, London: he believed the policy advocated was the only means by which accountancy could be raised to the status of a great profession. There were other speeches, which perhaps were not particularly high-minded; and that could equally be said of similar speeches at the Society's meeting. The draft Bill was not a confection which the Institute's members were willing to accept: it must be said with regret that the resolution was defeated by a large majority, a decision subsequently confirmed on a postal poll.

*   *   *

The Society's meeting got off to a good start by an able speech by the President, Frederic Walmsley, Manchester. He affirmed the continuous policy of the Society of statutory registration and consolidation of the profession, with effective control and discipline, and expressed some apprehension of 'officialism', the encroachment of which the Bill would resist. Arising from the Building Societies Act, which enjoined audit by at least one of the auditors being a person who 'publicly carried on the business of an accountant', counsel's opinion had not brought them any nearer the definition of a public accountant. This illustrated the unsatisfactory character of the situation then existing. In framing the Bill neither the Institute nor the Society had got all it wanted; but the Bill was the fairest compromise possible. It was the first time agreement had been reached, and he appealed to the members to look beyond personal considerations. Having moved the resolution authorizing the Council to proceed, the President called on R. E. Emson to explain details of the Bill and to second the resolution. Already informed of criticisms which had reached the Secretary, he specifically defended the various provisions as to categories; he did not ask the members to accept all the details but to adopt the main principles of the Bill. The Councils had found it very difficult to assimilate the categories of members in each body upon fusion; hence the provisions of the schedule dealing with that aspect, which he considered fair and reasonable. He strongly invited support from the members. If the report of the speeches from the floor of the meeting gives an impression of criticism, they were directed to details and not to the principle of registration: perhaps there were some members who on general grounds were reluctant to yield the independence enjoyed by the Society. There were objections that the Bill was entitled 'The Chartered Accountants Bill', that the Society should first know what the Institute was doing about it, that the conditions of admission of 'outside accountants' were not sufficiently stringent, that the provisions relating to Associates and non-practising members of the Society were too rigid. But the most serious opposition came from members who were corporate (municipal) treasurers: they objected to becoming Honorary Fellows and Honorary Associates of the Institute and considered they were entitled to be F.C.A.s or A.C.A.s. One such member moved an amendment, in effect, to place all Fellows and Associates of the Society on an identical footing with members of the Institute; which would have negatived the carefully negotiated categories in the Bill. After the amendment was seconded there were other speeches in support thereof and some vigorous replies from the Council. Whilst this opposition was developing, news reached the hall where the meeting was held—but quite unofficially—that the Institute's members had rejected the proposals. James Martin was put up on behalf of the Council to move the adjournment of the meeting for one month, to withdraw the original resolution, and to request similar withdrawal of the amendment. It would be unwise, in view of the opposition, to force the Bill on the members and the proposed course would leave the door open to amendment. But he asked members to realize the difficulties. In 1893 the Society had said to the Institute, 'You must take all our members or none.' The Council had now brought the members a Bill which in the opinion of the Council provided for every class of member: but as the meeting did not seem to agree, the proper course was to adjourn the meeting. The proposal was carried unanimously. At the adjourned meeting the President could only lament the rejection of the Bill by the Institute and the opposition of some members of the Society. But he declared emphatically the intention of the Council to pursue the purpose of protecting the profession by legislation.

Thereafter, the editor of the *Incorporated Accountants' Journal* delivered himself of a pungent editorial on these abortive proceedings. He commended and quoted with approval the moderate speeches of those who had supported the proposals, and, on the other hand, was severe towards the argument that the chartered accountants were satisfied and wanted nothing more. But he was even more critical of the member who had moved the amendment at the Society's meeting and who had threatened to block the Bill at every stage—and in fact had already claimed that he 'had obtained blocks before coming to the hall' Then the editor berated those who at the Institute's and the Society's meetings had produced lists of persons who they assumed would be admitted under the Bill by reason of some flimsy claim to accounting pretensions: 'a dressmaker, a collector of accounts, an ex-schoolmaster and a mystery', and others. Quoting from the Bill the definition of public accountant, one whose 'principal business or occupation was the performance of the functions of a public accountant', the article concluded: 'the admission therefore of the miscellaneous collection gathered together by M—— is not provided for by the bill but is the creation of his fertile brain'.

The article was certainly a forceful reply to those who had defeated the proposals.

*   *   *

In the course of the next thirty years or so there were members in both bodies who, recalling the events of 1897, in private sincerely deplored the fact that agreement was not then reached and amalgamation effected: yet they entertained little hope that a revival of those ideas was practicable. Happily they were wrong.

1898–1908

II. CONSOLIDATION AND EXPANSION

Membership and Examinations

UNDER a by-law of the Society operative in March 1898, articles of clerkship were made a condition precedent to the intermediate examination. At the same time the Council stated that it was not intended to discourage applications from those in the profession whose standing and experience entitled them to election upon such conditions as in the opinion of the Council afforded satisfactory evidence of training and general fitness, or from senior accountancy clerks to sit for the final examination. The immediate effect was restraint upon the number of candidates, while the number of articles registered showed a large increase.

In 1902 there was an extensive revision of the Society's articles, which was considered at extraordinary general meetings. The redrafted articles defining in broad terms the conditions for admission to membership were the subject of some discussion. Coupled with those conditions was the perpetuation of an article which defined precisely the power of the Council to make special elections to membership without examination. The Council did not feel that the time had arrived to make, without any exception, the passing of approved examinations by candidates an essential condition. Somewhat naturally this occasioned comment on the part of one or two younger members who had qualified by examination, as indeed at that time the majority of new members were doing. But the President explained that in any case the discretion of the Council was limited, and gave an assurance that it would be used in a conservative manner and only upon complete satisfaction in each case as to the length of experience and the professional standing and character of the applicants. In fact this power was exercised most sparingly; it gradually fell into desuetude and, except for those candidates who were members of other bodies of standing, was completely dropped by 1912. Up to 1902 those who under pre-1902 by-laws passed the intermediate examination were elected 'student members'. The revision of the articles in 1902 brought this hardly satisfactory arrangement to an end, a time limit being imposed within which existing student members must present themselves for the final examination.

In 1904 the Council took a decisive step which had favourable consequences in the immediate concerns of the Society and far-reaching effect in determining its ultimate destiny. For in that year the Council authorized what were then known as 'the special by-laws', applicable to non-articled examination candidates. The soundness of these by-laws may be judged by the fact that their main substance, with some modifications to meet war circumstances and some excisions, subsisted until 1948, and were the foundation of those in force till 1957. The special by-laws recited that articles of clerkship were a condition precedent to the intermediate and final examinations: but the Council approved important exceptions to cover the cases of clerks to public accountants, not serving under articles; the exceptions were in fact the substance of these regulations. Subject to passing or obtaining exemption from the preliminary examination, those having six years' service (as prescribed) and being twenty-two years of age could be admitted to the intermediate examination: after they had passed the intermediate examination they could be admitted to the final examination on completing nine years' continuous service (in effect six plus three years) and attaining twenty-five years of age. There was an additional facility for senior accountancy clerks of at least twenty-seven years of age, with not less than ten years' continuous professional experience, who might be admitted to the final examination direct; also an examination equivalent to the final for persons of mature age and exceptional experience. These were invaluable provisions available to the increasing number of accountants' clerks, and for the most part ensured a definite basis of professional experience on the part of those who later became members of the Society. The special by-laws expressed in practical terms one of the main objects of the Society, namely, to provide a means of qualifying to persons engaged in the profession who had not the means and opportunity to serve articles. At that time articles usually involved the payment of substantial premiums, and in England and Wales a practising chartered accountant or a practising incorporated accountant was limited to two articled clerks. For the purpose of the special by-laws a public accountant was deemed to include a municipal or county treasurer or accountant who was the head of his own department. The conditions as to professional service (and otherwise as to general education) as a requirement for admission to the examinations were now codified; and the special election to membership of candidates without examination was progressively and substantially reduced.

It is not possible to give precise statistical interpretation to the effect of the special by-laws (1904); but the following figures illustrate the situation in regard to examinations and membership for the five years 1 January 1905 to 31 December 1909:

724 candidates including articled clerks and by-law candidates sat for the final or equivalent to final examination (at ten half-yearly examinations December 1904 to June 1909), of whom 496 (69 per cent.) passed, and during the corresponding period 600 new members were elected. The total membership of the Society on 31 December in each of the following years was:

1904	. .	1,942	1907	. .	2,193
1905	. .	2,024	1908	. .	2,240
1906	. .	2,110	1909	. .	2,303

Simultaneously with the new by-laws changes were made in the examination syllabus, and auditing became a specific subject in the final examination. The Council also decided to award a gold medal and a silver medal annually to the two candidates who respectively presented the most meritorious work at the final examination. These medals were additional to honour certificates in the final examination (authorized in 1891), awarded to the four to eight candidates whose work was considered to be of honours standard: similarly 'place certificates' were given in the intermediate examination. By 1905 examinations were held half-yearly in eight centres in England and Wales, Scotland and Ireland, and overseas.

From time to time there had been informal contacts with the Scottish Institute of Accountants, established in 1880, a body which in Scotland was similar to the Society; a few of its members were also incorporated accountants. The Scottish Institute had endeavoured without success to obtain a royal charter. The circumstances led to suggestions that an arrangement should be effected between the Scottish Institute and the Society. In the year 1898-9, the President of the Society was a Scot—Andrew Wallace Barr, who practised in the City of London—a fact which maybe had some bearing on the proposal. Unhappily the abilities of Barr were lost to the Society through his early death during his presidential period. He and Martin negotiated an agreement which was confirmed on both sides. Members of the Scottish Institute upon application were elected members of the Society (123 were so elected; 8 were previously members); the Scottish Institute became the Scottish Branch of the Society while retaining its identity as the Scottish Institute of Accountants; and the Branch had the right to appoint two members of the Council. The Scottish Branch was to receive half the annual subscriptions of the members in Scotland, who felt this arrangement to be a mark of liberality towards England and Wales, but James Martin humorously observed that it gave the agreement quite a Scottish tang! The concentration of membership thus effected was celebrated at a conference in Glasgow in 1901 when the Scottish Branch entertained the visiting members. The first Scottish members of Council were Borthwick Watson, Falkirk, and James L. Selkirk, Glasgow, and the last two Mr. P. G. S. Ritchie, Glasgow, and Mr. Festus Moffat, Falkirk. The work of the Scottish Branch was largely associated with the name of James Paterson, who was Secretary of the Branch and a member of the London Council from 1906 to 1953 and who lived to be over ninety years of age. Having regard to the traditional position of the (then) three bodies of Scottish Chartered Accountants with their system of unrestricted apprenticeship and minimum premiums, the Scottish Branch had not the same kind of field for expansion as the Society had in England and Wales. It was a situation which the zeal and character of James Paterson refused to accept. With unprovocative tenacity, often he pressed his colleagues on the Council to permit a degree of flexibility in the examination and membership regulations when applied in Scotland; and there were lengthy and frequent communications with head office. But the Council took the view that in the interests of the whole Society, and notwithstanding practical difficulties, the regulations must be applied with little modification. Several younger members of the Society who qualified through the Scottish Branch pursued successful professional careers in the dominions, colonies, and the U.S.A. and owed much to the personal interest of the Scottish Secretary. James Paterson enjoyed the affectionate regard of his colleagues on the Council and was ever a charming host and good conversationalist.

*   *   *

An important development in Ireland took place in 1901. At the time the Society had a few members in Ireland, and there was a desire to form them into an Irish organization under the aegis of the Society. Preliminary conversations had taken place during the conference held in Leeds in 1900. As a result James Martin was invited to Ireland, and on 14 March 1901 a meeting of members was held in Dublin. The chair was taken by M. J. Stapleton, F.S.A.A., who practised in Cork, and those present included members who practised in Dublin, Belfast, and Cork, some of whom were also members of the Institute of Chartered Accountants in Ireland which had been incorporated by royal charter in 1887. Stapleton summarized the leading objects of the Society as the building up of a body of professional accountants whose status would be recognized throughout the world and obtaining from Parliament legislation to constitute a statutory register of professional accountants in the United Kingdom. The first of those objects was attained, but the second purpose remained unaccomplished. A resolution that the Society of Incorporated Accountants in Ireland be formed as a branch of the Society was adopted unanimously. Edward Kevans, who became a member of the Society in 1885 and was a member of the English Institute and of the Irish Institute, was elected the first President, and F. W. Kenny, A.S.A.A. (Messrs. Cooper & Kenny), the first Hon. Secretary. In the evening the first dinner of the Society's Irish Branch was given in honour of James Martin. This was the first of many dinners given in Dublin at which distinguished Irish guests have been present; the President and one or other of the officers of the Society were also entertained—both officially and with memorable personal hospitality. And after the formation of the District Society in Belfast the members in Northern Ireland indeed emulated the Dublin precedent. The members of the first Council of the Society of Incorporated Accountants in Ireland were: Edward Kevans, F.C.A. (*Ireland*), F.S.A.A., Dublin, President; M. J. Stapleton, F.S.A.A., Cork, Vice-President; H. B. Brandon, F.C.A. (*Ireland*), F.S.A.A., Belfast; Michael Crowley, F.C.A. (*Ireland*), F.S.A.A., Dublin; A. Killingley, A.S.A.A., Dublin; J. McCartan, A.S.A.A., Dublin; Stewart Blacker Quin, F.C.A. (*Ireland*), F.S.A.A., Belfast; F. W. Kenny, A.S.A.A., Dublin, Hon. Secretary. Although it was not a part of the constitutional arrangement, a welcome step was the election of Edward Kevans as a member of the Council of the Society: after his death in 1920 he was succeeded in 1923 by Mr. A. H. Walkey, F.S.A.A., Dublin, and an unofficial but valuable precedent of a member of Council from Ireland was established; Mr. Walkey remained on the Council until 1957. The four successive Hon. Secretaries in Ireland, the last of whom was Mr. John Love, were all partners in Messrs. Cooper & Kenny and rendered most acceptable service to the Society, particularly to their fellow members in Ireland. It is significant that the title adopted for the Irish Branch was 'The Society of Incorporated Accountants in Ireland' at a date when the Society itself was the Society of Accountants and Auditors. The title of the Irish Branch testified to the considerable use by members in practice of the designation 'Incorporated Accountant'—a fact which had increasing and valuable emphasis.

Since the Society of Incorporated Accountants in Ireland was formed, constitutional and historical changes have taken place and the country suffered much political vicissitude. Notwithstanding these changes, and happily, the Society of Incorporated Accountants continued uninterruptedly as an entity embracing members in all parts of Ireland with mutual understanding and cordiality, both at official and personal levels. The situation, however, was modified to the extent that there was independently a District Society in Northern Ireland—founded in 1913—which maintained cordial relationships both with head office in London and with the Society of Incorporated Accountants in Ireland.

*   *   *

The proposition that as a preliminary condition for admission to a professional body a candidate shall have a good standard of general education is beyond dispute. But its application and the definition of a good standard of general education are almost perennial problems. In the main, professional bodies have accepted the standard approved currently by educational authority while adding conditions as to details which seem to them desirable for their own special requirements. At times when changes have been under consideration discussion has become more vocal and even acute. The Society required that a candidate should hold one of the certificates awarded by the universities to pupils in public and secondary schools or that he should pass the Society's own preliminary examination. In the case of those of over school-leaving age, more general evidence of education in conjunction with professional experience was considered. At the beginning of the century the scheme of subjects, and possibly the standard, varied from one examining body to another: further, each body worked independently of others and was free to introduce changes from time to time. Whether justified or not, the London University matriculation examination seemed in public estimation to have a *cachet* of its own. It was an external examination and although taken mainly by sixth-form boys it was open to any candidate irrespective of the school he attended or whether he had prepared by private study. The choice among subjects required was comparatively restricted, and English, mathematics, and a classical language were compulsory.

At that time there was ferment of thought about secondary education and its extension: a legal decision had shown that certain expenditure by county councils on secondary education was irregular; elementary education administered by the old *ad hoc* elected school boards or denominational bodies left much to be desired. There had been a Royal Commission on secondary education in 1895 under the chairmanship of Lord Bryce, and its important report commanded attention in Government departments and educational circles.

These circumstances, among others, led to the Balfour Education Act of 1902, by which the school boards were abolished and responsibility for the local administration of education, both secondary and elementary, was vested in the county councils and county boroughs. The public schools and many of the old grammar schools retained their independence. The real merits of the 1902 Education Act seemed to be lost amid the angry controversies relating to religious instruction in 'provided' and 'non-provided' schools—the names given to the elementary schools, some of which had been under the previous school boards and others under the management and control of denominational bodies. The Act became known as the Balfour Education Act and was thus linked with the name of the Rt. Hon. A. J. Balfour, M.P., First Lord of the Treasury, who became Prime Minister in 1902. In force for more than forty years, the Act proved to be of great benefit, particularly to secondary education (the Fisher Act, 1918, turned out to be a dead letter). The religious controversy died down and great improvement in education was undoubtedly effected. It is sometimes forgotten that both before and, more extensively, after the Balfour Act there were scholarship facilities enabling elementary school children to attend grammar schools, to the life and repute of which they made notable contribution.

In the course of these and future discussions about secondary education, examinations in public and secondary schools were a continuous topic: too great a variety of examinations available for pupils in fifth and sixth forms was one question, and some educational opinion was critical of the comparative rigidity of such examinations as London matriculation and of the low standard of some others. An early change was made in 1902, when London University established a school-leaving certificate (matriculation standard): the examination permitted a wider choice of subjects than the external matriculation examination and was open only to pupils of schools inspected by the University. If the certificate covered prescribed subjects, it allowed the pupil formal matriculation. The London matriculation as an external examination, however, continued to be held.

Companies

During the early years of the Society's life, company law was spread over a number of Acts—and so continued until 1908: contemporary professional literature suggests that the general situation in regard to companies was far from satisfactory. Limited Liability had been established in 1855, and the main Companies Acts in force in the 1890's were dated 1862, 1867, and 1879 (limited banking companies). No less than sixteen amending Acts were passed between 1862 and 1907, and were consolidated in the Companies (Consolidation) Act, 1908.[1] There were a Directors' Liability Act, 1890, and the Companies (Winding-up) Act, 1890. The Winding-up Act placed heavy penalties upon promoters, directors, managers, or other officers of a company in respect of their misfeasance or other specified defaults. In the *London and General Bank*[2] case and the *Kingston Cotton Mills*[3] case the Court of Appeal considered whether an auditor was an officer of the company within the meaning of section 10 of the 1890 Act. In the respective circumstances of those cases, the court held that the auditor was an officer of the company. The auditor of the London and General Bank was found liable for misfeasance in respect of his certificate on one of the balance sheets. But in the *Kingston Cotton Mills* case, reversing the judgment in the lower court, the court decided that the auditors, having no reason to suspect the value of stock as certified by the managing director (which in fact was inflated), were not liable. The pronouncements of the judges in these and some other cases became authoritative in regard to the duties and responsibilities of auditors. Considerable concern existed at serious abuses in company finance and promotion, notably the frauds which had taken place in the Jabez Balfour group of companies in the early 1890's (out of which the *London and General Bank* case arose).

A Departmental Committee of the Board of Trade on Companies was appointed, the chairman being Lord Davey, a Lord of Appeal in Ordinary, and issued its report in 1895:[4] the report comprised a draft Companies Bill. Some of the provisions in the draft Bill seemed rather drastic: in responsible business and

[1] Gore-Browne on *Companies*.   [2] [1895] 2 Ch. 673, C.A.
[3] [1896] 2 Ch. 279, C.A.   [4] C. 7779, 1895.

professional circles a feeling existed that possible reforms, aimed at the unworthy minority, would curb enterprise and prevent reputable people from assuming the responsibilities of directors. James Martin had become a member of the Council of the London Chamber of Commerce in 1893 and he and Frederick Whinney (Institute) served on a committee of the Chamber appointed to consider the draft Bill in the Davey Committee's report. The Chamber convened a representative conference to discuss the draft Bill and among those present were representatives of the Institute, the Society, and the Scottish Chartered Accountants. In opening the conference the chairman, Sir Albert Rollit, M.P., who was a solicitor, said 'they must guard against endangering instead of protecting the public by illusory provisions, as no law could ultimately save careless shareholders and creditors from the consequences of their own negligence'. A suggestion that there should be added to the Bill provisions for filing with the registrar, either from time to time or annually, a balance sheet or statement of assets and liabilities was, by a narrow majority, not adopted. The chairman strongly expressed the view that the proposal would disclose the financial position of every company to the whole world: such a system would ruin a private trader, so why should a company be exposed to such risks? There was some variety of opinion on the severe penalties imposed by the Bill on auditors for misfeasance (in the absence of fraud). The representatives of the Institute and Society urged that the auditor should be held responsible for negligence only to the extent of such reasonable penalty as should be fixed by the legislature: the Scottish Chartered Accountants were less inclined to support an amendment to that effect, affording some relief to auditors from the onerous provisions in the draft Bill. But the amendment was lost by a substantial majority. It was agreed unanimously that the Board of Trade should be asked to appoint a committee of experts to formulate the principles and conditions on which revenue might be divided as profit; the state of the law was unsatisfactory, and many issues were involved. That was in 1895, and the question 'What is profit?' still endures with persistence in every accountant's mind.

Discussion on companies and company law continued, for in

1896, 1897, and 1898 there were Committees of the House of Lords which published voluminous blue books. Likewise there was considerable discussion in the profession. Before one of the House of Lords' Committees evidence was given by Frederick Whinney. The Bill was introduced into the House of Lords but was not then passed.

★   ★   ★

At a conference of the Society held in 1898, Harry Lloyd Price (Manchester) presented a paper on 'Proposed reform of the Companies Acts'. He stated the principal abuses to be over-capitalization, allotment with insufficient subscription, bogus directors, and promoters' methods. His forceful criticism was directed to attempts made to define the duties of auditors (instead of the old Table A) and to impose on auditors statutory penalties for breach. The suggestions were 'at once too much and too little'. James Martin was emphatic on the need for the registration of mortgages and debentures of companies, as to which a private Bill had been introduced into Parliament in 1894—without success. Debentures had become of importance since the 1862 Act; and it is believed the word 'debenture' was not to be found in any Companies Act. Further he favoured the prescription of an interval between two successive general meetings, but was opposed to the registration of balance sheets which he said were for the information of shareholders, not of competitors—a doctrine long since discarded. In the absence of more specific provision in a company's articles, the Institute and Society agreed to a proposal that one of the auditors of a company should be a professional accountant or, if only one, he should be a professional accountant. The comment of the Inspector-General in Companies Liquidation was, 'I agree if a professional accountant can be defined'—a problem which has persistently plagued the profession and its legal advisers.

The foregoing summary has interest as indicating views entertained in 1895 to 1900 upon certain aspects of the administration of companies and of the duties and responsibilities of auditors.

★   ★   ★

The Companies Bill was again introduced into Parliament in 1900 and became an Act in that year. Probably it was the most important factor in the immediate and subsequent fortunes of the profession. The stringent conditions in regard to auditors proposed by the Board of Trade Committee were struck out in Committee of the House of Lords; but the proposal of the Institute and Society about the qualifications of auditors was rejected in Committee of the House of Commons. The Act was of great importance, as for the first time it imposed a compulsory audit on all companies and made provision for the appointment of an auditor who was to have a statutory right of access to books and papers, and to require from the directors and officers such information and explanations as might be necessary. Previously, under the Act of 1862, the audit of accounts was provided only in the model set of regulations and the auditor was but a stepchild of Table A. In fact a company had been at liberty—within limits—to have special articles, and Table A became operative only if a company did not have them. Salutary though the Act of 1900 was, no qualification was provided for appointment as auditor. Nevertheless, it became the practice generally to appoint professional accountants; yet another forty-eight years were to elapse before a Companies Act prescribed in terms the qualifications essential for auditors of public and non-exempt private companies.

Richard Brown, C.A. (*Edinburgh*), Secretary of the Society of Accountants in Edinburgh, writing in his *History of Accounting and Accountants* published in 1905 after the fiftieth anniversary of his Society, said: 'The Companies Acts beginning in 1862 and ending for the present in 1900 have already been referred to as friends of the accountant and two ways have been particularized, auditing and liquidation, in which they bring grist to his mill.'

Before, and later as a consequence of, the Companies Act, 1900, much discussion in the profession, as well as articles in professional periodicals, was related to the auditing provisions of the Act and to the several judgments of the High Court—now become classic and venerable—bearing upon the duties and responsibilities of auditors. Was it not a period of discovery and of the formation of principles—limited, no doubt, if measured by currently accepted standards and requirements?

The End of the Nineteenth Century

The end of the nineteenth century and the beginning of the twentieth witnessed some great events in the nation's history—of rejoicing, of anxiety, and of bereavement: perhaps it is not an exaggeration to say that at that time one of the pages of history was turned. In these events the Society took its part.

The Diamond Jubilee of Her Majesty Queen Victoria was celebrated in 1897, when the aged Queen drove to a service of thanksgiving in St. Paul's and the Prime Ministers of the British Dominions assembled in London to pay their humble duty, with Her Majesty's subjects at home and from all parts of the dominions and colonies. Her Majesty was not only the Queen but a great figure venerated by her subjects, and in the course of her long reign had become an established institution. The soul of the nation was uplifted by her Diamond Jubilee and by the thought of the social, economic, and political progress—notwithstanding blots and neglect—of her reign. The celebration was made colourful by the brilliant cavalcade which accompanied Her Majesty to St. Paul's, including the uniforms of the armed forces and representative contingents from the British dominions and colonies. The assembly in London of the Imperial Conference of Dominion Prime Ministers and the other events of the Diamond Jubilee undoubtedly stimulated the imperial feeling in the British peoples, not merely in terms of territories and trade, but in a higher conception of public good and of British achievements towards more backward peoples. At dinners of the Society about that time the eloquence of public men, including members of Parliament and High Commissioners of the Dominions, was frequently directed to this theme.

The South African War which broke out in 1899 was an unhappy event to follow so soon after the Diamond Jubilee. Although the voice of criticism (in part directed against Joseph Chamberlain, M.P., Colonial Secretary, and Cecil Rhodes and led by David Lloyd George, M.P.) was heard, the war engendered patriotic feeling. This feeling found expression in the service of volunteers in the army, in the raising of funds to help the dependants of those on active service (fostered by Kipling's

Absent-minded Beggar), in admiration of some effective improvisation on the part of the Royal Navy and of other feats of endurance, and sometimes in more flamboyant forms. At the beginning of the war there was much ineptitude on the military side, and the nation endured depressing defeats: but later there was a favourable change in military operations under Lord Roberts and Sir Herbert (Lord) Kitchener, whose services were recognized by the British people and by Parliament. After the war two Boer generals, General Louis Botha and General Jan Smuts, emerged as great statesmen: General Smuts lived actively to a great age and became Prime Minister of South Africa and a world figure. His last visits to England were to carry out his duties as Chancellor of the University of Cambridge (1948 to 1950) where as a young man he had been an undergraduate at Christ's. Sir Alfred (Lord) Milner's efforts to avert war unfortunately failed and he did not avoid some criticism; but when the fighting was over and after the Peace of Vereeniging (May 1902) his brilliant administrative ability as High Commissioner was successfully exercised in the work of rehabilitation and restoration in South Africa.

The war was particularly brought home to the Society by reason of the valued connexion established with South Africa. Among losses of members of the Society, Major C. E. Taunton, C.M.G., Pietermaritzburg, a member of the Society's first South African Committee, was killed in action. In his memory members in the United Kingdom subscribed to a contribution to the Natal Volunteers Fund, and a memorial brass was presented to the cathedral in Pietermaritzburg. J. G. Hamilton, F.S.A.A., Johannesburg, was civilian director of the Imperial Yeomanry Hospitals in South Africa and received the decoration of M.V.O.

The death of Queen Victoria in January 1901 brought to an end the long Victorian age, and public grief and the obsequies, attended by the crowned heads and royalty of Europe, testified not only to the enduring strength of the Crown but to the heartfelt sense of loss among Her Majesty's subjects.

The death of the Queen and the Accession of King Edward VII were occasions of Loyal and Dutiful Addresses to the royal family and His Majesty from the Society.

The Coronation of Edward VII took place in 1902 after a postponement for a few months owing to His Majesty's regretted illness. The King was popular and after the long reign of Queen Victoria gave a new interpretation of the functions of a constitutional monarch. It has been said that the Edwardian period was one of extravagant gaiety in society, which has not escaped the descriptive and sometimes mordant pens of writers. The period was destined to lead to a time of acute political and parliamentary anxiety at home and serious international complications abroad, which His Majesty, in person and with constitutional propriety, did his utmost to avert.

It was at this period that the motor-car began to make its appearance and the aeroplane was in its experimental stage—with the promise of great industrial and social consequences for the future.

Two happy events which indirectly and subsequently had considerable effect on the accountancy profession in the two countries concerned were the Proclamation of the Commonwealth of Australia in 1901, when H.R.H. The Duke of York (George V) and the Duchess of York (Queen Mary) visited Australia, and the establishment of the Union of South Africa in 1910.

Audit of Local Authorities

It is a curious but material fact that almost from its foundation up to 1933—with intervals—the Society's external policy was largely directed to, and indeed was influenced by, the question of the audit of the accounts of local authorities in England and Wales: the term 'local authorities' is used comprehensively. Concurrently, that was in good measure the case with the English Institute.

The systems and procedure relative to the accounts of local authorities had behind them a considerable history, dating back at least to Gilbert's Act of 1782; the issues as to audit were finally settled by the Local Government Act of 1933. These matters were of much public importance, although the general public took precious little interest in them—except when some local irregularity or unjustified extravagance was brought to light, and later when public interest in municipal trading began. But it was otherwise for the Institute and Society in the period with which this chapter is immediately concerned and subsequently: there were several reasons. The great expansion of local government, beginning with the Poor Law Amendment Act, 1834, and the Municipal Corporations Acts, 1835 and 1882, and the growth of cities, boroughs, and urban areas and their finances presented a promising field for audit work of a highly responsible and remunerative character: from 1900 onwards municipal trading raised new accounting issues. Here was an expanding profession, evolving new accounting methods, the services of whose members were increasingly sought for business purposes and the audit of large undertakings such as railways and public utilities: was it not in the public interest that those services and enlarging experience should be utilized by local authorities, especially in view of the 'trading' which they undertook? These considerations were not absent from the minds of many engaged in municipal government and administration. It has already been noted that commencing in 1889 a number of cities and boroughs obtained powers from Parliament by local Acts to appoint professional auditors. The general policy was also marked by the appointment of municipal treasurers or accountants with professional qualifications. Moreover, the profession felt, not without justification, that the system of district audit was mainly concerned with legal issues, the legality of the raising of money and of payments, rather than broad accounting considerations, which in the opinion of the profession the situation demanded. The accountancy profession was not recognized or governed by a particular statute, and therefore specific recognition of the professional bodies in statutes and by Government administration became an issue of policy with high priority. Again, they were vigilant of any extension of 'officialism' in various forms. On the other hand, the fact that local services involved the expenditure of public money and increasingly of Exchequer grants from Parliament constituted a circumstance which to some sections of parliamentary and official opinion called for a Government audit in respect of the receipt and expenditure of ratepayers' money and of grants from the Exchequer. The power of 'surcharge' vested in the district auditors seemed to some people to be a curb on possible irregular payments and a deterrent on temptations to abuse: to others the effectiveness of surcharge was illusory as it was *ex post facto* and was often directed to trivialities, while surcharges were frequently remitted.

*   *   *

Some reference may be made to the evolution of district auditors and the District Audit Department of the (present) Ministry of Housing and Local Government. An interesting account is given in Professor William A. Robson's *Local Government Audit*, to which acknowledgement is made.

Wide change in the Poor Law was effected by the Poor Law Amendment Act, 1834. It aimed at the amelioration of destitution and provided for the care of the sick poor, the mentally afflicted, and the aged, at the same time imposing deterrents on the idle and vagrants. In the light of the prevailing philosophy of 1834 it was regarded as a great reform and removed some of the undoubted abuses which had grown up in the administration of the Poor Law in immediately preceding years. But it took more than three-quarters of a century before there was adequate realization of the stigma of the Poor Law and the workhouse, of the pauperizing effects of the system, and of its dreaded prospects for the aged poor. The reforms of 1834 have not withstood the judgement of history or of enlightened humanitarianism, and the system then introduced has few friends. The Act set up a highly centralized body, the Poor Law Commissioners, who directed the local administration of the Poor Law by the overseers of parishes and the guardians, with a view to securing a standard of uniformity throughout the country. By section 46 of the 1834 Act, the Poor Law Commissioners could direct guardians to appoint paid officers for examining and auditing, allowing or disallowing accounts. The boards of guardians appointed and paid their respective auditors, whose duties were laid down by the commissioners. There was an Amendment Act in 1844 which permitted Poor Law Unions in England and Wales to be grouped in districts for the purpose of the audit of accounts. Although power of appointment was left with the chairmen and vice-chairmen of boards of guardians, actually the auditors for the majority of the new audit districts were selected by the commissioners. The district auditors were empowered to 'surcharge' persons in respect of irregular payments: but persons surcharged had the right of appeal to the High Court or to the Poor Law Board. The High Court could not remit legally valid surcharges, but the Poor Law Board could, and frequently did so. By 1851 (and later) the audit system had been considerably developed by orders of the Poor Law Commissioners, and in that year one of the board's inspectors was appointed to supervise the whole system of audit. This post eventually became the office of Chief Inspector of Audit—now of the Ministry of Housing and Local Government. Two further steps led to greater centralization and independence of the auditors: for by an Act of 1868 power of appointment was entirely removed from the guardians and vested in the Poor Law Board, and district auditors became permanent civil servants; and by the District Auditors Act of 1879 the whole system was reorganized and appointments became the responsibility of the President of the Local Government Board (established in 1871) which was succeeded by the Ministry of Health and, more recently, the Ministry of Housing and Local Government.

*　　　*　　　*

The district audit system was extended, and by 1900 the position was broadly as follows. The county councils were created by the Local Government Act of 1888, and the metropolitan borough councils by the London Government Act of 1899; both Acts prescribed a district audit for the accounts. An Act of 1894 had a similiar provision for the urban, rural district, and parish councils. These Acts were to be followed by the Education Act, 1902 (the Balfour Act), and, after the conclusion of the First World War, by the Housing Acts.

In pursuit of its policy the Society took some action in Parliament in regard to the audit clause in the Bill of 1888 (county councils), and so did the Institute independently, but with no avail. To a rather obscure audit clause, apparently mainly prescribing an elective audit, in the London Government Bill of 1899, the Society suggested the addition of the words: 'Provided that at least one of the auditors so to be appointed shall be a qualified professional accountant, carrying on business in the Metropolis, and not necessarily a ratepayer in the particular district'; and this was agreed by the Institute. The

Council of the London Chamber of Commerce, at the instance of James Martin, agreed with the Society's suggestion and communicated the proposal to the Rt. Hon. A. J. Balfour, M.P., First Lord of the Treasury. But the outcome was the imposition of the district audit, a matter of much regret to the Society.

The Education Bill of 1902 placed the administration of secondary education in the hands of the county councils and county boroughs; and of elementary education with boroughs and urban districts with a population of over 20,000—and in certain circumstances a county council could become the authority for elementary education. Already by the 1888 Act the accounts of county councils were subject to the district audit. Apparently this covered the new education accounts of county councils. When the Bill made its appearance it was found that a clause provided that the education accounts of a borough under the Bill should be audited in the same manner as the accounts of a county council. This innocent-looking clause meant audit by the district auditor, and as the President of the Society stated: 'Once get the Local Government Board auditor into the county boroughs and we shall never get him out again.' The Institute made representations to the Vice-President of the Council of Education that there should be direct appointment of professional accountants as auditors under the proposed Act. The Council of the Society would have liked an amendment to that effect: but after the experience in relation to the London Government Bill it considered that an amendment on those lines would fail. Further, it was aware that the municipalities—acting through the Association of Municipal Corporations —favoured the existing provision in the Municipal Corporations Act, 1882, for borough auditors (the mayor's auditor and two elective auditors). Although this system was far from ideal, some professional accountants were, and might become, elective auditors; moreover, several municipal corporations had already obtained power by local Acts to appoint professional auditors, either in addition to, or in substitution for, borough auditors. The Society therefore supported an amendment to the foregoing effect proposed by the Association of Municipal Corporations and put down in the name of Sir Albert Rollit, M.P. Owing to Sir Albert's absence abroad, Sir James Woodhouse, M.P., took charge of the amendment. The Bill was very contentious and the Government imposed the closure. Unfortunately, the amendment fell under the operation of the closure and was never discussed. Thereafter, a deputation from the Association of Municipal Corporations waited upon Walter Long, President of the Local Government Board. He explained that the situation which would be created by the Bill was different from the receipt and expenditure of ratepayers' money; that was mainly a local matter, for which the audit provisions of the Municipal Corporations Act, 1882, were appropriate. But under the Education Bill grants would be made by the Exchequer to local authorities for the purpose of education: this was not a matter for local auditors but called for Government audit, that was audit by district auditors of the Local Government Board. He declined to alter his view as to the desirability of the audit clause in the Bill. Sir Albert Rollit again raised the question on third reading and made a protest at the action of the Government: but Mr. Long made a reply similar to that which he had given to the deputation from the Association of Municipal Corporations. The Education Act of 1902 became law with the provision for a district audit of all education accounts of local authorities.

*   *   *

The whole question of the audit of the accounts of local authorities was shortly to be considered authoritatively on another plane. It is probable that local administration and local elections attracted more public interest than they do today. Local politics were largely concerned with municipal trading and there was vigorous public opinion on the question. It was not concerned with metaphysical political considerations: the issues were more practical. There were people in all political parties who were favourably disposed to municipal trading within limits, although probably it was more strongly supported by people of progressive inclinations. On the other hand, there were those who were definitely of opinion that what are now called public utilities should be left to private enterprise. Generally there was variation of opinion as to what services local authorities should provide. There were notable examples of successful municipal trading—to mention a few:

the Glasgow trams, Birmingham gas, and the Leeds and Liverpool trams and electric supply. Electric traction was then coming into its own. Some provision of public utilities by private enterprise had not escaped criticism. The whole question called for consideration. The issues for the public were broadly the provision of cheap fares (there were $\frac{1}{2}d$. tram stages) and did the municipal undertakings 'pay'? The latter aspect was anything but simple and involved complicated accounting questions.

Accordingly, in 1903 Parliament appointed a Joint Select Committee of both Houses of Parliament 'to consider and report as to the principles which should govern powers given by Bills and Provisional Orders to municipal and other local authorities', under the distinguished chairmanship of the Earl of Crewe. As the committee had to complete its work before the end of the current parliamentary session (when all committees were dissolved), it decided to concentrate on the form of municipal accounts, the systems under which they were audited, and the right of access to them by ratepayers.

Able witnesses submitted evidence to the committee: they included a past President of the Institute of Chartered Accountants (T. A. Welton); the President of the Society, who was also Lord Mayor's Auditor of Leeds (Charles H. Wilson); the chairman of the Finance Committee of Glasgow (Alexander Murray, C.A.); several city comptrollers and borough treasurers; and J. M. Fells, F.S.A.A., who presented the point of view of private enterprise operating public utilities. The Secretary of the Local Government Board and the district auditor of the London County Council also gave evidence, particularly as to the work of district auditors.

Municipal undertakings were mostly financed by loans, which were redeemed by sinking funds operating over the period of the estimated life of the assets acquired by the loans. Much evidence was given upon the provision of depreciation where sinking funds were in operation. Some witnesses thought that sinking funds plus a reserve fund were sufficient; if the undertakings were also to provide full depreciation, the present generation of ratepayers would not get the full benefit of the undertakings, but in effect would be providing undertakings free of debt for succeeding generations. Other witnesses considered that the operation of a sinking fund extinguishing capital debt was entirely separate from depreciation, representing the wearing-out of assets, which ought to be charged against revenue. This is perhaps an over-simplification of the situation, as there were other factors which made it more complicated. The question formed the subject of an interesting paper and discussion at a conference of the Society held in Liverpool in 1903 at which the paper was read by F. Walmsley, past President, who was chairman of the Finance Committee of Bolton Corporation. Clearly the sinking fund–depreciation question involved important accounting considerations, but also questions of policy and the determination of objectives sought.

The committee devoted much time to ascertaining information about the different systems of audit, already described. The substance of the evidence is indicated by the committee's recommendations.

First as to the audit of the elective auditors under the Municipal Corporations Act, 1882: 'The evidence shows that no effective system of audit is thus supplied. The elective auditors are poorly paid, or are unpaid altogether, little interest is taken in their election. . . . No complete or continuous audit is ever attempted by them.'

The examination of witnesses in regard to the district audit of the Local Government Board, who claimed advantage for its extension to municipal trading accounts, was largely directed to the operation of surcharge exercised by district auditors; whether the district auditors would deal with such accounts on commercial lines; and whether they were qualified to do so. The committee, after indicating the authorities, the accounts of which were by statute subject to district audit (including four municipal corporations empowered in that respect by local Acts), stated:

District Auditors as a rule are not accountants and are not, in the opinion of the Committee, properly qualified to discharge the duties which devolve upon them. . . . The duties of the auditors seem to be practically confined to certification of figures and to the noting of illegal items of expenditure . . . the fact that District Auditors are not accountants seems to unfit them as a class for the continuous and complicated task of auditing the accounts of what are really great commercial businesses.

The committee's recommendations for audit were:

(a) The existing systems of audit applicable to corporations, county councils, and urban district councils in England and Wales should be abolished.

(b) Auditors, being members of the Institute of Chartered Accountants or of the Incorporated Society of Accountants and Auditors, should be appointed by the three classes of local authorities just mentioned.

(c) Appointment should be subject to the approval of the Local Government Board . . . and the auditor should hold office for a term not exceeding five years, should be eligible for reappointment and should not be dismissed . . . without the sanction of the Board.

(d) . . . (e) . . .

As to the duties of the auditor, the committee considered it should be made clear by statute or regulation that the duties were not confined to the mere certification of figures, and indicated under four headings particulars which he should certify. Further, 'Auditors should be required to express an opinion upon the necessity of reserve funds, of amounts set aside to meet depreciation and obsolescence of plant in addition to the statutory sinking funds and of the adequacy of such amounts.'

It is not surprising that the committee decided to leave the vexed sinking fund–depreciation question to the auditors within the terms of the particular recommendation. The committee were doubtful if standard forms of account were practicable but recommended that local government departments should confer on the matter with the Institute, the Society, the Institute of Municipal Treasurers, and the Scottish Chartered Accountants.

It should be added that the Lord Advocate gave evidence so far as Scotland was concerned, where the accounts of all local authorities were audited by professional auditors and there was (and is) no form of Government audit imposed upon them.

The report of the Joint Select Committee[1] was most favourable for the profession and particularly for the Society, which had consistently advocated the reforms recommended in the report. Unfortunately the Government did not take any action to implement the recommendations and the report was pigeonholed, notwithstanding protests from professional quarters. Afterwards there were conferences on the form of accounts as suggested. Ministers questioned in the House on implementing the report were evasive. Some people thought 'officialism' was rather hard at work. However, municipal corporations continuously sought power by private Bill to appoint professional auditors, but the audit of other authorities continued to be by district auditors, as laid down in the respective statutes (pp. 38–40).

Professional Discipline

As might be expected, the development of the Society's policy over some seventeen years called for reconsideration of its articles, which had been in force since 1889. The recommendations of the Council were laid before an extraordinary general meeting of members in May 1902.

The two principal points were: (1) a revision of the powers of the Council governing the admission of members, and of the general terms of eligibility for admission to membership; (2) the setting up of a Disciplinary Committee and a definition of its powers. (Question (1) has been discussed (pp. 21–25).)

As regards discipline, in the previous articles the powers to investigate alleged circumstances of unprofessional conduct were vested directly in the Council and, as the records disclose, were actively exercised as necessary. The earliest articles of the Society had provided that membership ceased if a member failed to pay his subscription by a given date in each year: also that a member suffering insolvency in any form *ipso facto* ceased to be a member. Upon proper evidence of a member's insolvency—happily in very few cases—it was the practice for the Secretary to give immediate notice by registered letter to the person concerned—without waiting for a resolution of the Council—that his membership had ceased and that he must not in future use any description implying that he was a member of

---

[1] *House of Commons Paper* 270, 1903.

the Society. Those provisions were naturally continued in the revised articles of 1902.

The new articles laid down that there should be a Disciplinary Committee of the Council, elected by ballot from among the members of the Council, except that the President and Vice-President were *ex officio* members; and, inclusive of them, should consist of not more than ten members, of whom five constituted a quorum. The Disciplinary Committee considered allegations of unprofessional conduct, of which due notice would be given to the member concerned. He was always afforded an opportunity of appearing before the committee to offer an explanation and, by permission of the Chairman (never refused), could be legally represented; or he could send an explanation in writing. Similar facilities were given to a complainant. In any case in which the committee was satisfied that a member had been guilty of discreditable conduct, it had the power to suspend him from membership for a period not exceeding two years or to censure him. Should the committee be of opinion that the member was guilty of dishonourable conduct or of conduct derogatory to the Society which rendered him unfit to remain a member, it was required to make a report to the Council accordingly, and formal notice of such report was sent to the member. The report had to be considered by a special meeting of the Council, before which (if he so elected) the member was permitted to appear and, if desired, to be legally represented. After hearing the report of the committee and any information from the member, the Council was empowered, if it thought fit, to exclude the member from the Society by a vote of two-thirds of a quorum of council members present.

The procedure thus laid down stood the test of long experience and—at a later date—favourable review by counsel. The number of cases dealt with was relatively small, having regard to the size of the Society's membership, and in no case was a decision of the Disciplinary Committee or of the Council challenged in the courts.

The Society did not at any time prepare a formal code of ethics—which some overseas bodies have done—but relied on the training and professional instincts of members to observe an unwritten understanding and to maintain a high standard of professional conduct. As time went on, however, the Council occasionally made pronouncements on specific matters for the information and guidance of members.

*   *   *

At the meeting in May 1902 an interesting part of the discussion was a suggestion by one or two members that the title of the Society might be changed to 'The Society of Incorporated Accountants', or some such title embodying the designation used by members. There were valid objections—mainly legal—at the time, especially as the name 'The Society of Accountants and Auditors' had been included in some Acts of Parliament and in certain Government regulations. The Council was not prepared to risk such substantial gains. But the members concerned had anticipated—however unwittingly—what happened in 1908, after the Warrington judgment, when the Society's name was changed.

III. RELIABILITY AND INTEGRITY

Income Tax Practice

SOME observations have been offered already on the early work of practising accountants and their staffs. Bankruptcy practice and deeds of arrangement constituted a more conspicuous proportion of professional work than is the case today: the private company accounts to some extent for the change. In the professional journals considerable space was given to information on insolvency practice relatively to that allotted to information on income tax. In fact the paucity of advice and comment on income tax is very noticeable. In particular, practically no information was given in the issues of periodicals following the introduction of the Budget each year by the Chancellor of the Exchequer. The attitude taken was indicated in an article in *The Accountant* in April 1902, 'Second Thoughts on the Budget' (apparently published with reluctance), which opened: 'It is not our custom to deal in detail with questions of national finance and taxation, but the somewhat exceptional circumstances obtaining at the present time have induced us to break through a rule which, under ordinary conditions, is we think a wise one.'

The exceptional circumstances were apparently the comparatively heavy Budgets (for that time) and the increase in taxation arising from the South African War. The article was somewhat critical of past Government policy which led to a standard rate of 1s. 3d. imposed during that war. The rate was reduced to 11d. next year!

In the *Incorporated Accountants' Journal* the first reference to income tax is in July 1893, reporting a reply from the Board of Inland Revenue to an inquiry on a practical point of detail. It was not until February 1900 that any systematic treatment of the subject was presented. In that month there was published a paper on 'Income Tax Schedule D', by George S. Pitt, London, which he had read to the London Students' Society. Between 1896 and 1905 there were only 43 items (including reports of decided cases) on income-tax matters: in the same period there were 310 items (including cases) on bankruptcy and deeds of arrangement: whereas between 1906 and 1915 the number of items on taxation had increased to 192, and the number of items on bankruptcy and deeds of arrangement was 324. Similarly, the corresponding figures for *The Accountant* in regard to taxation were 609 and 2,878. (Incidentally, the critical change made by the scheme of estate duties in Sir William Harcourt's Budget embodied in the Finance Act, 1894, received comparatively slight attention in the accountancy journals.) Nevertheless the settlement of income-tax assessments on behalf of clients from 1900 increasingly, if slowly, became a part of professional practice, stimulated no doubt by the increase in the rates of tax during the South African War (1899 to 1902). Those rates of tax in their modesty seem today to be fantastic.

*   *   *

Against that background consideration may be given to a new factor in income-tax practice in 1903 which indirectly had considerable influence—at first unobserved—on the organization and composition of the accountancy profession. Practising accountants and their clients had come to feel that when an appeal against an assessment went to the Commissioners of Income Tax there should be a facility to enable the taxpayer to be represented by the accountant who was handling his income-tax affairs. An interview was given by the chairman of the Board of Inland Revenue to representatives of the Birmingham Chamber of Commerce on the subject of frequent objections by General Commissioners of Income Tax to hear accountants who were advising appellants. The chairman did not think that any further burden should be placed on general commissioners, who were unpaid; but the law might be altered to provide that, if general commissioners raised objection to hearing an accountant, the appellant should have the right to remove his appeal to the Special Commissioners, who had no power to refuse to hear an accountant. Accordingly, in the Revenue Act, 1903, the following provision (section 13) was enacted:

If upon any appeal under the Income Tax Acts the Commissioners for the general purposes of the said Acts refuse to permit a barrister or solicitor to plead before them or to hear any accountant, the appellant may, in lieu of proceeding with the appeal before them appeal to the Commissioners for the special purposes of the said Acts, and the last-mentioned Commissioners are hereby required to hear the barrister, solicitor or accountant. The term 'accountant' in this section means a person who has been admitted as a member of an incorporated society of accountants.

The relevant words were 'a member of *an* incorporated society of accountants'.

The *Solicitors' Journal* was understandably critical, as in its view the presentation of cases for consideration by judicial or quasi-judicial bodies was the function of barristers or solicitors, and the inclusion of accountants in the section was not welcomed. Elsewhere, however, it was pointed out that the first part of the section referred to refusal to permit a 'barrister or solicitor to plead' while the words applicable to the accountant were refusal 'to hear'. The section occasioned little more than a brief note in *The Accountant*. The *Incorporated Accountants' Journal* went a little farther and quoted the section under the heading 'Recognition of Incorporated Accountants'. The heading was a pardonable if partial implication of the section, since in 1903 there was comparatively little recognition of accountants by statute. Moreover, the section was evidence of the growing activity of the profession in relation to taxation. In the next issue there followed an editorial on 'What is an accountant?' The editorial was not limited to the immediate issues arising from section 13, although it derived some encouragement from the provision. 'Here for the first time is a legal answer to the question "What is an accountant?" Parliament has left no room for doubt. We must regard the definition as satisfactory and the more so as it is given in connection with Acts of Parliament under which accountants' duties are constantly increasing.' This was a distinctly ingenuous comment. The concluding part of the editorial was a philippic against the failure to obtain and to pursue statutory regulation for the profession.

But if inference from this recorded if slight comment is correct, the accountancy bodies had not at first apprehended the *naïveté* of the section and the influence it was destined to exert on the formation of new bodies. In 1903 'an incorporated society of accountants' included the bodies of chartered accountants and the Society. Another body had been registered in Scotland in 1891 and its members were likewise covered. No doubt Parliament—and, it may be said, the Board of Inland Revenue—meant that at the time, but used phraseology which, avoiding discrimination and monopolistic intention, opened a wide channel of possibilities and provided no professional standard at all. Had the authorities realized the effect of the section? The accountancy bodies do not seem to have done so immediately. But the fact was that 'an incorporated society of accountants' meant for the future, besides the bodies already established, any body of accountants which might be formed by as few as two persons under the Companies Acts, with whatever standards or lack of them, short of illegal misrepresentation, it might choose. Even prior to the 1903 Revenue Act, attempts had been made to form new institutes: but either the attempts did not get very far or the formations seem to have disappeared from the scene.

The English Institute had its large and important share of the expanding field of accountancy and its system of admission after service under articles and the passing of examinations. The Society, the members of which were progressing in the practising sphere, had a similar system of articles and examinations, augmented by the new special by-laws for non-articled accountants' clerks who must also pass the examinations, and by a restrained facility to make limited special elections to membership. To the Society it seemed that existing bodies and arrangements offered all the facilities which the service of accountancy to the public needed at that time and in the foreseeable future. Already vigilance was exercised to guard against possible moves to form new bodies: extension of the then conceived area of accountancy as a profession seemed to be unnecessary and unjustified. It was not a question of maintaining a monopoly, which indeed the situation was far from approaching, but of guarding and improving hardly-won standards and public recognition—and, if possible, of obtaining statutory regulation for the profession. However, the progress of the established bodies and the beginning of a more general demand for qualifications set in motion attempts to extend the field from which recruits for accountancy were drawn; and during the next twenty-five years in this enlarged field, no less than ten new bodies were formed, including some which aimed at specialist qualifications.

It would be going too far to say that the formation of new accountancy bodies was attributable solely to section 13 of the Revenue Act, 1903: but when its implications were comprehended it became an invitation to do so. Among the new bodies were those which, having registered themselves under the Companies Acts, were not at a loss, in communications to members or when inviting applications from persons with accountancy aspirations, to claim that by their membership or by joining one of the newly formed organizations they were, or would thereby become, 'members of an incorporated society of accountants': thus, it was said, they would be recognized under section 13 of the Revenue Act, 1903. Leaving on one side the natural reactions of the Society, the situation led over a considerable period to sincere misgivings, not alone on the part of the Society. It seemed to portend the extension to uncertain boundaries of the area within which dwelt those who professed and called themselves accountants: that was the prospect which these developments foreshadowed.

The Designation 'Incorporated Accountant'

Each new body had to discover for itself a suitable title and a concise designation—with initial letters—for its members. One body, established in 1905, conjectured that as it was 'an incorporated society of accountants' its members were 'incorporated accountants'. Having upon consideration come to an affirmative conclusion on the point, it recommended its members to use the designation 'Incorporated Accountant (———)' with a suffix which, it was represented, differentiated the designation from that of members of the Society. But the recommendation could not fail to create confusion. For nearly twenty years the Society had been cultivating the use of the designation 'Incorporated Accountant'—in fact one of the earliest recommendations to the members made by the Council —and had already sedulously built up the reputation attaching to it. The proposal of the new body seemed outrageous to the Society, an invasion of its rights and certainly prejudicial to the members. Whatever the tense feeling at that date, the passage of time and longer reflection have probably induced general agreement as to the unwisdom of the suggestion: it was bound to be provocative. Thus challenged, the Society's powers of resistance were raised to a maximum. Legal advice was taken and it was decided to bring an action in the High Court. The Society sought an injunction to restrain an individual member of the defendant body from using the designation 'Incorporated Accountant' and an injunction to restrain the body itself from representing that its members were entitled to use the designation.

After some delay—in part occasioned by the indisposition of the Secretary and the death of the Society's solicitor (Turton Norton)—the case was heard in January 1907 by Mr. Justice Warrington (afterwards Lord Warrington, a Lord of Appeal in Ordinary) in the High Court of Justice (Chancery Division). The Secretary and Assistant Secretary, with Richard A. Witty, had collected a large amount of evidence as to the use by members of the Society of the designation 'Incorporated Accountant' and as to its recognition by people of standing who had business with accountants. The principal witness for the Society was James Martin, whose performance under cross-examination was both masterly and actuated by deep conviction. William Strachan also gave evidence on the facts produced by the Society. Altogether there were sixty-two witnesses for the Society, who included the Inspector-General in Bankruptcy, an official receiver, solicitors, chartered accountants, a member of Parliament, business men, a journalist, and the Secretary. A considerable part of the evidence concerned the regulations and examinations of the Society, procedure governing the admission of members and the exercise of professional discipline by the members of the Council. The Society was represented by C. M. Warmington, K.C., A. W. Rowden, K.C., and A. R. Kirby; and the defendants by H. Terrell, K.C., Ashton Cross, and F. T. T. Duka.

The profound judgment of Mr. Justice Warrington presents a subtle argument which calls for a complete reading: but three extracts may be quoted advantageously.[1] The first deals with the character of the designation 'Incorporated Accountant', the second with its significance (in fact the decision of the learned judge), and the third with observations on a case in the Court of Session (1893) relating to the initial letters 'C.A.' and to the rights of a professional body as regards the designation used by its members. (In 1893 the Court of Session in Scotland interdicted two persons not members of one of the bodies of Scottish Chartered Accountants from using the initial letters 'C.A.'):

Is the term 'Incorporated Accountant' a descriptive term or is it—to use a convenient phrase, though not I think quite an accurate one—a fancy term? I only use that phrase as opposed to the expression 'descriptive term'. In my opinion it is not descriptive.

What I am satisfied of is that . . . that designation denoted membership, not of any society of accountants which was incorporated, but membership of the definite Incorporated Society, which by its tests and examinations and by its rules and requirements as to qualifications, conferred on its members a status different from that of other members of the profession who had not the same qualification. In coming to that conclusion I am driven to hold that in the year 1905 the designation 'Incorporated Accountant' did mean a member of the Society and did confer on the members the privilege —which one cannot help regarding as a valuable one—of being looked on by persons who had dealings with accountants as holding a certain definite status indicating reliability and integrity.

Commenting on the previous chartered accountant case in the Court of Session, Mr. Justice Warrington said:

The Lord Ordinary and the Lords in the Inner House unanimously came to the conclusion that the Chartered Societies were entitled to prevent the defendants from using the letters C.A. or any similar designation which would lead people to believe that they were members of one or other of those Chartered Societies. It is true that in arriving at that decision the Lord Ordinary emphasised the fact that the plaintiff societies were chartered societies and that it might be said that what the defendants were doing was an infringement of the charters: but I think the judgments of the Court there—not only of the Lord Ordinary but especially the judgments in the Inner House—were put on a much wider ground, namely that a body

[1] [1907] 1 Ch. 489.

however incorporated has a right to prevent persons who are not members of it from representing themselves to be members of it. In the case before me there seems little difficulty in coming to that conclusion.

The injunction was granted in terms of the Society's statement of claim with the addition of a few words to make precise the scope of the decision and to indicate its limits. The defendants stated that they might take the case to the Court of Appeal, but after consideration decided to abandon any such intention.

The decision was a triumph, for not only had the Society secured for its members the legal and exclusive right to the use of the designation 'Incorporated Accountant' but it had obtained from the High Court a declaration that the designation conferred a certain definite status indicating reliability and integrity. James Martin always regarded the Warrington judgment as the great achievement of his life and as the most conspicuous milestone in the Society's progress. In later years to his friends in the Society, he delighted to refer to the able assistance he had received in regard to the preparation and marshalling of all the evidence from William Strachan, Assistant Secretary, and from Richard A. Witty, who was then one of the staff of his firm. Equally he recalled the valuable guidance and advice the Society had received from its solicitors from the inception of the Society in 1885, who had charge of the Society's case. Turton Norton had made himself responsible for the Society's business: after his death in 1906, the Hon. Bernard Barrington was the partner who advised the Society for many years.

At this distance of time, perhaps it can be said that the advice of counsel received before the action was by no means free from doubt as to the legal considerations. Fifteen years earlier, relative to a person who had lost his membership and who misdescribed himself as 'Incorporated Accountant', the opinion of counsel (one of whom became subsequently Master of the Rolls) gave no support whatever to the possibility of legal restraint upon the offender. But in the interval between that opinion and the action before Mr. Justice Warrington in 1907, the Society had made firmly based progress, the designation had become more widely known and recognized, and there was the precedent of the chartered accountant case. Thus urged by the President, past Presidents, and Secretary, the Council had taken its courage in its hands and, fortified by what it felt to be a paramount duty towards the members, it had pursued with unrelenting vigour the case, which was brought to such a successful conclusion and in terms which exceeded the best hopes entertained.

In the year or two following the action the Society's solicitors were instructed to communicate with a number of persons not members of the Society who were found to be using the designation, and undertakings were given by the offenders to refrain from doing so. Occasions arose from time to time, even as late as 1954, upon which the Society made application for an injunction to restrain a person wrongly described as an incorporated accountant; and the court invariably followed the decision of Mr. Justice Warrington, with costs against the defendant, which in terms of money, as may be imagined, had little practical value.

The Profession in South Africa

Although in the period 1898 to 1908 there were ample problems at home, fruitful attention was given to the Society's affairs in South Africa.

The South African War had inevitably arrested professional development in that country. But the Society was fortunate in having as the Hon. Secretary of the South African Committee a member of unlimited energy and perspicacity—Harry Gibson. Subsequent partners in his firm, Mr. Cyril Gibson (son) and Mr. Hugh Hyslop, have successively served as Hon. Secretary of the committee in Cape Town, with much ability. Harry Gibson paid a visit to England in 1901 and met the Council. He had won the complete confidence of James Martin and found in Charles Wilson (later Sir Charles Wilson), President of the Society from 1901 to 1904, a kindred spirit—progressive, forthright, and courageous, although not entirely conciliatory. Harry Gibson's visit enabled tentative ideas to be discussed, having for their purpose an extension of the Society's policy in South Africa at the conclusion of the war.

In 1894 there had been formed in Johannesburg a body known as the Institute of Accountants and Auditors in the South

African Republic, for the Transvaal was then governed by the régime of President Kruger. Before the South African War it appears that some communication had been established between that body and the Society—but any kind of definite link or affiliation was ruled out, if only for the reason that by its articles the scope of the Society's activities was limited to the United Kingdom, British dominions, dependencies, and colonies. The Council of the South African Institute had conceived the idea, and in fact had drafted a constitution, of obtaining a charter from the Volksraad (the Parliament of the South African Republic); but the suggestion perished with the coming of war. On his return to South Africa, Harry Gibson got into touch with the Johannesburg body (of which F. W. Diamond, a member of the Society's South African Committee in Cape Town, was a leading member). The distinguished figure of Alexander Aiken, who practised in Johannesburg, also took part in preliminary and later negotiations. Alexander Aiken was a Scot who went to live in South Africa because of the delicate state of his health and commenced practice in Johannesburg: he lived to be eighty years of age. A scheme was prepared to merge the South African body into the Society as the Transvaal Branch of the Society.

After a lapse of three years due to the war, a general meeting of the South African Institute was held in Johannesburg, presided over by W. H. Dawe. In the post-war reconstruction that Institute naturally desired to resuscitate its activities. In a clear statement W. H. Dawe put before his members the elements in the situation and the choice of becoming merged in the Society or of endeavouring to obtain as an independent body a charter from the newly established Government. The proceedings showed that the South African Institute aimed at high standards and at maintaining the progress which it had already made. A charter would involve a considerable intake of persons not then members of the South African Institute and Alexander Aiken, in a reasoned speech, claimed much advantage for merger with the Society. The meeting, under the lead of the chairman, voted in that sense and authorized its representatives to proceed with negotiations. Heads of agreement were drawn and, after approval by the Council of the Society and by the representatives of the

South African Institute, were submitted to and adopted at an extraordinary general meeting of the Society in London in 1902.

The agreement was welcomed by the profession in Johannesburg; particularly, having regard to the wide ramifications and finance of the mining industry, its members preferred to become part of a British Society with world-wide connexions, rather than remaining members of a body with local limitations. The main terms were that all existing members of the Institute of Accountants and Auditors in the Transvaal (formerly the South African Republic) should become members of the Society and that Institute should become the Transvaal Branch of the Society and as an Institute should cease to exist. New members would subsequently be admitted under the terms of the Society's articles and by-laws. The examinations would be held in Cape Town and Johannesburg on the questions set by the United Kingdom examiners, save that the legal papers would be in South African law, set and marked in South Africa. But the settling of the Pass List and the declaration of results was to be in the hands of the Council in London. The first examinations were held in South Africa in December 1905. This procedure, with inevitable modifications and change in the acceptance of candidates and examinations, remained in force till 1957 and for a time afterwards. It was made clear in Johannesburg that the new Transvaal Branch and its committee, while being in friendly association with the Society's South African Committee in Cape Town, would be constitutionally independent of it and would have direct access to the Council in London. Harry Gibson, with whom Alexander Aiken closely co-operated, was given a power of attorney to be the Society's Commissioner for enabling the agreement to be made effective and to admit as members of the Society the members of the South African Institute. In this way the Society included amongst its members all the leading practitioners on the Rand and a valuable and progressive branch of the Society was formed in the centre of South Africa's leading industry.

The establishment of the Transvaal Branch of the Society and the belief of leading practitioners there, no less than of the Society's Council at home, in the statutory regulation of the profession suggested consideration of such a possibility in the

Transvaal. The setting up of the new Government and the progress of reconstruction after the war created favourable opportunity. Under the prevailing régime what was in effect an Act was known as an Ordinance. At the instance of the Transvaal Branch of the Society, which gave formal notice in the Government *Gazette* of its intention, the Transvaal Accountants' Ordinance was promoted and became law in 1904. It was thought to be the first piece of comprehensive legislation for the profession in the British dominions and was hailed as a considerable achievement by the Society. The Ordinance set up the Transvaal Society of Accountants, which became the statutory body to control the register of practising accountants: and it became obligatory for a practitioner to have his name inscribed in the register. Members of the Society's Transvaal Branch, of the Scottish Chartered Accountants, of the English Institute, of the Irish Institute, and of the Society, subject to residence in the Transvaal and to being in practice at the date of the Ordinance, were entitled to be registered and to become members of the Transvaal Society. A section set forth a list of acts or practices which constituted offences for which a public accountant would be liable to be suspended or to have his name removed from the register. The Ordinance did not vitiate the constitution and work of the Society's Transvaal Branch. The facility for first registration to members of United Kingdom bodies was continued, subject to residence, by the by-laws of the Transvaal Society, which also became an examining body.

One of the sections provided that if the Council, after formal hearing of a member, considered him to be guilty of any act under the Ordinance or regulations, it could call upon such member to show cause to the Supreme Court why he should not be prohibited from practising and why his name should not be removed from the register. The court could suspend a member or order the removal of his name from the register. Experience proved that, from a general professional standpoint, this was a weakness. In a case in which a member of the Transvaal Society was convicted of misappropriating trust funds, he received a fairly light sentence. When the Transvaal Society petitioned the Supreme Court for the removal of his name from the register, the petition was refused on the grounds that it was unfair to deprive the person concerned of his livelihood.

D. P. C. Blair was the Hon. Secretary of the Society's S. African Northern Branch (formerly Transvaal Branch) and effectively conducted its business for about fifteen years. Then for a period between the wars, during the Second World War, and after 1945, the Branch had the advantage of the services of Robert B. Hogg, M.C., as Hon. Secretary; he was succeeded by his partner Mr. R. E. Grieveson, M.B.E., who continued in office until the date of integration.

Some Festive Occasions

The year 1904 also witnessed some memorable events in the profession of a more festive character than legislation.

The Edinburgh Society of Accountants, the most senior of the three bodies of Scottish Chartered Accountants, celebrated its Jubilee in Edinburgh, to which representatives of the other bodies in the profession at home and overseas were invited and were welcomed with much cordiality by the President, F. W. Carter. The Society was represented by the President, W. G. Rayner, London. Among the distinguished guests were Lord Rosebery, the Lord Justice-General of Scotland, the Lord Provost of Edinburgh, the Lord Advocate, and the Principal of Edinburgh University.

Shortly after the celebration there was published in Edinburgh a learned work, *The History of Accountants and Accounting*, by Richard Brown, C.A., the Secretary of the Edinburgh Society. The work discloses much research into the earliest origins of accounting as well as the development of the accountancy profession as it appeared in 1904.

*   *   *

An event having prolonged significance occurred in 1904, when the (then existing) Federation of Societies of Public Accountants in the U.S.A., President, A. Lowes Dickinson, M.A., F.C.A., C.P.A., organized a congress in St. Louis, Missouri, U.S.A. Guests came from many countries and the congress afterwards became recognized as the First International Congress on Accounting, to be succeeded after an interval of over twenty years by a series of international congresses held in some of the capitals of Europe and again in the U.S.A. James Martin and Mrs. Martin were the representatives of incorporated accountants and they established a friendly and valuable relationship between the American Association of Public Accountants (which became subsequently the American Institute of Certified Public Accountants) and the Society. Other guests included J. B. Niven, C.A., C.P.A., New York, who represented the Society of Accountants in Edinburgh, Francis W. Pixley, past President of the English Institute, and F. H. Macpherson (the Institute of Chartered Accountants of Ontario), John Hyde (the Dominion Association of Chartered Accountants), J. W. Ross (the Association of Accountants in Montreal), and Emanuel van Dien (the Netherlands Institute of Accountants), who in 1926 was the President of the Second International Congress held in Amsterdam. The chairman of the St. Louis Congress was J. E. Sterrett, C.P.A., Pennsylvania; the congress was made the more interesting by coinciding with the World's Fair in St. Louis, which was a great event in America at that time.

A major paper at the St. Louis Congress was on 'The C.P.A. movement and the future of the profession of public accountant in U.S.A.', which was introduced by George Wilkinson, C.P.A., New York, who was Secretary of the Federation. He reviewed comprehensively the pattern of the profession in the U.S.A. at that time, which necessarily was rather complicated. This arose from the comparative youthfulness of the profession in the U.S.A. (as elsewhere) and from the fact that any legislation was by States, which are characteristically independent and exercise a large measure of sovereignty. The 'Certified Public Accountant' was the creation of individual State legislation, which entrusted the issue of C.P.A. certificates to State universities or set up C.P.A. boards; and in both cases prescribed the conditions and qualifications required for the issue of C.P.A. certificates, as well as the power of cancellation. A number of States had adopted C.P.A. legislation, the first being the State of New York in 1896; but several had not, among them States which had definitely defeated such proposals: and there was considerable variety in the standards and procedures required from State to State where C.P.A. legislation had been passed. Critics of proposed legislation presented the fairly common view 'The penny accountant on the side streets will be placed on a legal equality with the best in the land'. The Acts protected the title of C.P.A. within each State but do not appear to have limited public practice to persons who were C.P.A.s: it was something of a legal problem whether a C.P.A. of one State could practise as a C.P.A. in another State, and, if permissible, what formalities were necessary: this was particularly acute in the State of New York, where there had been attempts to enforce restrictions. For some reason or another the New York State Society had in 1903 withdrawn from the Federation: whilst some new-born reciprocal facilities had recently emerged in New Jersey, on the whole the doctrine of reciprocity had not received much encouragement. The policy of the Federation was to bring societies of C.P.A.s into friendly contact, to influence the formation of further societies of C.P.A.s, to encourage the promotion of C.P.A. legislation on uniform lines, and in other ways to elevate the standards of the profession. Mr. Wilkinson insisted that in promoting these purposes a high moral standard and code for the profession and for individuals was vital in principle and in their own and the public interest.

Organized on a nation-wide basis, but on entirely different lines from the Federation, was the American Association of Public Accountants incorporated in the State of New York in 1887. In 1904 it comprised but 140 members, 100 of whom were practising accountants. Some thirty years later the American Society of Certified Public Accountants was merged into the American Association: and now as the American Institute of Certified Public Accountants it is a body of great importance and influence throughout the U.S.A.

Afterwards, James Martin and Mrs. Martin went to Canada for a short time and continued the connexion formed at St. Louis with leading members of the profession in Canada, notably with J. W. Ross and with his brother A. F. C. Ross, Montreal, and John Hyde, Montreal. James Martin was ever an ambassador for the Society and his Canadian visit had the happy result of the formation of a Canadian Committee of the Society with John Hyde as Chairman and A. F. C. Ross as Hon. Secretary.

From time to time the Canadian Committee presented the views of the Society to the bodies of Canadian Chartered

Accountants, facilitated by the close connexion of the members of the committee with those bodies; and occasionally took action in the provincial legislatures in the interests of incorporated accountants.

The Society's Twenty-first Year

1906 was the twenty-first year of the Society's history. The preparation of the Society's case to obtain protection for the designation 'Incorporated Accountant' engaged continuously the attention of the Council and the Secretary. The Public Trustee Act, setting up an official (Government) Trustee Department, received the royal assent, but scarcely the favourable acceptance of the accountancy and legal professions. The Act was applicable to England and Wales only and there is not a public trustee for Scotland, where trusts and executorship matters are largely, though not exclusively, in the hands of the legal and accountancy professions. A Bill to make the audit of trust accounts compulsory was introduced but not proceeded with, a Companies Bill was laid before Parliament and the President of the Board of Trade set up a Departmental Committee to inquire into the law and practice of bankruptcy and deeds of arrangement.

*   *   *

In the early 1900's correspondence with the Institute took place which aimed at starting conversations on registration. After preliminaries, a 'no useful purpose' reply was received. It was not a happy phase. The Society had produced a Registration Bill which the Institute did not like, whilst the Institute took a hand in promoting a 'Chartered Societies Bill' in which the Society sensed monopolistic intention. Neither Bill got anywhere. However, wiser counsels prevailed by 1906, when a quite private and unofficial event and other circumstances greatly assisted the relations between the Institute and the Society. William Lever, M.P. (afterwards the first Lord Leverhulme) invited to a private luncheon party a few leading members of the Council of each body. As far as is known, no specific proposal emerged, but personal understanding was fostered with favourable consequences. At the same time mutual regard and confidence between James Martin and the Hon. George

Colville, who in 1899 had succeeded W. G. Howgrave as Secretary of the Institute, grew from their frequent communication and talks about the profession—of continuous benefit to both bodies. It is not suggested that these circumstances led directly to any formal decisions: but a welcome invitation from the English Institute to the Society enabled discussions on registration to proceed once again (p. 70). Thus the year was characterized by preparations which, as will be seen, had important subsequent consequences in more than one field of professional interest.

★   ★   ★

For the Society, the year also included a period of rejoicing, as in the autumn of 1906, the twenty-first anniversary of the foundation and incorporation of the Society was celebrated in London. By kind permission of the Master, Wardens, and Court, the proceedings, part of which consisted of a conference, took place in the Hall of the Worshipful Company of Cordwainers, under the presidency of W. G. Rayner, London: the Vice-President was Harry Lloyd Price, Manchester. At the conference the President gave an address in which he reviewed the progress of the profession since the foundation of the Society; and there were adopted three formal resolutions, supported by several well-informed speeches, which point succinctly to what were at that time the main objectives of the Society's policy. The first called for the regulation and control of public accountants by statute of the imperial and colonial parliaments. This was followed by a resolution expressing regret that effect had not been given to the recommendations of the Joint Select Committee of the Houses of Parliament on municipal trading (p. 43) for the appointment of professional auditors of municipal accounts. The third resolution affirmed the desirability in deeds of arrangement of a majority of creditors, representing three-fourths of the liabilities, binding the assent to the arrangement of the remaining one-fourth, that the accounts of trustees should be subject to audit and that security should be required from trustees. After these more serious sessions, the members were entertained at the Mansion House at a reception by the Lord Mayor (Sir Walter Vaughan Morgan, Bart.) and the Lady Mayoress, supported by the sheriffs and attended by some of the high officers of the Corporation of London. The Society gave the twenty-first anniversary banquet at the Whitehall Rooms, Hotel Metropole (since acquired by the Government).

*　　*　　*

A Conservative Government had been in power since 1886 with the exception of three years from 1892 to 1895 of a Liberal administration. This period covered the South African War, the ascendancy of imperialism and attempted tariff reform, and the Balfour Education Act, the merits of which, for the accountancy profession, were obscured by the imposition of district audit for education accounts. Differences within the Government, which not even the brilliant mind of Arthur Balfour, Prime Minister, could resolve, the unpopularity of some of the Government's legislation and policy, and a good deal of prejudice, led to a great defeat of the Conservatives at the general election of 1906, and the formation of a Liberal Government under Sir Henry Campbell-Bannerman: upon his death a year or two afterwards, H. H. Asquith, K.C., became Prime Minister. Although the Ministry passed through stormy political times, tradition has attributed a high degree of ability to the Ministers of that period.

The assembling in London in 1907 of the prime ministers of the respective British dominions for the Imperial Conference was the occasion of a resolution of the Council offering respectful greetings from incorporated accountants practising their profession in all parts of the British dominions and expressing the hope that as a result of the deliberations of the prime ministers, 'the Empire would be still further united in prosperity and peace'. The Council was always conscious that its policy effectively extended to all parts of what were then known as the British dominions, dependencies, and colonies.

The Companies (Consolidation) Act, 1908

An important piece of non-political legislation was the Companies Act, 1907, followed by the Companies (Consolidation) Act, 1908, which was a much-needed measure, and consolidated company legislation stretching from 1862 to 1907. Prior to the introduction of the Bill there had been a Departmental

Committee to report on what amendments in company law were desirable:[1] the chairman was C. M. Warmington, K.C.

The Act, in effect, divided companies into four classes, expanded the previous provisions as to auditors and their duties, and enacted facilities for private companies. The four classes of companies were (1) public companies which issued a prospectus, (2) semi-public companies which filed a statement of prescribed particulars in lieu of a prospectus, (3) private companies, and (4) foreign and colonial companies which had a place of business in the United Kingdom. For the audit certificate prescribed by the 1900 Act was substituted a report by the auditors to the shareholders on the accounts and on every balance sheet laid before the general meeting: the auditors were required to state whether or not they had obtained all the information and explanations they had required and whether, in their opinion, the balance sheet was properly drawn up so as to exhibit a true and correct view of the state of the company's affairs according to the best of their information and the explanations given to them and as shown by the books of the company. The report could be a separate document or could be appended to the balance sheet—the usual practice—but there must be a reference to the report on the balance sheet, so that the two documents were definitely connected. Some limited protection was afforded to auditors by procedure in case of a proposal to elect a person other than the retiring auditor, to whom prior notice of such intention had to be given. Counsel's opinion was taken by the English Institute—who favoured the editors of the *Incorporated Accountants' Journal* with a copy thereof—which comprised a form of wording of the auditors' report to conform with the provisions of the Act.

The new provisions for private companies gave small companies relief from some of the more onerous provisions applicable to public companies, including the issue of a prospectus and the filing of annual accounts with the Registrar of Joint Stock Companies. On the other hand, some restrictions were placed upon them—on the right to transfer shares, by the limitation to fifty shareholders (exclusive of employees), and by the prohibition of invitations to the public to subscribe share

[1] Cd. 3052, 3053, 1906.

capital or debentures. These restrictions were fundamental to the 'private' element and differentiated private from public companies. This facility accorded with the economic trend of that and later times and gave impetus to expansion of smaller units in industry and trade. Capital could now be contributed by, or shares placed among, a small number of people, without the risks and severe consequences of failure, as in the cases of businesses carried on by individuals or partnerships, who would suffer bankruptcy or disabilities of a deed of arrangement: this facility was valuable to many family businesses, in the respect of succession or giving interests to members of the family. Few could have foreseen the extent to which the private company became increasingly a vital factor in the structure of British industry and commerce, and, if known by other names, in the Commonwealth and other countries.

If the Companies (Consolidation) Act, 1908, was a measure of first-rate practical importance, the Limited Partnerships Act, 1907, has proved to be of comparatively small consequence. The limitation of the liability of a limited partner to the amount of his capital was strictly upon the basis that he took no part whatsoever in the conduct of the business. Partnership continues to the present day to be governed by the Partnership Act, 1890, and the Limited Partnership Act, 1907, supplemented by the Registration of Business Names Act, 1916 (and as amended by the Companies Act, 1948). The private company rendered the Limited Partnerships Act of comparatively minor usefulness.

The Society in 1908

The Society continued to be known as 'The Society of Accountants and Auditors', but the decision of the High Court in regard to the designation 'Incorporated Accountant' renewed more hopefully suggestions made from time to time in the past that the word(s) 'Incorporated' or 'Incorporated Accountants' could be introduced into the Society's title. Counsel's opinion was taken, and a proposal that the title should become 'The Society of Incorporated Accountants and Auditors' was submitted to, and approved by, the Board of Trade and was adopted by the members at an extraordinary general meeting on 30 June 1908.

No change was made in the initial letters F.S.A.A. and A.S.A.A. Although the designation became comprised in the title of the Society, the amended articles still did not contain any reference to the actual designation of members.

★　　　★　　　★

Two events of 1908 in different parts of the world marked progress in the profession and were of interest to the Society. An Act of the New Zealand Parliament set up a register of accountants in 'the Dominion of New Zealand' and constituted the New Zealand Society of Accountants. Among those who took part in negotiations leading to the Bill in their capacity as members of the profession in New Zealand were W. H. Churton, F.S.A.A., Auckland, and Peter Heyes, F.S.A.A., Wellington: the Bill was in charge of the Prime Minister of New Zealand, Sir J. G. Ward. Necessarily the Act was drawn on broad lines and membership was divided into those who were 'public accountants'—engaged as practising accountants or as members of staffs of public accountants—and 'registered accountants'—engaged as accountants in Government, commerce, and industry. Practice was thus regulated by statute and disciplinary powers were vested in the Council of the New Zealand Society: the initial letters adopted for use by Fellows in practice were F.P.A.N.Z. and the initial letters of other classes of members were similar but modified to differentiate each class. Provision in the Act permitted the New Zealand Society to register as members persons who were members of bodies of accountants in the British Empire which were recognized in that behalf by regulations: thus approval was given to membership of the Society of Incorporated Accountants and Auditors. Prior to the constitution of the New Zealand Society, the two bodies in that Dominion were the Incorporated Institute of Accountants of New Zealand and the New Zealand Accountants' and Auditors' Association. The members of these bodies became members of the New Zealand Society: the New Zealand Accountants' and Auditors' Association was eventually wound up. But the Incorporated Institute remained in being: subsequently its Council promoted the idea of applying for a Royal Charter and desired a requirement of experience in a public accountant's office for practice as a public accountant.

The proposal to petition for a Royal Charter, however, was not implemented, and a revised New Zealand Society of Accountants Act was passed in 1958 (p. 297).

*   *   *

Generous in its hospitality to representatives from other countries, the profession in the United States of America has continually welcomed visiting members of the Society. A cordial invitation from the (then) American Association of Public Accountants to its twenty-first anniversary celebrations in 1908 held in Atlantic City was accepted by the President (Harry Lloyd Price) and the Vice-President (Arthur E. Green). The speeches of Harry Lloyd Price and his views made a specific contribution to the proceedings, and both he and Arthur Green enlarged friendships with American members of the profession. The visit to the U.S.A. was followed by a short tour in Canada, where warm hospitality was extended to the visitors. They had an opportunity of discussing advantageously the recognition by by-law of members of the Society proceeding to Canada by the Ontario, Quebec, and other provincial bodies of chartered accountants in Canada, for the purpose of membership, which was the proper qualification for public practice.

*   *   *

In the autumn of 1908 the members assembled in conference in Cardiff at the invitation of the South Wales and Monmouthshire District Society. This event, marked by civic hospitality and topical discussions at business sessions, was but one of a series of activities in the principality, where the members have shown sustained enthusiasm for the Society and its affairs. For several years those attending conferences enjoyed the brilliant oratory of Harry Lloyd Price, President 1907-10, as readers of the *Journal* enjoyed his penetrating writing. The conferences were also enjoyable social occasions, complete with top hats, frock coats (men) and long skirts, big hats, and feather boas (ladies). The ladies were not always amused at being conducted *en masse* to a theatre—as sometimes happened—whilst the men were dining well and long!

*   *   *

Viewed in retrospect the Society had good ground for a measure of satisfaction at the end of its second phase in 1908. It had established a sound examination and membership policy, the designation 'Incorporated Accountant' had received favourable judicial review, its qualification had won statutory and official recognition, and its influence had been extended in what was then the British Empire.

IV. THE STANDARD OF AUDITORS' QUALIFICATIONS

The Professional Accountants Bills, 1909 and 1911

To those who knew it in 1909, it seemed that the Society entered upon a new phase in its career. The effects of past achievements showed themselves in a more confident development of policy both in external relations and in the Society's own internal organization and arrangements. The Council could not, and did not, take a complacent view of its affairs; on the contrary, it had to face and deal with new problems, or continuing problems in a more intensified form. Reflection upon the years from 1909 to the outbreak of war in 1914 suggests that the Society had reached such a position that no major change affecting the accountancy profession could take place without the participation and assent of the Society.

To begin with, from January 1909 the Society for the first time had its own independent office, council chamber and library, and a small administrative staff. This was desirable after the conclusion of the convenient agreement under which accommodation and secretarial service had been provided by the Secretary's firm at 4 King Street, Cheapside, London. A small but pleasant office was leased at 50 Gresham Street, near the Guildhall; and in the same building was the office of the Secretary's firm, an arrangement which enabled James Martin, aided by William Strachan as Assistant Secretary, to conduct the Society's day-to-day business with convenience.

* * *

Reference has been made to the invitation from the Institute to the Society in November 1906 (p. 63) to start discussions with a view to the preparation of a Registration Bill. The invitation

GRESHAM STREET, LONDON, E.C.2, LOOKING WEST, 1914

By kind permission of the Librarian, Guildhall, London

itself was an indication of an improvement in relations which assisted materially the negotiations, conducted by a Special Committee from each Council. Early in 1909 a draft Bill—the Professional Accountants Bill—was agreed; and in April a copy was sent to the members of both bodies for consideration at general meetings. The Bill provided for the registration of practising professional accountants in England and Wales and for the constitution of a Register Committee (of members of the Institute and of the Society). At the opening of the register, all members of the Institute and the Society in practice were to apply to have their names entered on the register, and all other persons who could prove to the Register Committee that on the appointed day they were in bona fide public practice. Thereafter admission to the register was limited to members of the Institute and the Society who gave notice to the committee of their 'intention to practise as professional accountants': similar facilities were available to Scottish and Irish Chartered Accountants in England and Wales and to members of approved overseas bodies. Each body would retain its separate identity and designation. There were provisions for discipline and for the maintenance of examination standards. Practice in future would be restricted to persons who were registered, and there were penalties upon persons who, not being registered, held themselves out as being in practice. The Bill defined 'Professional Accountant' as being any person whose business or occupation was the performance of the functions of a professional accountant. This was a somewhat elliptical statement but was the most favourable definition which counsel could draft.

The Women's Freedom League was then aggressively active in endeavouring to secure votes for women. A communication from the League inquired as to the admission of women under the Bill; and while the Board of Trade did not officially sponsor the Bill it was interested, and it advised that women should be eligible. The Society gave an intimation that it would amend its regulations in that respect, and the Bill definitely provided for the admission of women to the register. It was a somewhat involuntary commitment.

       *   *   *

At the Institute's meeting the presentation of the Bill was in charge of W. B. (later Sir William) Peat. He referred to many abortive attempts at legislation in the past and to a notice given at the Institute's annual meeting in 1906 calling for registration, while he commended the advance made by the Society. There was the consciousness that an unsatisfactory position was developing through persons excluded from the Institute and from the Society establishing themselves under various descriptions, and others with qualifications below the standard of the Institute and Society practising as accountants. Stimulated by the provisions of the Revenue Act, 1903, there was a growth of new bodies, multiplying their membership, no doubt in view of the possibility of registration. In 1909 the membership of the principal bodies in Great Britain and Ireland was

Institute.	.	.	.	4,000
Society .	.	.	.	2,200
Scottish C.A.s		.	.	1,000
Irish Institute .		.	.	80
				7,280

and there were the members of the newer bodies and other practising accountants. From the Institute's point of view, the Institute would retain its own organization and the designation 'Chartered Accountant', and the Bill did not provide for amalgamation as was the case in the 1897 Bill. In time William Peat thought there would be only two institutes in England and Wales, namely the Institute and the Society, and other bodies would disappear. On the whole the Bill was well received; and Ernest Cooper, who had strongly opposed the 1897 Bill, said he saw no possible objection to registration while the independence of the Institute was preserved. The Bill was accepted with only three dissentients.

The Society's members considered the Bill at a meeting held the day after the Institute's meeting, under the presidency of Harry Lloyd Price, Manchester, who addressed the members. The primary object of the Bill was to differentiate among accountants, the competent from the ignorant, the upright from the unworthy; and as a secondary purpose to empower a profession with ideals of proficiency and integrity to prevent what a London journal had styled 'the gutter fraternity' from sullying the fraternal reputation. No person in bona fide practice was excluded from registration and no monopoly was sought. Every member of the Society without exception had the right of registration upon giving notice of his intention to practise; the Bill would not interfere with the privileges of incorporated accountants, and members who did not apply to be registered merely elected to leave a right in abeyance. A suggestion to set up another register of non-practising accountants was quite impracticable. Support to the proposals was given by the general body of members present, but there was considerable criticism from members who were municipal accountants. A principal municipal accountant considered that his position was analogous to public practice and that the Bill ought, by an extension of the definition of professional accountant, to express his corresponding right to registration. Called on by the President to deal with the question, the Society's solicitor, the Hon. Bernard Barrington, said it was perfectly clear to him—and the Bill was drafted having regard to the point—that any municipal accountant who gave notice that he intended to practise would be at once entitled to have his name entered on the register as a professional accountant: but the legal opinion hardly satisfied the critics, and the Council undertook to consider the points raised. The resolution for approval of the Bill was carried with but three dissentients.

*   *   *

The Institute and Society were fortunate in inviting the Earl of Chichester to sponsor the Bill as a private member's Bill, which was introduced by him into the House of Lords. On the second reading Lord Chichester made a comprehensive and temperate speech, in which he outlined the position of the profession, and indicated the standards of the Institute and the Society, which, however, were discounted by the fact that anyone could offer himself to the public as a public accountant. With some delicacy he referred to the new societies which had sprung up since 1903: he did not consider their status entitled them to be represented, but any of their members who could prove their qualifications as practising accountants would be registered on the setting up of the register. Some apprehensions on the part of the Scottish and Irish Chartered Accountants, and other details, he felt could be met at the committee stage: and he asked that the Bill be given a second reading and sent to a Joint Select Committee for consideration. Strong objection was made to the Bill by peers representing the views of the Scottish and Irish Chartered Accountants, who, if they did not maintain an office in England and Wales, were concerned that they would be unable to undertake professional business there, and lest the legislation would prejudice their use of the designation 'Chartered Accountant'. The Marquess of Salisbury objected on the ground that closed corporations were only justifiable if there was a great good to be performed or an evil to be remedied: that, he considered, had not been shown to be justified in the case of accountants. A peer, speaking on behalf of the Board of Trade, thought the Bill would be to the public advantage having regard to the very responsible duties of public accountants; but it was necessary to take the utmost pains to prevent injustice being done to any individuals or class of persons. Another Government peer believed the object was to prevent improper persons becoming accountants: he described the attitude of the Government as benevolent—cool but correct. In view of Lord Chichester's undertaking to meet the objections, the Lord Chancellor hoped to avoid a division, which, however, was pressed. The voting was 15 peers in favour of second reading, 14 against; but as 30 peers were not present, as required by standing orders, the debate stood adjourned. After another debate, in which a suggestion was made to bring up the matter again at a later session, a motion that the debate be adjourned was carried without a division.

Following the proceedings in the House of Lords, negotiations took place with the Scottish and Irish Chartered Accountants: a new Bill was prepared which met their previous objections, and some smaller but important points were clarified. The second Bill provided for three registers, and three Register Committees, one for England and Wales, one for Scotland, and one for Ireland, with reciprocal facilities for registration: but its fundamental principles remained unchanged. In March 1911 Lord Chichester again introduced the Bill into the House of Lords: peers who had previously opposed now gave the Bill their support, including Lord Salisbury, who said that having

Address to His Majesty the King.

It was reported that Mr. E. Kevans, J.P. President, and
Mr. M.J. Stapleton, Vice-President, attended as a deputation
and presented an Address to His Majesty the King on the
occasion of his visit to Ireland on behalf of the Society's
members in Ireland, and that His Majesty was pleased to receive
same and returned a reply.

Conference.

The Secretary reported that the arrangements for the
Autumnal Conference in Dublin had been completed and the
draft programme to be issued to the members was approved.

Professional Accountants' Bill.

The Chairman of the Professional Accountants' Bill
Committee reported that a Conference had been held with the
advisers of the Society and the Institute having regard to the
fact that Sir Frederick Banbury had blocked in the House of
Commons the motion of the President of the Board of Trade to
refer the Bill to a Joint Committee. The Parliamentary Agent
and Solicitors having consulted various officials, were of opinion
that it was inadvisable to move in the Lords for the rescission
of the motion referring the Bill to a Joint Committee in order to
have a Special Committee of the Lords set up during the current
session. It was resolved to adopt the advice given in which
it was stated that Lord Chichester concurred.

West Riding Asylums Bill.

The Chairman of the Parliamentary Committee reported that the
audit clause in this Bill specifically placed the audit in the
hands of Chartered or Incorporated Accountants.

National Insurance Bill.

Correspondence between Mr. C. Hewetson Nelson and the
Chancellor of the Exchequer was submitted, from which it
appeared that the intention is for the audit of the accounts of
approved Societies to be carried out by Government Officials.

A PAGE FROM THE COUNCIL MINUTE BOOK
20 JULY 1911

received further information he considered that Lord Chichester had prima facie made out a case for the Bill. Ministers indicated that, opposition having been overcome, the Government could now give warmer support: in addition Lord Alverstone (the Lord Chief Justice), and Lord Desborough, who had considerable influence in the City, spoke in favour. The Bill was read a second time and sent to a Joint Committee of both Houses for consideration. The next step was a message from the Lords to the House of Commons: the message was in charge of the President of the Board of Trade, who moved the reference of the Bill to a Joint Select Committee. The motion required the unopposed assent of the House, as the Bill was not a Government measure, and the Government were not prepared to put on the Whips. Sir Frederick Banbury, M.P., who had a reputation for much skill in parliamentary obstruction, opposed the motion three times. Although representations were made to him, he declined to alter his attitude. In consequence the motion was not carried and the Bill had to be dropped. Subsequently it was believed Sir Frederick Banbury's opposition was inspired by the railway accountants, who objected to the Bill.

Consultation with Lord Chichester, the authorities of the Houses of Parliament, and the Board of Trade led to the conclusion that in the political atmosphere in Parliament—which at that time was tense—it was not expedient to attempt to reintroduce the Bill. The situation was a cause of much disappointment in the Institute and the Society that after agreement had been reached between the principal bodies, the opportunity to put the profession on a statutory basis had been frustrated. There was good ground for thinking that had the Bill gone to a Joint Select Committee, before which interested parties would have been heard by counsel and evidence submitted, and had the principles of the Bill been accepted, serious opposition would have been overcome, although doubtless the Bill would have emerged with a number of changes incorporated therein.

*   *   *

Affairs of the profession overseas also engaged the attention of the Council. The Natal Accountants Act, 1909, reproduced many of the features of the Transvaal Ordinance of 1904 and was pleasing to the Society. After the constitution of the Union of South Africa in 1910, representatives of the profession prepared a Bill for registration throughout the Union, but in 1912 it was rejected in Select Committee of the Union Parliament on the preamble on the ground that compulsory registration was not desirable. In Queensland, by proclamation under the Local Authorities Act, 1902, the qualification of the Society was recognized, with other qualifications, for the purpose of exercising the office of auditor; and under the Indian Companies Act, 1913, the Governor-General notified the name of the Society as one of the bodies of which members were held to be fully qualified auditors throughout British India.

A rather troublesome problem arose in regard to the profession in Australia. Many of the practising accountants in Australia had formed themselves into the Australasian Corporation of Public Accountants, the policy and membership of which was limited solely to the practising side of accountancy. In pursuance of that policy—no doubt inspired by the policy of the English Institute—the Australasian Corporation in 1909 presented a petition to the King in Council for incorporation by royal charter. The draft charter gave a right to chartered accountants of England, Scotland, and Ireland resident in Australia to apply for membership of the proposed Institute of Chartered Accountants in Australia. The omission of the Society from this facility raised a point of general principle and a particular question, having regard to its membership in Australia and its two Australian Committees. Reluctantly the Council presented a petition to the Privy Council against the grant of the royal charter. There was also opposition from other bodies in Australia. Although various proposals and suggestions were made to the Society, they fell short of the Council's definite view of the inclusion of its name in the proposed charter; and its opposition stood. The petition for the charter did not succeed, but the matter was revived some twenty years later, when a revision of views and mutual concessions enabled the Society to withdraw its opposition.

The Lloyd George Budget, 1909: National Insurance

It is well to view the immediate concerns of the Society

against the larger background of affairs in the country at that time and to consider how the profession and its future were affected.

The climax of 'imperialism', the better side of which informed the policy of the Society in its overseas relations, had passed at the end of the nineteenth century. On the death of Edward VII the Society submitted a resolution of humble duty and sympathy to Queen Alexandra. Succeeding to the throne in 1910, his son, George V, entered upon a period of anxiety in international affairs, of political and constitutional tension at home, and later of war, in which His Majesty brought to bear his unostentatious qualities of character, duty, and wisdom.

In 1906 the Campbell-Bannerman Government with its large majority in the House of Commons had embarked on a policy of social and financial reform. The Chancellor of the Exchequer, H. H. Asquith, in 1908 introduced non-contributory old-age pensions (5s. a week for single persons, 7s. 6d. a week for married couples); and a differential rate of income tax between earned (if under £2,000, 9d.) and unearned income (1s.) first obtained in 1907–8. Becoming Prime Minister in 1908, Asquith appointed David Lloyd George Chancellor of the Exchequer. His Budget of 1909, intensely radical in content and politically acrimonious, had far-reaching consequences, both from the financial and constitutional points of view. The additional revenue was required to meet the extra costs of defence—mainly on the Navy in view of the increasing menace from Germany—and of projected social reform. But there were more controversial aspects of the Budget, sharpened by the fiery speeches of Lloyd George and by the bitter opposition of his critics, particularly in the House of Lords. Its somewhat elaborate provisions comprised four rates of income tax and the first supertax—if income exceeded £5,000, supertax was payable on the excess over £3,000—and there was an extension of the death duties, introduced in 1894. In 1909 the editors of the accountancy journals confined themselves to a mere recital of the rates of tax: the political atmosphere was such that comment on the Budget, however circumspect, would have seemed like playing with fire, and the editors were undoubtedly correct in their judgement. A legend gained some currency that one of the District Societies devoted an evening to a discussion of the provisions of the Budget, and that it ended in a bear-garden! Judged by modern standards the burden of the taxes imposed in 1909 may seem not unduly heavy and the claims of social reform comparatively modest. But in 1909 the Budget to many appeared to be almost revolutionary both by its financial implications and by the bitter attacks made on the better-off sections of the community, who wondered where further in-stalments of this policy might lead.

For the accountancy profession, the more complicated taxes had special importance, although it may be doubted whether the profession had appreciated their immediate and future sig-nificance in regard to its work. The minutes of the Council disclose consideration of questions arising from the administra-tion of income tax, not directed to the 1909 new taxes, but as to the inadequacy of rates of depreciation allowed by the Inland Revenue; and as to the practice, to which exception was taken, of some Surveyors of Taxes[1] to call for the production of balance sheets in relation to the taxation of individuals and firms. (This objection did not extend to companies.) These matters were not dealt with direct, but were referred to the London Chamber of Commerce, where they received the con-sideration of commercial men and of the representatives of the profession.

*   *   *

The philosophy of the 1909 Budget found further expression in the first National Insurance Act of 1911, which, if it was accepted with some hesitation, has proved of immense benefit. Insurance became compulsory for all manual workers and for others earning under £160 per annum, at a cost of 3d. a week to the employer, 4d. to men employees, and 3d. to women, whilst the State contributed 2d. In terms of the political arithmetic of that day, it was presented as 'ninepence for fourpence'. Under Part I of the Act, the insured enjoyed medical, sickness, disable-ment, and maternity benefits. Limited unemployment insur-ance was provided by Part II, mainly for seasonal trades. The principle and practice established in 1911 have been extended from time to time until in 1948 National Insurance became

[1] Until 1919, H.M. Inspectors of Taxes were known as Surveyors of Taxes.

universal, with the addition of contributory retirement pensions (established earlier, however, on a more restricted basis).

The operation of the 1911 Act involved building up a great administrative machine. Part II was administered by the Unemployment Insurance Department, Board of Trade, which controlled the first labour exchanges (1909): the two functions were complementary. Part I covered a large section of the population, each of whom was a separate case. By the Act the Insurance Commissioners (the principal administrative organ) and Commissioners for England, Wales, Scotland, and Ireland were set up to control the scheme: some devolution was effected through 'Approved Societies', which were *ad hoc* sections of Friendly Societies or similar sections of certain insurance companies, associated with the scheme. Nearly every insured person became a member of one of the 'Approved Societies': those who did not so join were in the 'Post Office' section. Contributions were paid by the now familiar method of affixing insurance stamps weekly on each contributor's card, the responsibility for so doing being on employers, who deducted from salaries or wages the employee's portion. Benefits were paid by the approved societies, which, if by selecting 'better' lives they showed surpluses, could within limits give extra benefits. These insurance responsibilities upon employers brought a new component into accounting and auditing and new duties fell to accountants and auditors.

But as the Bill was passing through Parliament, the accountancy bodies watched with some concern the provisions for auditing in relation to the scheme, which meant the audit of the approved societies. The Bill provided for audit by 'auditors appointed by the Treasury'. Hope that under this provision the audits would be entrusted to practising accountants—perhaps by an extension of the system of public auditors applicable to Industrial and Provident and Friendly Societies or otherwise— was modified by the possibility of some system of official audit and the enigmatic language of the provision. The Council of the Society made several representations to parliamentary and official authorities; the replies received were very uncertain and indeed vaguely suggested official audit. After the Act became law, the Treasury set up an Inter-departmental Committee of officials to consider the system of audit, and Charles H. Wilson, past President of the Society, gave strong evidence in favour of professional audit, not least on the grounds that the Friendly Societies were already familiar with professional auditors who understood local conditions, and that the Friendly Societies were unlikely to view with favour an official audit. However, the committee reported against professional audit, and recommended the formation of a National Insurance Audit Department, in the first instance to be staffed mainly by men trained in the profession and holding qualification as chartered or incorporated accountants: the recommendations were adopted. The Society found some consolation in the fact that, of seven Inspectors of Audit appointed, five were incorporated accountants as well as a considerable number in the next senior grade: one of the latter eventually became Accountant-General to the Ministry of Labour and National Service. Others were appointed in the Unemployment Insurance Department of the Board of Trade. Perhaps some vague idea was entertained by the Society that future appointments to the National Insurance Audit Department would be made from among accountants holding professional qualifications: but this was not to be, as the department's staff in future was recruited through the normal Civil Service channels.

Examination and Membership Policy Reviewed

Concurrently with the heavy responsibilities in Parliament—and there were others (pp. 82–86) in addition to those already discussed—the Society's own activities were expanded, while the evolution of policy in regard to examinations and membership occupied much of the attention of the Council and Secretary.

Between 1909 and 1914 five new District Societies were formed, including the Belfast District Society, which would act in co-operation with and continue to be part of the Irish Branch. With much cordiality the members in Ireland entertained the Society at a conference in Dublin in 1911, and in 1913 there was a conference in Liverpool at which liberal hospitality was extended by the Lord Mayor, Sir John Harmood Banner, M.P., F.C.A., a past President of the Institute. It is noteworthy that at each conference the administration of income tax—including 'fair play for commercial interests'—was a subject for discussion. Clearly income tax was becoming a more important element in the practice of the profession and demanded increasing knowledge on the part of members.

*   *   *

The period immediately before the outbreak of the First World War in 1914 was crucial in the development of membership policy. The general scope of membership and its limitations outlined in the Society's articles was administered by the Council, mainly under the guidance of the by-laws for the examinations, and with such closely guarded latitude as was permitted by the articles. The Council was concerned to maintain and raise the standards of the Society, which had received judicial approval in 1907 and recognition in increasing parliamentary precedents. Equally there was the need from a public point of view to combine a good standard of professional training and experience as a basis for admission to the examinations with opportunity, unhampered by restrictions, to obtain a recognized accountancy qualification. The great majority of candidates were covered by the regulations for service under articles with an incorporated accountant in practice or by the special by-laws governing admission to the examinations after professional training without articled service.

The articles of the Society vested in the Council power, in special cases, to elect to membership without examination persons having exceptional qualifications. These elections required an affirmative vote of three-quarters of those voting, who must comprise not less than half the total membership of the Council. The Council had undertaken some years previously that the power would be used infrequently and with restraint. At that date there were a comparatively small number of practising accountants and managing clerks to firms, of mature age and with substantial professional experience, some of whom from time to time applied for membership. Mainly the candidates were required to pass an examination equivalent to the final, which was a practical and exacting examination conducted separately from the normal examinations. There were a few other practising accountants, some principal borough treasurers and persons who already held a qualification from a recognized overseas body or who were chartered accountants of England and Wales, Scotland or Ireland—whose special election was believed to be in the interests of the Society. But the application of the power of special election became increasingly infrequent and difficult and the Council was set on bringing it to an end. After considering outstanding cases, the Council in 1912 made its last six elections without examination. At the same time a resolution was passed instructing the Secretary not to bring before the Council any application unless the candidate was prepared to sit for examination or unless he had already passed the examinations of another body of good standing. Further, it was decided that, as convenient, the articles should be amended in that sense. Actually between 1908 and 1912 (five years) twenty-seven persons only were elected to the Society without examination—and none in the succeeding forty-five years.

Bills in Parliament—Audit Clauses

A large number of private Bills were before Parliament from 1909 to 1914: they were mainly promoted by municipal corporations and by public utility companies. The interest of the Society was to see that the audit clauses provided for the appointment of incorporated accountants along with chartered accountants. In the earlier part of the period action here and there by the Society—by negotiation with promoters through the Society's solicitors and parliamentary agents—was necessary and was usually successful. Mostly the audit clauses were satisfactory to the Society and did not call for amendment.

Towards the end of the period the position became more involved. One of the newly formed bodies of accountants endeavoured, by requests to promoters or by petitions in Parliament, to secure that the clauses be in the form 'Such auditor or auditors shall be a member or members of an incorporated body or society of accountants', so that its members would be eligible for appointment. The Institute and the Society joined together to resist changes in the precedents and in the audit arrangements thereby enjoined. They did this not solely from monopolistic feeling or intention; but from a conviction, justified in the

result, that the proposed amendment offered no standard whatsoever, since 'an incorporated body of accountants' could consist of any few persons who chose to register themselves as a
company with some appellation of being a body of accountants. It would also cover all the recently formed bodies, the
standards of which fell below the standard of the Institute and
the Society; and this was ·not warranted. The issue was not
concerned with what particular accountants secured the appointments, but with the standard of audit approved by Parliament, in the absence of a specific statute governing the
constitution and functioning of the accountancy profession;
also it was desirable that there should be some guarantee of
the method of auditing the accounts, for the satisfaction of
ratepayers, consumers, shareholders, and managements.

In cases of public utility Bills, the main audit clause provided
for the appointment of members of the Institute or the Society:
there was also a clause relating to a special purposes fund, which
was applicable to meet such charges as 'a chartered or an incorporated accountant, being an auditor of the company or
appointed for the purpose by the Board of Trade, shall approve':
this clause had regard to the interests of consumers. In 1913,
after some opposition to the clause, the authorities of the House
decided that in the 'model Bill' the words 'a chartered or [an]
incorporated [accountant]' be deleted. These matters were considered on the Whitwell Gas Bill, 1914. The original Bill in both
audit and special purposes fund clauses followed precedents;
but owing to objections at the preliminary stage, the promoters,
desiring to avoid opposition, substituted the model Bill clause,
and in the audit clause provided for the auditor to be a member
of 'an incorporated body or society of accountants'. The Institute and Society lodged a petition in Parliament for the re-
insertion of the clauses as originally drafted. The Bill came before
a Committee of the House of Lords, which considered the
petition and heard counsel for the Institute and the Society and
counsel for the other side. The committee were given full information about the membership of the Institute and the Society
and their respective conditions of admission. Counsel pointed
out that four other bodies of accountants had been formed comparatively recently and that it was possible that other persons

would form themselves into further bodies by becoming registered under the Companies Act. Thus the suggested words 'member of an incorporated body or society of accountants' offered no safeguard or guarantee at all. Counsel said that there was not so much objection to the alteration in the special purposes fund clause, if still approved by the authorities of the House, as to the suggested alteration in the main audit clause, since in the special purposes fund clause the Board of Trade was the dominant authority in the matter. Arguments and facts were presented in support of restriction both in the main audit clause and in the special purposes fund clause. The Hon. George Colville gave evidence on behalf of the Institute, James Martin for the Society, and evidence was submitted by the other side. In the circumstances, and having regard to all the facts, the Committee of the House of Lords decided, not unexpectedly, that the amendment to the main audit clause would not be inserted. The special purposes fund clause was passed to correspond with the model Bill. The confidence which the Institute and Society enjoyed in Parliament was witnessed by the fact that in proceedings on private Bills at that time and after 1919, the hearing on the Whitwell Gas Bill was the only occasion on which evidence was required from them.

*   *   *

The question of the standard of auditors' qualifications was carried a step farther in the following month by the Local Legislation Committee of the House of Commons. The Ossett Corporation promoted a Bill in which the corporation sought power to appoint as auditors persons, being members of the Institute or of the Society, additional to the auditors appointed under the Municipal Corporations Act, 1882 (the elective and mayor's auditors). The clause followed a precedent in some thirty Acts of Parliament passed in the preceding twenty-five years. Another body presented a petition that the qualifications of the auditors in the clause should be omitted on the ground that the clause conferred a monopoly on members of the Institute and the Society. In the Local Legislation Committee counsel for the petitioners submitted that either the clause should leave the audit to an accountant approved by the Local

Government Board, or the qualifications for the appointment should be those laid down for the position of Assistant District Auditor under the Local Government Board (a whole-time official). No evidence was called, and counsel for the Institute and Society addressed the committee on the position and precedents, and on the question of the qualifications of the members of the bodies then before the committee. Ossett Corporation through counsel had submitted that they desired to have the clause without any alteration. The committee declined to grant the prayer of the petitioners, and in giving the decision of the committee, the chairman, Sir William Middlebrook, M.P., said:

> There must be some standard of some sort. . . . We all know the standing of the Institute of Chartered Accountants and the Society of Incorporated Accountants, and that those two societies are suitable societies to whom we can give the corporation power to entrust their audit. Knowing that, we have no evidence or suggestion of any other body or persons to whom such power might be given.

The committee indicated that they were not in a position to put an obligation on the Local Government Board that the audit might be entrusted to some accountants sanctioned by that department, as had been suggested. The chairman added that the committee would very carefully consider on their merits any other standards comparable with those put before them.

*   *   *

The decisions on the Whitwell Gas Bill and the Ossett Corporation Bill were reflected in other Bills. In the 1914 session of Parliament no less than fourteen private Bills were passed containing audit clauses in terms satisfactory to the Society. Whilst municipal corporations mainly favoured professional audit, there were a few instances of appointment of auditors of the District Audit Department, sometimes as a result of action by the Local Government Board arising from irregularities which had taken place, or possibly local pressure. There were those who felt there was some safeguard of the ratepayers in the power of 'surcharge' vested in the Local Government Board auditor, which was not vouchsafed to professional auditors. The Society watched these appointments with some regret; but unless there were local action to the contrary the Society could not take any effective action in specific cases. It relied on the general desirability of professional audit as recommended by the Crewe Committee of 1903 (p. 43).

Professional Education Discussed

Intense though parliamentary preoccupations were, they did not exclude the development of policy and of activities: but on the contrary tended to stimulate new ideas and purposes, on the part of the Council and elsewhere in the Society. The evolution of membership policy, already discussed (p. 81), was accompanied by a feeling on the part of some leading members that the means and substance of professional education merited attention by the Society. There was the essential purpose of providing for the accountancy profession young men of broad outlook and understanding as well as adequately equipped with professional skill: and there was the fact that candidates were left absolute freedom in the choice of methods of study for the requirements of the examinations. The London Students' Society and some students' societies in other parts of the country provided useful facilities for lectures (mainly arranged on an *ad hoc* basis) and discussions. In these ways students met one another and senior members, and were brought at an early stage of their professional careers into the life of the Society. Yet their studies were a responsibility for themselves, guided by their principals and aided by the helpful services of private coaching organizations. This individual responsibility and the practical training in the office had merits in character formation and self-reliance, and students were assisted by guidance from seniors and mutual discussion of problems at students' meetings. On the whole that procedure suited the circumstances of the profession and of students reasonably well and was practicable. It was reinforced by the importance rightly attached to practical training in the profession. Nevertheless, there seemed a gap through the lack of recognized and systematic facilities for study at a high level. The standard of qualification—to which proceedings in Parliament gave added significance—had to be maintained and raised: the strengthening of the critical faculties, creative power, and personality of the men qualifying in the Society claimed consideration.

In 1911 at the Dublin Conference, C. Hewetson Nelson, Liverpool, brought before the Society the question of professional education. In a closely reasoned address, backed by considerable research, he put the case for the higher education of accountant students in the Faculties of Commerce of the modern universities—of comparatively recent formation—with some modification in the period of training in the profession. The subject was presented with considerable imagination; but Hewetson Nelson emphasized that mere theoretical training without practical experience could never evolve the true accountant, who must be a man of affairs. Enlarging on the possibilities contemplated, he indicated developments taking place in the Universities of London, Birmingham, Manchester, Liverpool, Leeds, and elsewhere. Professor Lawrence R. Dicksee, M.Com., F.C.A., had been the first Professor of Accounting in Birmingham University (1902 to 1906), and after being a lecturer at the London School of Economics for several years he was elected Sir Ernest Cassel Professor of Accountancy and Business Organization, University of London (1919 to 1926). In Manchester there was an Advisory Committee to the Faculty of Commerce of which Harry Lloyd Price, F.S.A.A., was a member. Hewetson Nelson submitted that the Council should establish closer relations with the universities and request them to introduce such changes in the curricula of the Faculties of Economics or Commerce as would be appropriate for undergraduates who proposed to enter the accountancy profession: the relevant degrees would be accepted in lieu of the Society's intermediate examination and there might be some modification in the period of practical training. Some members of the conference received the proposals favourably; others found them very perplexing and maintained that there was adequate strength in the Society by the Council insisting on its present requirements for practical training and adhering to its own examinations. His mind receptive to ideas, James Martin gave a sympathetic but cautious response and promised that the proposals, in the first instance, should be brought before the Committee of the London Students' Society; also he thought of their bearing on the mission of the Society to offer facilities for obtaining a good accountancy qualification to men whose livelihood was in the profession. Moreover, he could not disregard the feeling of a good many students who awaited the examinations as some people contemplated the day of judgement!

The Committee of the London Students' Society considered the proposals for university training and prepared a report on them. Its general purport appealed to the Council, which set up a Special Committee, under the chairmanship of C. Hewetson Nelson, Vice-President. Recommendations were made and envisaged co-operation between the profession and the Faculties of Commerce in order to arrange a suitable university degree. This degree would confer exemption from the Society's intermediate examination, but without modification of the practical training prescribed by the Society's by-laws. Not out of harmony with opinion at that time, the Special Committee, in making its recommendations, was possibly thinking of evening studies—but not exclusively. Some regrouping of subjects for the final examination and the addition of economics and statistics were suggested. The report was accepted by the Council, and instructions were given to the committees concerned to prepare the necessary changes in the examination arrangements and, as convenient, to open negotiations with the universities. Unfortunately, owing to the outbreak of war in 1914, the whole question was shelved.

The proposals in substance were similar to those which formed the Universities Scheme of 1944, although it is right to say that the discussion of the 1944 scheme started of its own motion and was not consciously influenced by the proposals made some thirty years earlier. But acknowledgement should be made to those who in 1914 intensified, if they did not altogether initiate, thought and interest in the profession on the question of professional training, education, and studies, which later became perennial throughout the profession. Looking back, no doubt in the light of much subsequent experience, people today may well think that the enthusiasts of 1914 had unconsciously over-estimated the probable response among candidates and principals to their proposals. Nor perhaps had they quite appreciated that the Faculties of Commerce were comparatively new institutions and that the proposals would have to satisfy critical university opinion, particularly that they were sufficiently academic in purpose: the universities were hesitant towards what might have appeared to them as 'vocational' education.

*   .   *   *

Two incidents which had a permanent effect on professional education should be mentioned. In 1911 a voluminous report was made by the Consultative Committee of the Board of Education, to which the Society had given information. The situation of an excessive number of examining bodies, each acting independently and somewhat in competition, indeed called for rationalization. In 1917 the Board announced a scheme for examinations in secondary schools inspected by the Board, the examinations to be conducted by the universities.

The School Certificate was established, the examination for which called for a pass or failure in the whole test based on a group of subjects. There was also to be a second and higher examination for more advanced pupils. The scheme was a great and welcome reform; and at the end of 1918 the Board advised that it had approved School and Higher Certificates to be awarded by seven universities. Some purely external examinations continued to be available. In Scotland and Ireland similar changes were made, although the systems and descriptions of the certificates were different. From 1917 there was this established system of examinations; yet professional bodies continued to find the need for a preliminary (educational) examination conducted by themselves.

A resolution from the Incorporated Association of Headmasters (secondary schools) was forwarded to professional bodies urging that the standard for preliminary examinations and exemption therefrom, on the basis of the official school certificates, should be passes in English, arithmetic, mathematics, one language, and one other subject. The Society gladly accepted the recommendation, which, with perhaps some variations in emphasis, informed its policy for the preliminary examination from then onwards.

A scheme of constitution for the City of London College—

a unique City institution mainly devoted to education for commerce—comprised a provision for nomination of governors by various interests, which included a nomination by the Society. James Martin was the first representative of the Society, and the last two were Mr. Walter Holman and Mr. E. Cassleton Elliott, who was chairman of the governing body: a former chairman was Lord Plender. The City of London College has always had a department of accountancy studies which has functioned with much usefulness.

The Bankruptcy Act, 1913

In addition to the legislation of 1909 to 1914 already reviewed, there were other Acts and Government action which received the attention of the Society.

The Bankruptcy and Deeds of Arrangement Act, 1913, comprised several amendments which had received the support of the Society, mainly in conjunction with action by the London Chamber of Commerce. Penalties were imposed upon a bankrupt if he had failed to keep proper books of account for two years previously *and* if he had on a former occasion been adjudged bankrupt or had entered into a private arrangement with creditors. While welcoming the provision, some people saw no reason why the penalty should be limited to a second insolvency only; but in Committee of the Lords, the Government declined an amendment extending the provision to a first bankruptcy. In the Commons, the Board of Trade, after representations from the Chambers of Commerce, greatly modified onerous penalties in the Bill upon a trustee acting under a void deed of arrangement, provided his action was confined to taking such steps as were necessary to protect the estate. Generally the position of a trustee under a deed of arrangement was strengthened by an obligation to give security, which was a check upon undesirable persons being appointed trustees; and by the time to be allowed for obtaining assents of a majority in number and value of creditors and for filing with the registrar a declaration of the assents thus given. The Act of 1913 was followed by the Acts of 1914 which have remained in force ever since, save for the period of the Second World War, when special legislation was passed.

Speaking in Manchester in 1913, William Eaves, F.S.A.A., drew attention to the considerable decrease in bankruptcies and deeds of arrangement. In 1904 (a high-water mark), failures under both headings numbered 8,631 with liabilities of some £12,000,000 and assets £5,800,000, whereas in 1912 the corresponding figures were 6,351, liabilities £8,000,000, assets £3,500,000. This decrease was mainly attributable to the prosperity of the country as well as to the tendency of creditors to extend the practice of informal insolvencies and to the conversion of private firms into limited companies. The figures were not only a statistical record but indicated a considerable change in the practice of the profession. Insolvency business declined, auditing increased in importance and responsibility, direct taxation became more complicated and onerous; also an increasing share of the country's manufacturing and trading was carried on by private limited companies, which called for the professional advice both of accountants and of solicitors.

*   *   *

The increase in trading by co-operative societies had given new emphasis to the question of audit. By the Industrial and Provident Societies Act, 1913, the accounts of every registered society were required to be audited by public auditors appointed by the Treasury under the 1893 Act, instead of two or more persons as provided in the rules of such societies. A consequence was some tightening of the regulations for appointments as public auditors.

The great army reforms instituted by R. B. Haldane, K.C., M.P., Secretary of State for War in the Asquith administration, included the formation of the Territorial Army and of County Territorial Force Associations: the audit of the Associations was controlled by a Joint Committe consisting of five members of the Institute and three of the Society.

*   *   *

In January 1913 William Strachan relinquished the appointment of Assistant Secretary and the Council recorded in the minutes its great appreciation of his valuable services to the Society. In accepting the resolution, William Strachan assured the Council of his continuing interest in the Society, which assuredly was much more than a formal response. He continued to co-operate with James Martin in the editorship of the *Incorporated Accountants' Journal*. Mr. A. A. Garrett, who had been on the Society's staff since 1909, was appointed Assistant Secretary and continued his work until 1915: given leave of absence, he received a commission as Assistant Paymaster, Royal Naval Reserve, and served, inclusive of active service in the war, for fifteen years, until his name was placed on the retired list with the rank of (now) Commander (S), R.N.R. (The scheme for commissions as Assistant Paymasters, R.N.R., had been established by the Admiralty in 1904, and had been forwarded to the Bank of England, the Institute, and the Society with a view to applications from young men qualified for appointment.)

1914–1918[1]

V. THE FIRST WORLD WAR

The Outbreak of War and its Immediate Consequences

THE aggressive and expansionist ambitions of Germany, theatrically exhibited by Kaiser William II, were accentuated by the German Naval Law of 1898: this law resulted in menacing additions to the German Navy: there was also great expansion of the German Army. Apprehension had already brought forth the Franco-Russian Alliance (1893): the Anglo-French Entente, fostered by Edward VII, was completed in 1904 and stood *vis-à-vis* the Triple Alliance of Germany, Austro-Hungary, and Italy (from which afterwards Italy broke away). A series of European crises, Balkan wars, and incidents in North Africa caused mounting tension. A tragic climax was reached by the assassination at Sarajevo, Serbia, on 28 June 1914, of the heir to the Austrian throne. In consequence there followed peremptory demands and exchanges between the Foreign Offices and Chancelleries of Europe, the mobilization of Germany and Russia, and an attack on Serbia. The strenuous efforts of Sir Edward Grey, M.P., Foreign Secretary, to save the peace and call a conference; and finally the personal communications sent by King George V to Prince Henry of Prussia and to the Czar of Russia unhappily failed to avert the menace which threatened Europe. France, troubled politically and anxious for her safety, sought assurance of help from the British Government. Germany and Austro-Hungary declared war on France and Russia. At first uncertain, the attitude of the United Kingdom was finally determined by the German

[1] In respect of parts of this chapter, acknowledgement is made of references in *The Annual Register*, *The Memoirs of David Lloyd George*, Carter and Mears's *History of Britain*, and C. R. M. F. Crutwell's *History of the Great War 1914–1918*.

invasion of Belgium, contrary to treaty obligations: this, followed by the dispatch of an ultimatum to Germany, entirely
unheeded, caused the formal declaration of war on Germany
by His Majesty's Government.

Inured by crisis succeeding crisis in the previous decade and
diverted by intense political questions and differences, the
British public had probably failed to be conscious of the dramatic and dangerous situation which by the Sarajevo assassination
had all too rapidly developed. Who, in the middle of June 1914,
would have contemplated war? And yet strangely when the
situation became known, crowds, patriotically stirred, cheered
and sang in Whitehall and outside Buckingham Palace on
Sunday and Monday, 2 and 3 August. But their exuberance was
reflected only by oppressive gloom in the Foreign Office, where
Sir Edward Grey remarked: 'The lamps are going out all
over Europe; we shall not see them lit again in our lifetime.'

*   *   *

And in the City there was grave anxiety and bewilderment
as the delicate machinery of finance and international trade,
almost precipitately, ceased to function. The Government acted
with promptitude and judgement, and its decisions undoubtedly averted a financial panic—possibly a run on the banks. The
normal bank holiday of Monday, 3 August 1914, was extended
by three days; to discourage the hoarding of gold (available as
sovereigns and half-sovereigns then in free circulation) notes of
£1 and 10s. denominations were issued and postal orders were
made legal tender; a moratorium covering bills of exchange
was immediately declared by royal proclamation; on 3 August,
the Postponement of Payments Act was rushed through Parliament and confirmed the royal proclamation: the Act gave
power to the Crown to postpone payments of bills of exchange
and of other obligations in pursuance of contracts, subject to
such conditions as might be specified. The Stock Exchange
(on which in July there had been large sales by continental
holders, and a few not unexpected failures) was closed on
1 August to avoid heavy sales of securities, particularly sales
on enemy account; meantime, minimum quotations were fixed
for trustee securities. It was not reopened until January 1915,

and transactions were subjected to stringent measures of control. On 30 July the bank rate had been raised from 3 to 4 per cent., on 31st to 8 per cent., and on 1 August to 10 per cent.: but on 7 August when the banks reopened, it was reduced to 6 per cent. Parliament voted the Government a credit of £100 million to carry on the war. To keep shipping moving, the Government offered to insure ships carrying food supplies at special rates—a risk later undertaken by Lloyd's and companies. A first war loan of £350 million—3½ per cent. at 95—was raised when David Lloyd George was Chancellor of the Exchequer.

In the first week of war there was a strange and ominous atmosphere in the City: instead of the normal bustle of people going about their business and of the usual traffic, the 'square mile' seemed listless and forlorn. This, however, was a passing phase as, due to the immediate and subsequent steps taken by the Government, the City gradually began to function again—but on a war-time basis. Simultaneously, elsewhere there was great activity with mobilization as reservists and Territorial soldiers reported to their units; Mr. (later) Sir Winston Churchill, was First Lord of the Admirality, and the Fleet was already at sea; that splendid expeditionary force under Sir John French was successfully transported to France; it was soon to take part in the historic Battle of the Marne which saved Paris from the rapidly advancing German Army.

Shortly after the outbreak of hostilities, Field-Marshal Lord Kitchener became Secretary of State for War and immediately launched an immense recruiting campaign to obtain voluntary enlistment in Kitchener's army; for conscription had not then been adopted, nor was it likely to have obtained public support. Early enthusiastic recruits suffered from lack of accommodation and equipment, but the position improved as time went on: even the most staid among them quickly acquired the customs and jargon of army life as well as its fine traditions of discipline and courage.

★   ★   ★

What was the effect of this unprecedented situation upon the Society and its members? First, there were the younger men among members, articled clerks and examination candidates who were called up as Territorials or early responded to Lord

Kitchener's call. Concern for their future did not deflect them from their patriotic action; correspondingly both the Society and employers were anxious to mitigate in the future, as far as practicable, the abrupt disruption of the careers and immediate prospects of these men—and to give some early assurance of the determination to meet these proper obligations. Practising accountants were immediately and increasingly affected by staff joining His Majesty's forces, and were undoubtedly concerned at the effect of the war upon the affairs of their clients and indirectly upon their practices. At the same time they accepted many new responsibilities in the application of emergency legislation and regulations to business affairs: and throughout the war they adapted themselves and their organizations to the inevitable attenuation of staff and to the training of such substitute staff as could be found. Secondly, the Council was firmly determined that the organization of the Society should be utilized in every way possible to support the Government in the endeavour to bring the war to a successful conclusion. This object was to be accomplished, not by an emotional if well-meant abandonment of much of its work, but by wise judgement as to what should be done and what should be dropped. The Society had to be in a position to respond to what might be requested, either under general arrangements and regulations or by specific calls upon it by Government departments. If immediate requirements were uppermost, the Council had also to think of its eventual obligations—particularly to members and examination candidates on active service—and of the consequent need for maintaining as far as possible the structure of the Society's organization. A third important function fell on the Council, and especially on the Secretary, to keep members informed of the changing situation as it affected the personnel of the profession; and, as touching professional practice, of emergency legislation, royal proclamations, changes in taxation, memoranda and statutory rules issued by Government departments and the Bank of England. The *Incorporated Accountants' Journal* and *The Accountant* served a singularly useful purpose by making this information available to members.

At the same time—and for many years to come—members of the profession, especially those in practice, were dealing with a variety of new problems, particularly arising from emergency legislation and statutory and other Government regulations. The Postponement of Payments Act, 1914, and royal proclamations thereunder (in effect the moratorium), supplemented by the Bills of Exchange Act, 1914, were applicable to complicated circumstances: an invaluable address on this topical question was given to the Liverpool members by A. J. Ashton, K.C., and was published for more general information. The Government, however, were determined to bring the moratorium to an end as soon as possible. Relief was given in several ways. The breakdown in the foreign exchanges was mitigated by the Bank of England agreeing to provide funds to enable acceptors to pay approved pre-moratorium bills. The Courts (Emergency Powers) Act, 1914, afforded protection to debtors who could prove that their position had arisen from war circumstances; the Act gave greater stability than the moratorium. To encourage trading—especially export business and the import of cargoes of grain and produce—advances under Treasury authority were made to traders against debts due from abroad by foreigners. On 4 December 1914 the moratorium was finally determined.

The world-wide connexions of the United Kingdom called for strict measures of control to frustrate and to prevent the enemy deriving advantages by subterfuges in international trade and finance and from companies in the United Kingdom under the control of enemy aliens. Wide powers were given to the Government, mainly through the Board of Trade, by the Trading with the Enemy Act, 1914, and subsequent similar measures. The Board of Trade was enabled to appoint representatives to investigate the affairs of companies the activities of which gave proper ground for suspicion: and the Board could apply to the High Court for the appointment of controllers of enemy concerns in the United Kingdom. These investigations were frequently made by practising accountants nominated by the Board of Trade, who were likewise appointed controllers. Notably there were three large German banks in London, of which Sir William Plender was controller—a task of great complexity and responsibility, which did not escape some ill-informed press criticism; he made specific replies with much force and he was stoutly defended by the *Incorporated*

Accountants' Journal. A committee appointed by the Government found the allegations totally unjustified.

The spate of emergency legislation, its complications and uncertainties were such that a Court of Appeal composed of seven members, presided over by the Lord Chief Justice, was specially constituted to hear appeals on questions of law which had arisen through the outbreak of war.

*   *   *

A special meeting of the Council was held in October 1914 to deal with immediate matters, at which messages of good wishes were sent to Captain Charles H. Wilson and Major G. A. Evans, members of the Council serving with His Majesty's forces. The Examination and Membership Committee had already studied in some detail the needs of articled clerks and by-law candidates on active service at that time or in the near future, and brought up a report. The Council resolved that:

1. As regards articled clerks, the Council would recognize the period of service during the war as service under articles: but, as articles were a matter of contract between employer and clerk, it should be left to the employer and clerk to arrange voluntarily for any further time considered necessary to complete the clerk's professional training.

2. In dealing with by-law candidates, the Examination Committee be given discretion to consider each case on its merits, regard being had to the training specified in the special by-laws, provided that no candidate should be prejudiced by reason of service with His Majesty's forces during the war.

3. To avoid any lowering of standard, all candidates must pass the prescribed examinations, and no relaxation could be made by reason of candidates having been on active service.

It was also decided to continue to conduct the examinations half-yearly.

It may seem that in relation to the sincere spirit of helpfulness which actuated the Council, the assurance afforded by the terms of these resolutions was somewhat general, although there was acceptance of the principle that war service would be integrated with requirements of professional experience: this was inevitable in the situation as it was at that time. Buoyed up by hope, though not by complacency, the public mind—in spite of Lord

Kitchener's warning of a long struggle—could not at that time envisage the duration of the war, its continuous and persistent call on the active personnel of the nation, or its grim and heavy toll of casualties. Moreover, the individual circumstances of candidates varied considerably and it was hardly possible to reduce war-time relaxations to a code of regulations: the Council had to think not only how the Society could help its young men, but of the need—in the interests of the men themselves—to maintain its standard. The framework thus devised gave guidance to all concerned: towards, and at, the end of the war other modifications were introduced, to establish minima for professional service and examinations, whether by specific regulation or administrative process.

War Measures Affecting the Profession

The intensification of the war effort at home directed by the Government and Parliament necessarily involved new and growing burdens on the industrial, financial, and commercial activities of the nation, with corresponding responsibilities on all organizations and on the professions—not least on the accountancy profession.

In its desire to support the war effort, the Council caused communications to be addressed to the Admiralty and War Office and, later, to the Ministry of Munitions, offering to place the Society's organization at the disposal of the departments concerned.

Some reference must be made to specific legislation, which was of immense importance to the accountancy profession, and to Regulations under the Defence of the Realm Acts (which became known as D.O.R.A.).

Prohibition of trading with the enemy was a vital factor in defence and in the conservation of resources for the war. It was the subject of royal proclamations and then of the Trading with the Enemy Act of September 1914, supplemented by four further Acts up to August 1918. The Acts covered a variety of transactions and imposed essential obligations upon traders, companies, financial institutions, and the Stock Exchange. Considerable machinery was set up to deal with the dangers which existed, and included the appointment of a Custodian of

Enemy Property, a definition of his powers and duties, and of the duties of others concerned with dividends, trusteeships, enemy property, debts, and shares. There was much difficulty in applying and understanding all the requirements, and clients sought advice from solicitors and accountants.

Taxation soon became both heavy and complicated. The pre-war Budget of 1914 had proposed a rate of income tax of 1s. 4d. amended to 1s. 3d. by the Finance Act of that year. After the outbreak of war the tax was doubled for the last four months of the fiscal year 1914-15, giving a substantive rate of 1s. 8d.: there were special provisions for reduction in assessments of businesses whose profits had been severely hit by circumstances which it could be proved arose from the onset of war. Supertax was likewise doubled. The 2s. 6d. rate of income tax, repeated by the first Finance Act of 1915, was not to last very long, for by the Finance (No. 2) Act, 1915, the rate was raised to 3s. 6d.; in later war years it became 5s. and finally 6s. The exemption limit was reduced from £160 to £130 per annum and maximum abatement from £160 to £120; there was graduation in the rates applicable to earned income and to unearned income: the averaging of salaries over three years was dropped, and the basis for schedule B (farmers) became one year's rent instead of one-third: supertax was further increased.

But two new taxes were introduced as war measures and were based on an entirely new principle, namely a tax on excess profits. The earlier of the two taxes was the munitions levy, applicable to Government-controlled establishments—under-takings producing munitions of war. More general, however, was the excess profits duty, imposed by the Finance (No. 2) Act, 1915. This war-profits tax was designed to bring into the Exchequer (at first) 50 per cent. of exceptional profits, derived from the manufacture of war supplies or from trading and business gains above the normal, whether they were directly attributable to the war or not: agriculture, employment, and the professions were excluded. The rate was raised subse-quently to 60 per cent. and then to 80 per cent.: in 1916 the munitions levy was merged into the excess profits duty. The Act prescribed the method of calculating standard profits or that the standard could be a statutory percentage on capital employed; 6 per cent. for companies, 7 per cent. for other businesses. To mitigate anomalies as far as possible, the statute directed that a Board of Referees be appointed by the Treasury, which became a permanent organ in the administration of taxation. Upon application and consideration, the Commissioners of Inland Revenue could refer the circumstances of cases or of groups of trades to that Board. The Board could increase statutory percentages or vary the statutory standard, and could deal with technical matters such as depreciation, wear and tear, and exceptional capital requirements. Announcements were made from time to time of decisions to increase statutory percentages. It is obvious that in the application of the Act and regulations thereunder, there was necessarily a great deal of work and difficulty in preparing accounts for excess profits duty and of negotiation in agreeing assessments with the Inland Revenue. Among the members of the Board of Referees, over which a K.C. presided, were chartered and incorporated accountants; and the first two members of the Society appointed by the Chancellor of the Exchequer (Reginald McKenna, M.P.) were C. Hewetson Nelson, Liverpool, and W. T. Walton, West Hartlepool.

Eventually it became an open secret that the construction of the excess profits duty was largely the work of Josiah Charles Stamp, D.Sc. (Econ.), then an Assistant Secretary of the Board of Inland Revenue. Hastily devised though it was, and unavoidably an improvisation, as Stamp thought, it served the broad purpose for which it was intended, in spite of difficulties and anomalies. As the professional journals observed, however, if the excess profits in part arose from stock values inflated by war demand, it was one thing to agree an excess profits duty computation, it was quite another to be sure that the concern had the wherewithal to pay the duty—or would have it after the war when war materials might be at a discount. Early in 1917 Stamp's work on *British Incomes and Property* was the subject of a review in the Society's *Journal*. This review seems to be the first reference in the Society's records to this brilliant man, with whom members of the Council had recently been brought into contact through having business with the Board of Referees.

Munitions

The first year of the war brought the beginning of the long and grievous period of trench warfare, and a lamentable lack of shells and other munitions was disclosed. A great drive was made by the Government by the setting up of a Ministry of Munitions in 1915 under David Lloyd George, M.P., with wide powers. Quite early 'The Munitions (Limitation of Profits) Rules' were issued, governing the ascertainment of divisible profits in controlled establishments and the determination of profits to be retained by the controlled owner and the excess—the munitions levy—to be payable to the Exchequer. The rules provided for accounts audited by 'a chartered or incorporated accountant or an accountant approved in any particular case by the Board of Trade'; and for accounts and statements to be subject to examination by an accountant nominated by the Minister. The extension of manufacturing capacity, large output, and rapid production had to be conjoined with economy in manufacture, experiment, and limitation of profits in this paramount effort of organization and improvisation. In addition to the Ministry of Munitions, there were the contract departments of the Admiralty and War Office, similarly engaged.

Closely linked with the limitation of profits was the pricing of contracts; and quickly the question of costing came to the front in the great munitions effort. For one thing the limitation of profits on individual contracts was as necessary as the more general statutory limitation through the surrender of excess profits: and for another, information as to the costs of the vast variety of munitions, guns, vehicles, tanks, ships, and eventually aeroplanes, was essential for orderly administration and programmes of commitments, materials, and labour. To achieve these purposes the Ministers concerned appointed as heads of, or advisers to, accounts, finance, and costing divisions, partners in practising firms of accountants; and staff was found from among qualified accountants and senior clerks over a certain age whose military service had been postponed. There were also advisory committees of accountants invited by Ministers to give their assistance. Among others, James Martin was so appointed for a period as Director of Contract Costing at the Ministry of Munitions, whilst W. G. Rayner, past President of the Society, was a member of one of the Advisory Committees.

This work continued for a long time and there was a considerable amount of winding-up required at the end of the war, when some of those who were normally engaged in the profession were drafted to the departments or were given temporary—in some cases permanent—appointments to find or adjust the basis for settlement of many war contracts. A member of the Society was the (permanent) head of the Professional Accountancy Division of the Admiralty. The situation also engaged the attention of many practising members who had clients, engaged in war production, whose costings were required by the authorities. It is perhaps a far cry from the costing of 1915–18 to the highly evolved technique of costing and budgetary control of 1960. Certainly there were people with experience in costing: yet on the whole the evolution of methods during the First World War was by the application of basic accounting principles in organizing data and systems and in eliciting the cost of war production. Undoubtedly the war quickened interest in this branch of professional work, yet its later possibilities were not then adequately recognized.

Accountancy of National Importance

The shock of war in 1914 was accompanied by a general fear of social distress and unemployment, and patriotic feelings quickened the charitable impulses of the nation. Existing charitable funds were extended and others organized, notably the Prince of Wales Fund, an appeal for which was made to the whole country. The departure of men for the front and others leaving civilian employment to join His Majesty's forces created some hardship among their families, frequently mitigated by goodwill allowances from employers: and the impact of the war on the economic life of the country was at first severe, giving rise to some pockets of unemployment. But although early fears of widespread social distress became resolved, there was ample room for helpful organized efforts in many directions.

The Society and its members became particularly interested in contributing to these efforts. New responsibilities fell upon the Incorporated Accountants' Benevolent Fund; and, upon the formation of the Professional Classes War Relief Council, the Society was invited to nominate a representative on the Council; he was Arthur E. Woodington, London, then Vice-President. In co-operation with professional benevolent funds and other organizations, the P.C.W.R.C. gave much help to families, widows, and children throughout the war. Later it became a permanent organization under the title Professional Classes' Aid Council, with which the Society has continued to identify itself. For many years it received valued advice from the Hon. George Colville, Secretary of the Institute of Chartered Accountants: Lady Cynthia Colville, G.C.V.O., is President at the present time. Outstanding among many voluntary war efforts—although closely linked with the Government and the Services—was the Joint War Organization of the British Red Cross and St. John; the chairman was the Hon. Arthur Stanley, C.B., M.V.O., M.P., brother of the Earl of Derby. Its activities included the control and organization of voluntary war hospitals, for which many large houses in the country were lent, often with the personal services of the lady of the house and her friends. Through the agency of the British Red Cross and St. John the Society was able to send textbooks to students who had become prisoners of war. Approached by C. Hewetson Nelson, President of the Society, the Hon. Arthur Stanley gladly accepted a suggestion that the Society should nominate, when requested, incorporated accountants to be the honorary auditors of these hospitals. Nominations were also made by other bodies. These services were rendered all over the country and were gracefully recognized by the election of those appointed as honorary life members of the British Red Cross Society. Similar services were given voluntarily to War Savings Associations and to other war organizations. By the War Charities Act, 1916, the Charity Commission exercised control and made rules, among which was the obligation of each registered war charity to render audited accounts once in every twelve months, or at any time upon request. The opportunity for abuse had not been overlooked.

With the intensification of recruiting and of the manufacture of munitions and the extension of the administrative machine of Government, manpower and its deployment, instead of unemployment, became a major question of Government policy: this had implications throughout the country's activities at home.

★   ★   ★

In 1916 Lord Kitchener's army had reached seventy divisions —a remarkable achievement of voluntary recruiting, aided in its later stages by the influence and personality of Lord Derby through the Derby attestation scheme. There had also been a poster campaign. Viewed in retrospect some of the posters may seem to have been a little ridiculous; but ridiculous or not, they were undoubtedly effective. By December 1916 upwards of one thousand members, articled clerks, and by-law candidates of the Society were serving with the forces.

Yet the country was in a chastened but determined mood. The stalemate of trench warfare on the western front, the evacuation of Gallipoli, and the heavy losses at Ypres and Neuve Chapelle—to be followed later by the even more disastrous losses on the Somme (1916) and Passchendaele (1917) (still the subject of military controversy)—had resulted, and continued to result, in calls for more and more men, guns, and munitions. The outcome of the great naval action at Jutland (1916) was presented to the public in—as it seemed—unnecessarily stark terms: for if the German High Seas Fleet escaped destruction and the British Grand Fleet suffered considerable losses in ships and men, the strategic result was that the German Fleet seldom put to sea again, except to surrender at Scapa Flow after the end of the war. The tactics of Sir John Jellicoe (Commander-in-Chief) were strongly defended in the light of the fact, as it was truly said, that he was the only man who could have lost the war for the allies in an afternoon. Submarine warfare, later intensified and indiscriminate, caused heavy losses of shipping, and the food situation became serious. To add to the general strain, there was the Easter rebellion in Ireland with its aftermath of bitterness. A Coalition Government had been formed under the Rt. Hon. H. H. Asquith in 1915, followed in 1916 by political reconstruction of the Government when the Rt. Hon.

D. Lloyd George became Prime Minister, not without some feeling and repercussion.

Against a rather grim background of military and political events, Parliament in 1916 passed two Military Service Acts, imposing conscription upon a country mainly although not entirely convinced on the subject: but on practical grounds and in the circumstances of the time, conscription was unquestionably necessary, and came to be accepted. The Council of the Society had previously passed a resolution assuring the Government of the Society's determination to support by every means the measures deemed necessary by Parliament to bring the war to a successful conclusion. A conference at the Home Office had discussed steps to replace men in clerical and commercial employment withdrawn to serve with the forces. As a result of this conference, and in other ways, information was given to the authorities of the needs of the profession, and representations were made for the retention by firms of some proportion of experienced and qualified assistants, but only under pressing necessity or serious hardship. To give rationality to the scheme of conscription, the Acts authorized rules under which provision was made for tribunals to consider requests for postponement or exemption from military service; advisory committees in different parts of the country consulted representatives of trades and professions; and applicants and employers and the local military representative were heard by the tribunals. The authorities issued a 'list of certified occupations': some pride was taken in the profession through the inclusion in the list of chartered accountants and incorporated accountants, by reason of their work being declared 'of national importance'. This did not give them automatic exemption from military service; but in cases of married men over 31 and single men over 41 so qualified, the onus of proof before tribunals that their current work was not required in the national interests was upon the military representative. For some rather obscure reasons the inclusion of chartered and incorporated accountants attracted criticism and they were omitted from the second revised list; any necessary relaxation was effected under the general powers of tribunals. However, the situation developed, and when a third revised list was published (1917) the accountancy profession was again included; but the conditions for exemption were more onerous. Heavy casualties and the German onslaught in March 1918 were the cause of two Military Service Acts, the second of which raised the age limit for conscription to 51. These Acts, however, do not seem to have altered the previous (1917) position of those in the accountancy profession, as it was well understood that the Inland Revenue and Government departments were dependent on their work. Further, the Government departments were requisitioning the services of qualified members of the profession to deal with the accumulating work of cost investigation, the audit of factory accounts, and examination of contractors' books. The President of the Society appealed to members to offer their services to the Government—a responsibility which arose from their work being of national importance.

* * *

Much illumination on the importance of accounting and costing was given by the first report[1] early in 1918 of the Select Committee on National Expenditure upon the Ministry of Munitions; this, being an independent and authoritative report on the functions of accountancy, was of absorbing interest to the profession. There had been press allegations of waste and extravagance, arising from facts revealed by cost investigations. But there was much risk of doing less than justice to a number of able officials hastily got together, who, confronted with national danger, had to organize the production of the largest supply of munitions possible at great speed, whatever the cost. It was no wonder that anomalies arose. The Select Committee did, however, call for a greater degree of co-operation between the contract, supply, and finance divisions of the Ministry. Expressing themselves as impressed by the excellent work of officers who reorganized the accounts of the Ministry, the members of the Select Committee said:

The importance of this accounting work cannot be overestimated; it is not merely essential that the accounts should be on a proper basis for the purpose of accurate payment and prevention of waste. It is also important from an administrative point of view that the accounts and balance sheets of the Ministry should be upon a perfect footing.

[1] *House of Commons Paper 23, 1918.*

The report comprised a critical review of 'costs' and 'costing' and particularly of the relation between the technical costing sections and the accountants' cost investigation sections. The committee came down heavily on the *bête noire* 'cost plus', but drew favourable attention to the work of the Joint Committee of Accountants of the War Office, Admiralty, and Ministry in settling in principle the treatment of wages and oncost. Complications arose from capital expenditure on new plant, rate of profit on capital employed, and turnover. It was necessary that the rate of profit in different industries should be settled as early as possible. One example quoted by the committee indicated that a saving of £3,000,000 in the supply of cordite had been effected as a result of cost investigations. Having called attention to the inadequate staff of qualified accountants for the work, the committee, at a time when the army was clamouring for more men, recommended that the War Office should order the release of qualified accountants from the army for service in the Ministry.

*   *   *

At the annual meeting of the Society in the following May, the speech of the President (Arthur E. Woodington, London) and the discussion indicated that, in spite of private sorrows and public anxiety, these circumstances had made a great impression in the Society. Anticipating changes in commerce, finance, and economics, the President foreshadowed the necessity of strengthening the Society's constitution and recasting the examination syllabus in order that the evolving methods of accounting and costing should be part of the equipment of incorporated accountants in the future. Lieut.-Col. James Grimwood, D.S.O., F.S.A.A., then on active service, addressed the meeting with force and humour. He knew something of the inside of the War Office and warned incorporated accountants to be circumspect in discussing accountancy problems with civil servants. 'The last way to treat a Government servant', he said humorously, 'was to tell him that he knew nothing about accounts. A Government servant was an artist at defence.'

Somewhere a reminder appeared of Strachan's comments of sixteen years earlier. Had they been taken to heart? 'Generally speaking—there are of course notable exceptions—it is an un-doubted fact that there is in this country a great need of the fuller appreciation of the advantages of cost accounts.' The Select Committee's first report was indeed significant, and not least in regard to the future development of accounting. The question of costing recalls two comparatively early works on the subject: one by Garcke and Fells, *Factory Accounts* (J. M. Fells, C.B.E., F.S.A.A.), 1st edition, 1887, and the other by William Strachan, F.S.A.A., *Cost Accounts*, 1st edition, 1902.

*   *   *

A few events outside the immediate urgency of the war call for notice. An Act for the Registration of Accountants in Southern Rhodesia was passed in 1917 and followed closely the lines of the Transvaal Accountants Ordinance of 1904.

The intensive steps which had been taken to counter trading with the enemy gave rise to reflections upon the employment of foreign capital in British industries and upon control by aliens. Consideration was given to this and certain other details of company law by a Departmental Committee under Lord Wrenbury. Appointed in February 1918, the committee issued its report as early as the following August. The members in-cluded Sir William Plender, F.C.A., James Martin, F.S.A.A., A. W. Tait, C.A., and G. W. Currie, M.P., C.A. The com-mittee declined to be over-influenced by the emotions of that time and, looking ahead, emphasized the importance of main-taining London as the financial centre of the world. Generally the report was against severely restrictive measures on aliens and foreign capital in companies, but favoured disclosure of the nationality of alien directors and shareholders and alien owner-ship, and some control in the case of 'key industries': the com-mittee drew attention to practical difficulties in securing full disclosure. Three topics were of particular interest to the pro-fession. The committee did not feel justified in opening such a large question whether auditors should have some, and what, professional qualifications, nor was a suggested omission of 'as shown by the books of the company' from the auditor's report accepted. Curious as it may seem today, the committee could not recommend that a profit and loss account be required: to insist upon it would have given individuals as competitors in trade with companies an unfair advantage. Useful as the report was, it did not lead to a new Companies Act. At that time there were some 66,000 companies on the register, of which no less than 50,000 were private companies. The private company was a creation of the Act of 1908 and it had been on trial for about ten years. The committee expressed the opinion that it had justified its existence and should be left undisturbed.

The impetus given to costing during the war, and its relationship to progress in industry, led to the formation in 1919 of the Institute of Cost and Works Accountants as a specialized body which became well established with growing membership and organization.

Progress of the profession in India had been stimulated by the Indian Companies Act, 1913, and the rules thereunder, prescribing the qualifications of auditors. A number of incorporated accountants practised in India and they were able to take articled clerks, who towards the end of their articled period came to the United Kingdom for study and to take their examinations. In this way the Society contributed to the development of the profession in India, where steps were taken by the Government of India towards establishing an Indian diploma in accountancy.

In 1917, on the entry of the United States of America as a belligerent in the war, the following messages were exchanged with the American Institute of Accountants:

From the Society to the American Institute:
Society of Incorporated Accountants and Auditors send greetings to their brethren in war as well as in peace.

From the American Institute to the Society:
American Institute cordially reciprocates. Accountants here having watched with admiration splendid efforts of their British brethren rejoice in opportunity to co-operate.

The Armistice, 1918

As the war continued, increasing numbers of the personnel of the Society, particularly among the younger men, joined the forces. Lists of those serving were regularly published, and by

1918 about 1,300 members, articled clerks, and by-law candidates were in His Majesty's forces. At general meetings the President referred to those who had distinguished themselves in the field and had the melancholy duty to pay the Society's tribute of respect to the fallen.

A new feature in the profession was the employment of a number of women as audit and accountancy clerks: they took the place of men withdrawn and earned the gratitude of employers. It was said that they became inured to the lingua franca of Smithfield and Billingsgate when on audit work in the markets! In fact, throughout the country's activities and in the theatres of war women had distinguished themselves by their adaptability and enthusiastic work on tasks hitherto undertaken almost exclusively by men. The work of women and the valour of the young men of the country were recognized in Parliament by the passing of the Representation of the People Act, 1918, by which the vote was given to all men of 21 years of age and upwards and to women of 30 and upwards. The President of the Society had already on more than one occasion declared the Society's intention to open its doors to women, and preparations for the necessary amendment of its constitution commenced in the summer of 1918.

Preliminary consideration was given to arrangements for special lectures and courses of instruction to members and students after their return from the forces; also to the modification of the by-laws to cover the admission of articled clerks and by-law candidates to the examinations in more specific and relaxed terms than the resolutions passed in the early days of the war. Equally important was the question of the re-employment of the returning men; and the establishment of the Ministry of Labour in 1916 and its Appointments Department provided machinery for co-operation with the profession. The purpose of the Appointments Department was to give assistance to ex-service men of suitable education and experience for appointment in, or training for, higher employments and the professions.

In 1918 Parliament found time to pass a much-needed Income Tax Act consolidating up to that date income tax legislation which was otherwise spread over a large number of statutes.

The position had also become considerably complicated by the changes in income tax introduced during the war.

Nineteen-eighteen was the year in which, regrettably, the famous penny postage, inaugurated at the suggestion of Rowland Hill in 1840, was increased to 1½*d*.

The onslaught of the German armies on the western front in the spring of 1918 when the Allied armies were pushed back gave cause for grave anxiety about the safety of the Channel ports. The thrust spent itself with heavy German losses; Marshal Foch was appointed Generalissimo of the Allied armies, the American armies were arriving, munitions, guns, and aeroplanes multiplied, the submarine menace had been met, though not eliminated; and in July the Allied armies began to move forward until, with unexpected speed, Germany surrendered and an Armistice was signed on 11 November 1918. The country gave itself to almost unrestrained jubilation, perhaps unmindful for a time of the stupendous tasks ahead, and was uplifted in spirit by the hoped-for new order of international affairs. To these things President Woodrow Wilson had devoted himself, particularly to the project of the League of Nations, of which General Smuts and Lord Robert Cecil, K.C., among others, were also part-authors. Victory, however, had been purchased at a terrible cost in human life, bereavement, and ability, for, alas, there were no less than 3,068,929 casualties (947,023 killed or died, 2,121,906 wounded)[1] among the armed forces of the British Empire and India; and the economic and financial consequences were but barely represented by the addition of £4,000 million to the national debt, by a level of taxation previously unimaginable, and by evident signs of inflation and of increases in prices. Among financial achievements were the raising in 1917 of a 5 per cent. war loan of £2,000 million at 95, converted in 1932 to the familiar 3½ per cent. war loan; and the first issue of national savings certificates.

In a London rather worn and shabby, with its people exhilarated but very modestly fed, the Society's members assembled at extraordinary general meetings on 17 October and 12 November 1918. Not without some critical discussion, the meetings adopted amendments to the Society's constitution providing

[1] Crutwell, *History of The Great War*.

for the admission of women and formally removing the power, long fallen into disuse, to grant membership by special election only: in future no person could apply for special election to membership unless he or she had passed such examinations as might be approved by the Council. The amended provisions were subsequently confirmed by Mr. Justice Eve in the Chancery Division of the High Court.

Throughout the war the Government had called upon the services of members of the profession for unprecedented tasks of much responsibility; and Parliament had directly and tacitly acknowledged the importance of accountancy to the country. Several members of the profession received recognition in His Majesty's Honours Lists. In addition to discharging duties arising from relations with Government departments, the Society had conducted its examinations half-yearly, had published regularly the *Incorporated Accountants' Journal*, and by frugal management had lived within its attenuated income and emerged with its finances in reasonable shape.

And so the Society turned to meet the formidable tasks of peace.

1919–1930

VI. POLICY AND PROGRESS AFTER
THE WAR

Demobilization

AT the Front, the Armistice of 11 November 1918 brought the advancing armies to a halt, an unwonted silence of the guns, the end of fighting; at home, inexpressible relief. Masses of soldiers had known the agony of the trenches, of long and indecisive battles, of comrades killed, of bitter retreat: then happily the *élan* of rapid advancement became hope triumphant and victory. Civilians at home, although freed from immediate anxieties and the inexorable pressure of war conditions and work, were suffering from poignant personal losses, and many were wondering what the future held for them. Reaction to the early bewilderment of the armies and to civilian exuberance soon began to manifest itself. An urge to demobilization among the armed forces became assertive, a restlessness of spirit prevailed amongst civilians. The excitement of a general election followed before the end of 1918, an election in which the earlier and more realistic intentions of the Government became swamped by understandable but extravagant demands for the punishment of Germany and the Kaiser, and for war reparations: unrealizable commitments were made in response to public clamour.

Meantime, the policy of demobilization formulated in 1917, and having for its purpose the rehabilitation of the country's economy, was slowly applied. But it gave too little weight to the feelings of soldiers, and, as a result of civilian priorities in manpower, led to some belief among His Majesty's forces of 'last in, first out': the pivotal men in civilian life were wanted first and those of the early volunteers who were still mobilized thought the best jobs were being snapped up before their turn came. The situation has been vividly described by Sir Winston Churchill in his book *The Aftermath*. There were some ugly incidents at home and abroad among disaffected soldiers, but fortunately of limited extent and consequence. On Sir Winston becoming Secretary of State for War in the new Government, a revised scheme of demobilization was promulgated, in which the dominant considerations for demobilization were length of service, age, and wounds. The policy was made known among the armed forces and the agitation subsided. Provision was made for the strength of the armies of occupation, in part by conscription for two years of younger age-groups already called up—a measure of necessity accepted by the country with little enthusiasm: but for these younger soldiers and for other troops retained, more favourable rates of pay helped to ease the situation. A loan amounting to £360 million 4 per cent. Victory Bonds was launched by the Government in the summer of 1919 while the effects of war finance, the expenditure of well-earned war gratuities, and shortages of goods combined to produce an inflationary rise in prices: there were boom conditions until 1921.

That broadly was the situation in the country when the Council turned its thoughts to the immediate and urgent work facing the Society.

Practising members of the profession and members holding senior appointments were as anxious for the return of partners and staff serving with the colours as the men were themselves. A Committee of the Ministry of Labour, including representatives of the Society, advised the Ministry on the release of some pivotal men: there was no special facility for the release of others or of articled clerks. Another factor was the considerable number of members temporarily in the service of Government departments; their services were still required to complete costings, the adjustment of war contracts, and other matters. However, during 1919 the position improved as men became demobilized and returned to the profession.

*   *   *

During the first half of the war, the presidency of the Society was filled by C. Hewetson Nelson, Liverpool, whose energy and ability responded to the burden which the problems of the war cast upon him: his imagination and literary gifts were used in the service of the Society, not least after he had vacated the presidential chair. In 1916 he was succeeded by Arthur E. Woodington, London, a man of genial temperament and quiet decisive judgement, who carried the members with the Council in the amendment of the articles in 1918. These changes crystallized previous decisions on membership policy, the admission of women, and the Society's administration; and were followed by a strengthening of the by-laws, but with latitude towards candidates who had served with His Majesty's forces. In 1919 the Council elected William Claridge, Bradford, as President: he was greatly interested in education, and during his period of office the business of the Society's examinations and the admission of candidates under after-the-war circumstances assumed both intensity and greater volume. His Vice-President was George Stanhope Pitt, London, and it was favourable to the Society that the three Presidents mentioned and the Vice-President either were, or had been, examiners.

The Secretaryship of the Society

There was considerable change in the administration of the Society. James Martin had been Secretary since 1886 and it had been known for some time that he wished to relinquish his duties as soon as convenient. It fell to Arthur E. Woodington as President to receive Martin's resignation from that office in a letter dated 15 January 1919:

My dear President,

I desire to place in your hands my resignation of the Secretaryship of the Society, and thereby return to the Council the trust which has been reposed in me for nearly thirty-three years. I have been anxious for some time past to seek relief from this office, but I felt bound to keep to my post so long as I could be of use to the members in connection with military service and other matters arising out of the war. Although the end has not yet been reached, demobilisation and a return to peace conditions are within sight, and I shall be available to give assistance until the difficulties of the situation are cleared away. This is not the time to review my connection with the Society, which has been continuous since its incorporation. I cannot, however, refrain from saying that every Incorporated Accountant has reason to be proud of his Society, as it has won not only public

SIR JAMES MARTIN
After the portrait in oils by Solomon J. Solomon, R.A.

confidence, but legislative and judicial approval. As to the future, this is assured so long as the members uphold their diploma as a certificate 'indicating reliability and integrity'.

Yours sincerely,

(Sgd.) JAMES MARTIN.

The resignation was accepted by the Council with many expressions of regret, and a formal resolution was adopted recording the great indebtedness of the Society for his services.

For twenty-eight years James Martin had been a member of the council of the London Chamber of Commerce as the representative of the Society; from 1918 to 1921 he was the chairman of the Council of that body: he also held some appointments in the City, for the traditions and business of which he entertained high regard. It was with much pleasure that his friends in the Society and elsewhere learned that in the New Year Honours List of 1919, His Majesty intimated that the Honour of Knight Bachelor would be conferred upon him. A Testimonial Committee was formed under the chairmanship of Arthur E. Woodington, who in March 1920, at a reception held in the hall of the Worshipful Company of Cordwainers, presented Sir James with his portrait in oils by Solomon J. Solomon, R.A., and Lady Martin with a suitable gift. Sir James accepted the portrait in a charming speech, in which with elegant conciseness he reviewed some of the principal achievements of the Society during his secretaryship. The speech is printed as Appendix III in this book. The portrait was subsequently hung in the Incorporated Accountants' Hall and a replica was executed by Solomon J. Solomon for the family.

Acknowledgement was made of the services of the Hon. Secretary of the committee, Mr. Herbert Vinall, who had been acting as Assistant Secretary of the Society during the war.

To enable the experience and connexions of Sir James to be at the disposal of the Society, he was appointed to be Adviser to the Council, for which position provision had been made recently in the Society's articles. His appointment was particularly relevant to parliamentary and other public business affecting the Society's interests and to relations with other bodies of accountants at home and overseas. Later Sir James consented to be elected a member of the Council.

Having announced the vacancy in the office of Secretary in the press and considered applications, the Council appointed as Secretary Mr. A. A. Garrett, who was previously Assistant Secretary and who was about to be demobilized after service in East and South Africa in the Royal Naval Reserve. The Society's chief clerk, James C. Fay, was concurrently the Secretary of the London Students' Society, to the work of which he brought enthusiasm and ideas, with advantage and acceptability to the large number of students in the metropolitan area. The office of the Society continued to be at 50 Gresham Street in the City.

War Candidates: First Women Members

The immediate and considerable task which faced the Council and the administration in 1919 was to facilitate the return of members to the profession and to promote arrangements for the studies and the examinations of articled clerks and by-law candidates upon their release from active service. Anticipating the situation which would arise at the end of the war, the Council had previously set up a Special Committee to consider the examination of navy and army candidates and provision for their professional training. The committee was influenced by the considerable developments in accountancy during the war: costing and taxation practice had acquired greater significance; there were new forces in the economy of the country which affected business and finance and the scope of professional practice. The training and studies of candidates called for review from that standpoint. The chairman was C. Hewetson Nelson, past President, who was singularly zealous in advancing the proposals before the committee. The committee produced its report in July 1918. It recommended the provision of a series of lectures at seven centres, attendance at which was to be obligatory, and that students should divide their daily time between practical work in the office, attendance at the lectures, and studies. The lectures were to be focused on a revised final examination in which more time was to be given to advanced accounting and auditing than hitherto, and costing, statistics, and economics were to be new subjects. The committee stated:

Every indication points to the lesson that in the future the accountant who is devoid of a wide range of knowledge, including Economics and Statistical Methods, will be greatly handicapped in the prosecution of his profession. The day of the accountant as a mere checker of postings and additions has gone, and the future lies with the creative and constructive brain. The promotion of such faculties will in our opinion be greatly aided by the introduction of the subjects here recommended.

The Council gladly adopted the report, and the minutes show that its members considered these ideas should influence examination policy in the future—as well as meeting the specific needs of students whose contacts with the profession had been broken by the war. When, however, demobilization gained some momentum, it was found that the recommendations were rather too idealistic to be applied in the circumstances which prevailed, and a modified report was adopted in April 1919. The alterations in the examination syllabus were postponed, but lectures for the benefit of students were to be organized by district and students' societies, although attendance was to be voluntary: grants were made available to articled clerks towards coaching fees if they had been on active service for a considerable period. In addition to the efforts of the Council, a good deal of responsibility for the training of these men rested with principals.

The decision made in the early days of the war to grant relaxation in the length of professional service normally prescribed took effect: each candidate was required to give satisfaction that he had completed a reasonable period of professional experience: in practical terms, if candidates had served some three or four years with the forces, the period of articled service in the profession accepted was three years (provided the candidates were 21 or over) in lieu of five years; and correspondingly the minimum by-law service was to be six years, if the candidates were 25 years of age. They were also permitted to present themselves for the final examination without having passed the intermediate, a concession which the length of absence from the profession made desirable: however, this had not been contemplated during the early period of the war. In cases in which the length of active service was shorter and the candidates were younger, the concessions were reduced proportionately and exemption from the intermediate examination was permitted only within narrower limits.

The policy of the Government through the Ministry of Labour was to offer grants to demobilized officers and others of suitable education to obtain training for callings of a professional type which prior to the war they had not contemplated. It was sound policy for the men and for the country to ensure as far as possible that those who had shown character and ability in the war should be enabled to give the best account of themselves in the future. There was a Committee of the Ministry of Labour including representatives of the profession to give effect to this policy. As a result, a somewhat unexpected problem arose. It was found that a large number of men concerned desired to qualify for accountancy. Accordingly, the Council modified the by-laws to enable men over twenty-one years of age to serve articles reduced by the period of war service up to a maximum of two years. In practice nearly all these men served three-year articles and were able to make application for special exemption from the preliminary examination. There were advisory panels throughout the country of members of the Society who stimulated interest among practitioners to accept articled clerks under the scheme, a condition being that those accepted received grants from the Ministry, but premiums would not be paid; the articled clerks were required to pass both the intermediate and final examinations. The panels interviewed candidates and made recommendations to the Ministry. Arthur E. Green, past President, a man of practical mind and sympathetic in these matters, gave a large amount of time to interviewing and advising these demobilized men on their future with much comfort and assurance to them. The Council aimed at maintaining proper standards: at the same time, but with due regard to that purpose, it accorded to war candidates modifications in the normal regulations in order to facilitate the resumption of their studies. These arrangements enabled them to qualify as incorporated accountants with as little delay as possible. A revised examination syllabus, projected during the war, was put into final shape and brought into force in 1920.

Appointing Josiah Charles Stamp, C.B.E., D.Sc. (Econ.), to be an examiner, the Council received his advice in the formulation of the syllabus, particularly on the introduction of economics and statistics: he examined in those subjects for some time, being succeeded by Sir William Coates, Ph.D., LL.B.

The return of men to the profession and their eagerness to obtain their qualification resulted in a great increase in the number of examination candidates, indicated in the following figures for the preliminary, intermediate, and final examinations taken together:

Year			Total	Passed	Failed
1913	.	.	552	378	174
1914	:	.	465	317	148
1920	.	.	953	665	288
1921	.	.	1,393	957	436
1922	.	.	1,441	944	497
1923	.	.	1,500	918	582
1924 ·	.	.	1,457	888	569

In parenthesis, it may be mentioned that in May 1926, on the dates fixed for the examinations, the country was convulsed by a general strike—a serious affair. Public transport was suspended and at that date private motor-cars were by no means common. G. S. Pitt, President, decided without hesitation that the examinations must proceed. In the result over 92 per cent. of the candidates who had entered found their way to the respective examination centres. This incident was a demonstration of character and of physical effort on the part of the students, following upon weeks of intensive study.

*   *   *

There was early, although inevitably limited, response to the opening of the examinations and of membership to women. Miss H. M. Claridge had for several years been in the service of a firm in Bradford, and she was the first woman to pass the final examination and to be elected an Associate (1920). By a happy coincidence, her father, William Claridge, was at that time President of the Society. The first woman articled clerk to qualify was Miss Phyllis E. M. Ridgway, B.A., who, articled to her father, G. A. Ridgway, F.S.A.A., Hull, passed the examinations and was elected an Associate in 1922 and afterwards became a partner in her father's firm. Miss Ridgway was elected to the Council of the Society (1949) and had the distinction of being its only woman member. In 1922 Miriam M. Homersham, M.A., who was with a London firm, passed the final examination and subsequently commenced practice. The number of women members increased over the years but rather more slowly than had been expected. Even after the lapse of some thirty-five years, at the date of Integration, the number of women members of the Society was about one hundred. But if their number was comparatively small, they showed themselves to be interested in the affairs of the Society and took considerable part in its activities. In consequence of the new power to admit women to membership, the Council in 1919 received a renewal of the application, first made in 1888, from Mary Harris Smith, who had practised in London for over thirty years. The amendment of the Society's articles had eliminated the hitherto limited power to admit to membership persons without having passed approved examinations. The Council was in a dilemma but met the difficulty by electing her an honorary member in recognition of her being the first woman to be a practising accountant. This election brought the number of honorary members to four only. Subsequently to the Society having taken power to admit women, the Sex Disqualification (Removal) Act, 1919, had been passed by Parliament, whereby a person was not to be disqualified by sex for admission to any incorporated society. It then transpired that the royal charter and by-laws of the English Institute permitted its Council to elect to membership a person who had been in practice as long as had Mary Harris Smith. In this way she was elected to the Institute and became a chartered accountant.

*   *   *

A satisfactory feature of the ten years succeeding the conclusion of the war was the fact that on the whole the large number of men who then qualified and became junior members of the Society were absorbed in employment: there was not a serious problem of unemployment in the profession.

Accountancy in Government Departments

In an earlier chapter attention was called to the extensive problems of accounting which arose in Government departments during and after the close of the First World War. Following a report of the Select Committee on National Expenditure,[1] early in 1918 Lieut.-Col. James Grimwood, D.S.O., F.S.A.A. (afterwards C.B.), received an appointment as special assistant to the Financial Secretary of the War Office to take charge of the extension of cost accounting to army establishments. At the end of 1919 the King by royal warrant authorized the formation of a Corps of Military Accountants, the first officers of which included men who prior to military service had qualified as members of the profession. There was already a Professional Accountancy Division of the Admiralty, and an extensive organization to control contracts and costing had been built up at the Ministry of Munitions. On a broader front, the seventh report[2] on National Expenditure gave emphasis to the inadequacy of Government estimates and accounts on a cash basis and the need for the application of income and expenditure principles to promote sound administration and economy.

By 1919 indications of post-war inflation included a troublesome rise in prices, and people became emphatically 'profiteering conscious'. Perhaps it had been hardly realized that profiteering was as much an outcome of inflation as its cause. Some profiteering there certainly was, and an attempt to arrest it was made by the Profiteering Act, 1919. Part of the machinery was an Investigation of Prices Committee, and a Costings Department, the chief officers of which were a chartered accountant and an incorporated accountant. There was attached to the Costings Department an Advisory Committee, of which those who directed costing at the War Office (Sir Nicholas Waterhouse, F.C.A.), the Ministry of Food (Sir Harry Peat, F.C.A.), and the Ministry of Munitions (Sir John Mann, C.A.) and the President of the Institute and the President of the Society were members. A report at the end of 1920 recommended the utilization—as far as propriety and respect for confidence permitted—of the vast amount of accumulated information about

[1,2] *House of Commons Papers* 151, 1917/18; 98, 1918.

the costs of many articles in common everyday use. And to maintain this information up to date, a permanent Costings Department of the Board of Trade was proposed.

These matters were significant indications in a wide field. It seemed to many in close touch with the situation that considerable impetus had been given to accountancy as a factor in Government administration; particularly this applied to those sections in which accountancy as understood professionally was operative, whether internally or to control the external functions of the departments. Already there were members of the Society (and chartered accountants) who held appointments in the Civil Service, some permanent and others temporary. The question arose whether the position which had developed between the profession and Government departments in the exigencies of recent years could, with advantage, be maintained in the future. The extension of accountancy in Government departments would call for qualified men, and the interest of the departments was made known to the Council of the Society. The practical question was, should the Council now consider the admission to the Society's examinations of candidates in Government service who were engaged in the echelons of higher accountancy; and, concurrently, would appointments to accountancy posts in the Civil Service be made from among men trained in the accountancy profession and holding a recognised qualification?

Semi-official conversations between the Treasury and representatives of the Society took place. In 1921 the Council—not without some hesitation—adopted a scheme. The scheme provided that a Special Committee was empowered to consider applications for the examinations from candidates in Government service, normally of executive rank, whose experience was considered to be equivalent to that required from accountancy clerks to public accountants, and who otherwise complied with the regulations. The committee had the advice of three higher civil servants nominated by the Treasury—later by one Treasury official—and the committee was furnished with detailed information as to each applicant's experience and work. The scheme was dovetailed into the general policy of the Society without impairing the main professional basis of admission. A number of those admitted under the arrangement were promoted to positions of high responsibility in the public service. Some pleasant relationships grew up between the members of the Special Committee and the successive advisers, whose knowledge and helpfulness were invaluable.

After a few years and in the process of army reorganization, the Corps of Military Accountants was disbanded: a part of its work was relinquished, and its more important functions and some of its officers were transferred to other regiments. This step was viewed somewhat critically by the Society, but was taken by the War Office after inquiry by an expert committee. It seems that the Corps of Military Accountants attempted to do too much, and there was some anomaly that the work of a military corps was largely planned at civilian level.

The Challenge of Sir Josiah Stamp

The responsibilities of the Council towards ex-service men and the work involved—slightly dislocated by a railway strike in 1919—did not obscure the need to reinvigorate activities throughout the Society. On the contrary, they emphasized the importance of extending the Society's own organization at home and overseas. Therefore, initiative on the part of District Societies and of London members in undertaking the arrangements for conferences periodically was welcomed by the Council, as well as the hospitality extended in each city by the Lord Mayor and Lady Mayoress. Visits by representative members from overseas permitted helpful consultations concerning the Society's branches in the dominions and their presence as guests afforded additional interest at the conferences. Reciprocally there were visits to South Africa by Sir James Martin and George Stanhope Pitt.

The series of conferences held more or less annually in the autumn enlivened the Society in both the social and intellectual senses. It was opened by the gathering in Liverpool in 1921.

Here Mr. E. Cassleton Elliott, London, surveyed 'The work of the accountancy profession from the standpoint of recent experience'. His main theme was the constructive functions of practising accountants as advisers in business affairs, and he pointed to the ample problems which were then, and would continue to be, entrusted to them—subsequently to the early post-war inflation—particularly the complications of four forms of direct annual taxation imposed on an economy then affected by falling prices.

After the practical approach made in this paper, there was lively antithesis in the succeeding paper given by Sir Josiah Stamp, K.B.E., D.Sc. (Econ.), 'The relation of accountancy to economics'. In a subtle exposition presented with flashes of humour, he invited accountants to extend their interest and apply their first-hand knowledge in the sphere of economics. And then he fluttered the dovecots by a challenge:

I doubt not that economics will have a salutary influence on accountancy. But what I am much more concerned with is, what is accountancy going to do for economics? The keys to many doors are in its hands, and there alone.

I make this serious indictment of accountants. Scientific accountancy has now been developing for some fifty years, but I cannot trace that it has yet made a single substantial contribution to economic science over its own field of the analysis of the results of industry, although it has practically a monopoly grip of the required data.

To illustrate, Sir Josiah indicated specific objectives in his larger field of inquiry—the nature and origin of profits, the reasons for marginal and intra-marginal undertakings, the relation of profits to capital, of profits to output and price, the capitalization of business profits as a factor in estimating the national capital. The material for these purposes was in the hands of accountants; they knew as others did not the bases of, and the considerations affecting, its compilation; and accountants equipped with economic knowledge were the people best qualified to pursue these objectives, which in Sir Josiah's view were of high importance. 'You suggest the economist can see what is wanted or draw up and initiate it himself. He cannot. It is only the professional accountant who knows what can be done, what can be found, what is practicable and what is not.'

He went further and, thinking of the economic conception of capital and income, he asked his audience to deliberate upon 'the sorry figure that is cut in the light of it by . . . a safe or sound balance sheet . . . which overstates no assets and understates no liabilities'. He knew they were against him to a man.

There were vigorous replies—in the immediate discussion as well as in subsequent discussions elsewhere and in the professional journals. The business of accountants was towards their clients individually, it was a highly fiduciary relationship; accountancy was but a small part of the economic field. If they attempted to enter it, were they not liable to be shot at by the economists? Was it not better that they should mind their particular concerns? Subject to their professional responsibilities, accountants would be glad to supply economists with the material needed for research: but already was there not considerable material unused. And Arthur Collins pointed to the amount of published information in regard to municipal accounts and trading of which the economists had not (then) made use. For all its critical burden, the discussion produced a faint glimmer of possible future research—not by individuals but by groups, in which economists and accountants would co-operate. Both criticism and response were offered by the *Incorporated Accountants' Journal*—criticism that Sir Josiah had been less than generous to the profession, which in the course of half a century had built itself up to a calling of national importance, had had to create its professional literature, and had provided itself with a code of ethics, while considerable effort had necessarily—and regrettably—been given to the protection of sectional interests. And as to 'sound' and 'safe' balance sheets, was it to be wondered at that, having regard to leading cases in which damages had been sought against directors and auditors, balance sheets if they erred did so on the side of prudence? Perhaps in 1960 in retrospect, it might be asked whether Sir Josiah spoke with rather more discernment than was appreciated at the time. But less critically and by way of favourable response, the *Journal* recognized that the horizon of too many members of the profession was limited by the walls of their own offices and those of their clients; and it welcomed the appeal of Sir Josiah to the rising generation to produce at least 1 per cent. 'who have the real itch for knowledge and whom the microbe of curiosity will give no rest'.

Other preoccupations and the level of thinking at that time scarcely left room for any development, in whatever degree might have been acceptable, as a result of Stamp's ideas. But the seed he sowed germinated slowly and in the course of about fifteen years some younger men in the Society embarked on an effort of research until it became a recognized function of the accountancy bodies. Some research took the direction Sir Josiah apparently had in mind; other efforts have been concerned with the problems and needs of the profession itself than with those he adumbrated. Accountants were apt to be shy of going too far in a field in which, with the passage of time, the professional economist has progressed and the professional statistician has evolved. Strict demarcation there is not, for indeed if knowledge is conveniently divided by subjects it is not broken into compartments. And so within useful but limited degree accountants, economists, and statisticians have in various ways co-operated: true, there are a few accountants who in the Stamp tradition have betaken themselves to the neighbouring field and brought their expertise to useful purpose, while some reciprocal effort has been wisely planned. Further, Sir Josiah thought that accountants if called upon to deal with large questions for the nation, or with higher policy in industry and finance, could the better approach those problems if guided by broad economic considerations: his belief has found ample justification and notable examples.

Conferences

Much encouragement was given by the success of the Liverpool Conference and an *ad hoc* Reception Committee of London members was formed to organize a London Conference in 1922. (There was not a London District Society at that time.) Sir James Martin had accepted an invitation from the Council to be President, an invitation which he humorously said might more conveniently have waited until 'trade, industry and commerce had settled down and until political crises were things of the past: but he supposed that if they were to wait for all these things, they would have to wait until the wicked ceased from troubling and then probably they would all be at rest!' By kind permission of the Corporation of London, the President's address and a paper by G. S. Pitt, London, Vice-President, on 'Accountancy as the first-aid to commercial recovery' were given in the historic council chamber at Guildhall (unfortunately destroyed in the Second World War by enemy action); and the Lord Mayor courteously lent the Egyptian Hall at the Mansion House for a dinner. A distinguished company included the Lord Mayor and Sheriffs, the Minister of Health, the Dean of Westminster, the heads of City institutions and of the legal and accountancy professions, and a number of senior members of the Civil Service.

Although the 1922 Conference did not mark any particular anniversary in the Society, the President in his address gave some interesting information about the profession of accountancy since the Society was established in 1885. At that date the Chartered Societies of Scotland for some thirty years, and the English Institute for five, had been laying foundations which 'it had been the privilege of the Society to widen in order to build thereon temples of varying design but possessing similar characteristics'. On 31 December 1885 the aggregate membership of the chartered bodies in Scotland, England, and Wales and the Society was 2,099, whereas by 31 December 1921 that membership, with the addition of members of the Irish Institute, had reached 10,928. The Bankruptcy Act, 1883, introduced the system of official receivers and affected the work of practising accountants: but it eliminated a number of men who would not be considered a credit to the profession, for whom the previous Act of 1869 had provided a happy hunting ground. The more significant changes, however, had occurred in regard to companies, taxation and the extension of local authorities. In April 1885, 9,344 companies in England, Wales, Scotland, and Ireland represented paid-up capital of £495 million. By 1921, 82,636 were on the register (two-thirds of which were private companies) and the capital recorded was about £4,200 million. The weight of taxation, only too familiar to the present generation, seemed scarcely less a burden to the generation of the 1920's. Sir James Martin found that the weight of taxation had lent itself to the formation and activities of a variety of income-tax agencies and advertising accountants: they offered their services to a suffering public, often on terms of commission on repayments effected, and sometimes they made claims to special expert knowledge. The proponents, unlike the chartered and incorporated accountants, were not subject to disciplinary control,

were untrammelled by rules, and complied with no professional standards. To have a cash interest in the result of any
claim could but colour the action of the person representing
a claimant and impair his usefulness as a reliable and impartial
authority. On the other hand, members of a recognized profession must be paid proper remuneration for their services and
should not be dependent upon results.

*   *   *

In succeeding years the members were invited to Cardiff
(1923), Leeds (1924), and Manchester (1927). The Cardiff
Conference was an opportunity for the abundant enthusiasm of
the South Wales and Monmouthshire District Society and the
organizing ability of the committee and of Percy H. Walker,
who for a long period was Hon. Secretary: he subsequently
became one of the auditors of the Society at head office. J. M.
Fells, C.B.E., explored the functions of accountancy in relation
to costs and market prices and the elusive problem of stable
prices.

Travelling north to Leeds and Bradford the following year,
the conference was marked by the presence of two members
of the Council who were also members of Parliament—Sir
Charles Wilson (a Leeds Division), and Thomas (afterwards
Sir Thomas) Keens, (Buckinghamshire Division)—and by a
consideration of 'The Accountant and public life' in a discussion
opened by C. Hewetson Nelson, Liverpool. The assistance of
Mr. T. W. Dresser, who had given much help to students in
Yorkshire, was enlisted as Hon. Secretary for the Leeds Conference.

Manchester had been a focal point in the formative years of
the Society and the only conference which had been held there
was as far back as 1899. The services of the same Hon. Secretary,
Arthur E. Piggott, were again devoted to the arrangements for
1927. The members had the honour of entertaining Lord
Hewart of Bury, Lord Chief Justice, and the occasion became
memorable by his concise observation: 'I suspect that even
now, for reasons not easy to understand, the great profession
of accountancy has not a register, from which for good reasons
a man's name could be removed.'

A perusal of presidential addresses at these conferences and at the Society's annual meetings at this and subsequent periods impresses the fact that, while dealing with matters of strictly professional importance, Presidents increasingly commented on aspects of public affairs from the angle of the accountancy profession.

The record of these meetings of members must include the celebration of the Society's fortieth anniversary in 1925 when, by the kindness of the Lord Mayor, a dinner was given by the Society in the Mansion House, London. At this function the President, G. S. Pitt, had the honour of receiving the Lord High Chancellor (Viscount Cave).

★   ★   ★

An active adjunct to the social life of the Society was created in 1921 by the formation of the Incorporated Accountants' Lodge of Freemasons, Number 4255. Among the founders were Sir James Martin (Worshipful Master), Mr. M. J. Faulks, Henry Burgess, Richard A. Witty, and James C. Fay. Members of the Society from all parts of the country have participated in the Lodge, which has afforded regular opportunities for maintaining friendship amongst them. Its title is now 'The Sir James Martin Lodge'.

VII. AT HOME AND ABROAD

The Branches and District Societies

DURING the First World War the organization of each Branch and District Society had been maintained, but necessarily on a restricted basis. Thereafter, revival of activities had been encouraged by requests from the Council to provide lectures for students and ex-service members and by the local panels of members concerned with advice to the Ministry of Labour on grants to ex-service students and new articled clerks. There had, however, been no definite steps to develop further their organization and work; and there was undoubtedly some variation in the level of activity. By 1923 it was felt that something further should be done and, during his year of office as President, Sir James Martin invited each Branch and District Society and the London Students' Society to send two or three representatives to a meeting in London for an exchange of views. The meeting was a great success in stimulating interest and raising morale. Hitherto the Presidents and Secretaries of District Societies had met each other and members of the Council somewhat adventitiously at local dinners, at conferences, and perhaps at annual meetings of the Society. Communication was maintained with head office through the Secretary or through a member of Council from the district. Now the London meeting placed District Society policy on a higher plane: it manifested a community of interest among all who worked actively in the district organizations and gave the representatives assurance of direct interest on the part of the Council and of its members individually. The step thus taken most favourably modified an unconscious sense that the Council, energetic though it was in promoting the interests of the whole Society, was, nevertheless, a rather remote entity.

Impressed by the value of these considerations, the Council decided to hold each year a conference between representatives of district organizations and members of the Council on the day after the annual meeting in May. The District Societies were invited to propose subjects for the agenda, which was put into shape by the District Societies' Committee of the Council, with as little pruning as practicable: and at the conferences the President, who took the chair, gave the utmost latitude to discussion. The fact that these conferences were closed meetings facilitated a greater degree of confidence than was possible at public meetings of members. The opinions expressed enabled the Council to be aware of the views of members throughout the Society; and representatives were afforded information by the Council on current policy and proposals.

At one or two of the earlier meetings, after the experimental stage of this initiative had passed, a few of the more zealous amongst the representatives suggested that procedure should be by way of resolutions submitted by the District Societies; and there was possibly a hint that a pre-conference meeting among the representatives would enable them to put forward concerted rather than individual views. In the nature of things, proposals made or representations presented could not always be accepted by the Council, which sustained responsibilities for the whole Society; moreover, however sympathetically inclined the Council might have been to representations made, it had to consider them in a wider setting of the whole profession and was aware of situations elsewhere, in the light of which proposals had often to be judged. This applied particularly to the question of registration for the profession (pp. 162-80) which time and again was brought forward, but its promotion was not possible on the initiative of the Society alone: and in any case the difficulties of legislation were perhaps inadequately appreciated by those to whose views the Council would like to have given positive response. Thus on the question of procedure the Council in a conciliatory but definite way intimated to the representatives that the conferences were meetings of professional friends for an exchange of views, that the proceedings must be deliberative only, and that unequivocally the governance of the Society by its constitution was vested in the Council. This attitude was supported by Fred Woolley, Southampton—not then a member of Council—who had unofficially become regarded as the principal spokesman at the early conferences. The policy stated by the Council was accepted, and no major question of procedure or status arose thereafter. At the conclusion of each conference the representatives were entertained to luncheon by the Council, and on these pleasant occasions they were able to meet successive Presidents and Vice-Presidents immediately after their election by the Council every two or three years.

*   *   *

A further major step was completed in 1928. On his becoming President in 1926 Thomas Keens was convinced that there should be further integration between the Council and the Branches and District Societies without prejudicing, but rather to encourage, District Society initiative. Up to that time membership of the District Societies was entirely voluntary; the rates of subscription were fixed locally and varied considerably from district to district: each society made its own rules, subject to formal approval by the Council, and local revenue was supplemented by small annual grants from head office. Under a proposed scheme each member of the Society in England, Wales, Scotland, and Ireland would automatically become a member of a Branch or District Society, local subscriptions would cease, subscriptions to head office would be increased, and the Branches and District Societies would be financed by annual grants from the Council, the assessment of grants to be on a scale with supplements according to special circumstances. Students' sections of Branches and District Societies would be formed and every student would be required to join and maintain membership by a small subscription paid locally as a condition of entry to the examinations: this was proposed as a matter of administration, but the real purpose was to enlist the interest of students in the work and organization of the Society so that they would derive benefit from meetings and from association with other students. With much skill, Thomas Keens evolved the scheme with a small committee of District Society representatives and with the Council and made visits to the District Societies accompanied by Mr. J. R. W. Alexander, who had recently been appointed Parliamentary Secretary (p. 138). The proposals were received with somewhat open minds: at first the District Societies wondered if their independence would be impaired, whether the concentration and control of finance to be vested in the Council would be to their advantage and whether there was a slight implication of compulsion which might not bring with it the desired stimulation of personal interest. In the administration of grants, was there a likelihood that head office finance might benefit indirectly at the cost of the provinces—an idea that arose from the recent additional commitment of running Incorporated Accountants' Hall? There was a substantial answer: the higher subscriptions to be paid by practising members in London and the large London membership would result in London's joint contribution under the scheme being very considerable, while the relative expenses and London's share of grants would not be *pro tanto*. After all the issues had been considered, the scheme was accepted by the districts and by Scotland and Ireland, which, together with the London area, were the subject of special provisions: and the members at extraordinary general meetings approved the necessary alterations to the articles to increase annual subscriptions.

It would be going too far to suggest that all the District Societies were invariably and completely satisfied with the grants voted to them; and the commendable interest of Honorary Secretaries was shown by requests from time to time for augmentation of the amounts their committees received. But once the scheme was accepted and put into operation (1928), all doubts were resolved: it proved to be an unquestioned advantage and fulfilled the promises claimed for it during the course of the negotiations.

As an outcome, a London District Society was formed, of which Thomas Keens was the first Chairman. It was anomalous that there had not been a London District Society earlier: meetings of London members arranged from time to time had been in the hands of London members of the Council and the secretariat at head office. There was, however, a somewhat delicate phase when the London District Society was formed, as the London Students' Society, founded in 1890, had attained a position of much usefulness in its own right: its work was financed from students' subscriptions with a small grant-in-aid, and its administration was at the parent Society's head office with James C. Fay as Secretary. At the time of these developments its President was Sir Stephen Killik, who led conversations with members of the Council, and it was agreed that the special position of the Students' Society should be recognized alongside that of the London District Society. Happily that situation continued without difficulty, and indeed with a large measure of co-operation between the two London organizations, which were mutually represented on the respective committees.

For many years Thomas Keens was chairman of the District Societies' Committee of the Council, and it was a source of immense satisfaction to him that his scheme, for which he had laboured with unwavering conviction, was accepted and became an essential part of the Society's organization.

*   *   *

A continuing task of the committees and Hon. Secretaries of the Branches, District, and Students' Societies was the arrangement from year to year of a programme of lectures and meetings for discussions. This task was undertaken with enthusiasm and was done supremely well. So far as students were concerned, the arrangements did not comprise systematic and complete courses in preparation for the examinations: students made their own arrangements with specialist coaching organizations, or attended evening classes provided by the educational institutions of local authorities. But many of the District and Students' Societies' lectures were upon examination subjects, intended to supplement systematic instruction obtained elsewhere. In a few instances in the provinces, on an *ad hoc* basis, some senior members were good enough to undertake revision classes particularly directed to the examinations: and from time to time the London Students' Society arranged series of three or four lectures, among which may be mentioned those given by Lawrence R. Dicksee,F.C.A., Professor of Accounting at London University, by Dr. Hugh Dalton, then Professor of Economics at London University, and by C. A. Bennett, K.C. (afterwards Hon. Mr. Justice Bennett), who practised at the Chancery Bar. However, it should be said that the purpose of all these meetings was on a higher plane than simply the pursuit of examination studies, important though they were: for instance, the formal objects in the constitution of the London Students'

Society included the promotion of proceedings having relation to the training of members for the examinations of the parent society and for practice in professional accountancy, and others of a social character. But no formal statement of objects could do adequate justice to the advantages of professional association and to the elevation of status which resulted there and elsewhere from the whole of these activities. For the qualified members of the Society the District Societies' meetings were occasions for the discussion of professional questions, particularly those having topical significance as the work and the problems of the profession developed.

The committees were fortunate in receiving the honorary services as lecturers of members of the accountancy profession, both in practice and engaged in industry and commerce, of barristers and solicitors, bank managers, financial journalists, and university lecturers, as well as of professional lecturers, usually members of the tuition staffs of the coaching organizations. These arrangements were made locally, sometimes with assistance from head office. There gradually evolved a helpful system known as 'the panel of lecturers scheme' under which head office secured annually the services of suitable people qualified to give lectures who made visits to the District Societies, frequently on short tours, where they were welcomed by the members and students. The panel of lecturers grew out of the better organization developed by the Branches and District Societies Scheme.

Most of the Branches and District Societies arranged an annual or bi-annual dinner at which the Lord Mayor and a distinguished figure in public life, as well as public people in the particular city and the President and Secretary of the Society, were entertained. There was usually an informal meeting between the President and the local committee; and, when time permitted, the President and Secretary were entertained personally in such interesting and varied ways as visits to works in the neighbourhood, an opportunity to see the surrounding country or an international or other football match. These visits were indeed stimulating occasions in the life of the Society, and successive Presidents spared no efforts to fulfil these engagements.

Increasing momentum in the Society's affairs as well as in the volume of administrative and parliamentary work led to the appointment as Parliamentary Secretary in 1927 of Mr. J. R. W. Alexander, M.A., LL.B., barrister-at-law, and to a more active presentation of the Society to the public. Proceedings in Parliament (p. 160), which were continuous, the promotion of the District Societies' Scheme (p. 134), and prospective arrangements relative to the purchase and opening of Incorporated Accountants' Hall were matters to which Mr. Alexander mainly devoted himself. He remained with the Society until 1931, when he took up another similar appointment and was succeeded by Mr. Ernest E. Edwards, B.A., LL.B., barrister-at-law, who later went to practise at the Bar.

Incorporated Accountants' Hall

Walking on the Embankment with Sir James Martin in 1920, the newly appointed Secretary noticed a 'For Sale' board affixed to the railings of what was then Astor House, and remarked enthusiastically: 'By Jove, if the Society wanted a place of its own, there's the building.' But Sir James, conservative in temperament and practical-minded, replied: 'Yes, a fine building but the Society has plenty of business at present without thinking of a building.' Intuitively he realized that at that time, resources and work were needed for other purposes—and it was the correct view. However, in a few years, when this casual conversation was quite forgotten, some members of the Council brought up the question of the Society having a building commensurate with its standing and progress. In any case an administrative problem was looming ahead, for the accommodation then occupied at 50 Gresham Street, near Guildhall, had become quite inadequate and the lease was due to expire in 1929. For some fifteen years at that address, the Council had had a comfortable council chamber and committee room and the Secretary and staff used a small but suitable office of three rooms, whilst a fourth room housed the library. For students' meetings there was a room on the top floor, the austerity of which was the subject of frequent complaint by students; occasionally, special meetings were allowed to be held in the council chamber instead.

By 1924 the Council had reached a decision to implement the proposal to obtain a building; and, in anticipation of the necessary financial provision, secured the concurrence of the members to increases in the rates of entrance fees and subscriptions and to borrowing powers being vested in the Council. It was brought to the notice of the Council that the Sun Life Assurance Company of Canada, which had acquired the former Astor House, were considering the disposal of that property, situated on the Embankment at the border of Westminster and the City of London. Negotiations ensued but proved abortive. Other less satisfactory proposals were considered. George Stanhope Pitt, then President, was unwavering in his belief that the building on the Embankment would again come on offer, since the owners showed no signs of being in a hurry for its disposal: this view proved to be correct. In 1928 the property was advertised for sale and the Council gave Henry Morgan full power to conduct the negotiations. At a crucial stage of the negotiations, courageously he took upon himself considerable personal responsibility which enabled the purchase to be assured. His action was gratefully confirmed by the Council. Some internal alterations—mainly to convert a ground-floor office into a library—and restoration work were required. F. L. Pearson, F.R.I.B.A. (son of the architect of the building), was retained and the contract was placed with John Thompson & Sons Ltd., Peterborough: the foreman who carried out the joinery work had been engaged on similar work when the building was first erected. The work proceeded in 1928, after vacant possession had been obtained, and with the furnishing was completed by the end of January 1929.

To finance the purchase the Council made an issue of £70,000 5 per cent. debentures to members and applied the accumulated fund, represented mainly by trustee securities some of which were realized. The issue was over-subscribed, a fact which showed the goodwill and confidence of the members, especially as the terms were barely competitive in the conditions then prevailing in the money market. Some voluntary contributions were also received, including much-appreciated gifts from overseas committees. The total cost involved, including alterations and restoration work, was about £110,000. It must be admitted that in consequence of the purchase the Society was carrying a heavy liability. At an early date the Council resolved that each year a contribution to a sinking fund should be made from revenue. From time to time debentures were redeemed by drawings, and in 1943 outstanding debentures had been reduced to £30,000. Unfortunately the outbreak of war, and subsequent events, necessitated the maintenance of liquid resources which prevented further reduction of the liability. Debentures were seldom offered for sale, and buyers at par were always found for the small amounts which occasionally became available.

Few events in the history of the Society appealed to the imagination of members as much as the purchase of the building, which became known as Incorporated Accountants' Hall. This feeling was further stimulated by the fact that His Royal Highness the Duke of York (later King George VI) honoured the Society by consenting to open the Hall. The function took place on 19 February 1929, in exceptionally cold weather. His Royal Highness was received at the front gate by the President, (Sir) Thomas Keens, who presented Sir Charles Wilson, M.P., LL.D., past President, G. S. Pitt, chairman of the Hall Committee, C. Hewetson Nelson, chairman of the Finance Committee, and the Secretary: the guests included His Worship the Mayor of Westminster and the Dean of Westminster (the Very Rev. W. Foxley Norris, C.V.O., D.D.). After an inspection of the guard of honour, present by kind permission of the Officer Commanding the London Scottish, the company proceeded to the Hall where speeches were delivered. At the conclusion of the proceedings His Royal Highness signed the President's visitors' book and he spoke to the foreman and other workmen who had been engaged on the work. The visitors' book was lost after the blitz of 1944, but fortunately was found some years later.

The arrangements had been admirably organized by Mr. J. R. W. Alexander, who also wrote a booklet descriptive of the Hall.

The Hall was built in 1895 for the first Lord Astor and the architect was J. Loughborough Pearson, R.A. Its elevation was in Portland stone and there was much fine craftsmanship in the

OPENING OF INCORPORATED ACCOUNTANTS' HALL, 19 FEBRUARY 1929
H.R.H. the Duke of York being received

OPENING OF INCORPORATED ACCOUNTANTS' HALL, 19 FEBRUARY 1929

W. Claridge.[1]
A. E. Woodington.[1]   A. A. Garrett, *Secretary*.
Sir Charles Wilson.[1]   H.R.H.   The Dean of Westminster.   The Mayor of
C. Hewetson Nelson.[1]   Sir Thomas Keens, *President*. The Duke of York. Lady Keens.   G. S. Pitt.[1]   Westminster.

[1] *Past Presidents*.

interior. The accommodation included a library, hall for meetings, a President's room, and administrative offices.[1]

Although the purchase of the Hall had the unanimous support of the Council, there were one or two City of London members who wondered whether the Society's head office ought to be outside the City: and a small number of senior members had slight mental reservations as to the commitment incurred and as to the—for them—considerable extent of the accommodation. But in a year or two the value of the Hall for practical use and as enhancing the dignity of the Society removed any minor personal doubts and all were enthusiastic about the step taken.

In keeping with the dignity enjoyed by the members at the Hall, the Society received, under the authority of the Earl Marshal, a Grant of Arms[2] including the motto *Fides atque Integritas* ('Reliability and Integrity'—the words of Mr. Justice Warrington in 1907).

In May 1929 the Society held its annual meeting—the first to take place in its own premises. A function given in July of that year afforded much pleasure to the President and Council when they entertained at dinner in the Hall, General Charles Gates Dawes, Ambassador of the United States of America, and Sir Josiah Stamp, G.B.E., who had just returned from the successful conference in Paris appointed to find a solution, which became known as the Young Plan, of the German reparations problem. The company on that occasion included Sir Herbert Samuel, G.C.B., M.P. (Lord Samuel).

If not used for meetings of the Society the hall upstairs was let from time to time for company meetings, and for many years the board of the Thames Conservancy held its weekly meetings there. A courtesy which the President and Secretary enjoyed was an annual invitation to be guests at the July inspection—Windsor to Teddington—by the Conservators of the River Thames, over whom a great Thames oarsman, Lord Desborough, K.G., G.C.V.O., presided: the occasions brought out his Leander tie and Oxford Blue straw boater.

*   *   *

[1] A short description of the Hall is given in Appendix IV.
[2] See Plate facing p. 142.

Sheffield District Society was the second in date of foundation among the District Societies and entertained the Society at a conference in the autumn of 1930. Mr. Percy Toothill, who was the local President, and Mrs. Toothill welcomed the visitors and they and the committee were admirably supported in all the arrangements by Mr. J. W. Richardson, Hon. Secretary. The Lord Mayor; Arthur Greenwood, M.P., Minister of Health; and H. Fitch Kemp, President of the Institute, were among the guests: the visitors were greatly interested by visits to Thomas Firth & Sons Ltd., one of the large steel works, and to the workshops of the renowned silversmiths, Walker & Hall Ltd. The Sheffield Conference was an enjoyable event—can it be said an occasion of some relaxation?—after the more strenuous occupations of the Society, which are reviewed in the next chapter. It marked the end of the decade after the First World War in the annals of the Society.

Overseas Affairs

Replete though the Society was with problems at home in the 1919-30 period, its interests in the dominions were actively maintained; and elsewhere its representatives participated in some international occasions, which were expressions of the world-wide scope of the accountancy profession.

In the oldest Branch of the Society—Victoria, Australia (1886)—George S. Anderson, Melbourne, became Hon. Secretary (1918) on the death of Charles A. Cooper, who was an original member of the Society. In New South Wales, Herbert Priestley and Alexander Rattray, each of whom visited the United Kingdom, maintained communication with head office and took action locally on some matters of consequence.

Harry Gibson, Cape Town, had played a leading part in establishing the Society's interests in South Africa: he died in 1920 and was succeeded as Hon. Secretary in Cape Town by his son, Mr. Cyril Gibson, who in later years relinquished the office to his partner, Mr. Hugh Hyslop. Expansion in South Africa was marked by the formation of a Branch in Natal (1928), whose members had previously been under the jurisdiction of the committee in Cape Town: Douglas Mackeurtan, Durban, was the first chairman.

THE ARMS OF THE SOCIETY, 1929

Argent, an open book, issuant from the dexter chief a Sunburst proper, all within
a bordure Sable charged with six Bezants and six Plates alternately. *And for the Crest
on a Wreath of the Colours* a demi-figure of a Scribe proper habited Sable, holding
in the dexter hand a Pen, and in the sinister an Ink horn also proper.

For several years the chairman of the Cape Town Committee was Sir Harry Hands, K.B.E., who had been Mayor of Cape Town during the war. His three sons—regrettably now deceased—were Rhodes Scholars at University College, Oxford. All of them were Rugby Blues; one subsequently played Rugby for England; the other two played cricket for South Africa: these two qualified as incorporated accountants and chartered accountants (S. Africa). This is a remarkable record.

Notable constitutional development took place in the British dominions—as the self-governing overseas countries were then known—by the declaration at the Imperial Conference of 1926, followed by the Statute of Westminster, 1931. This development was reflected in the evolution of accountancy bodies in those countries. Whilst the Society did not abate its overseas interests, they were influenced by this changing situation and those interests were increasingly concerned with relations with the overseas bodies.

*   *   *

The petition of 1909 for a royal charter by the Australasian Corporation of Public Accountants had met with opposition—including opposition from the Society—and had not proceeded. Other opposition was overcome and the petitioners decided in 1928 to renew their submission to the Privy Council. Their representatives made a visit to London, in the course of which they met the President and some members of the Council. The Society's previous opposition had arisen from an absence in the draft charter of facilities for membership of the proposed new Australian body to members of the Society resident in, or who would become resident in, Australia. The visitors were keen to get a charter, and after discussion they recognized the standpoint of the Society: the Society's representatives on their part were conscious both of the Society's claims and of the constitutional situation, considerably changed since 1909. Happily a solution was found by an undertaking on the part of the visitors to include in the by-laws of the proposed Institute of Chartered Accountants in Australia an absolute right on the part of a member of the Society resident in Australia to apply for membership, as if the name of the Society had been mentioned in the charter in which were set forth the names of the chartered bodies of the United Kingdom and Ireland. The Society withdrew its opposition, the Privy Council advised His Majesty to grant the charter, and an era of cordial relationship between the Society and the Australian Chartered Institute was initiated.

*   *   *

In South Africa a Bill was introduced into the Union Parliament to incorporate a body of accountants for the whole Union (1923). So much was the Bill amended in committee that the promoters decided to withdraw it (1926)[1]. Later attempts at legislation also did not succeed. Thus the then existing position continued—and continued for twenty-five years—that there were in South Africa separate bodies for each of the four provinces, in two of which, the Transvaal and Natal, statutory registration was in force. The Society had a *de facto* position with influential membership, but not a statutory position, except that its members had registration facilities under the Transvaal and Natal Acts. Most members of the Society in South Africa were also members of one of the Union bodies. They greatly valued their status as members of a body having worldwide connexions, while upholding unquestioned loyalty to their own South African bodies. It was their desire to harmonize these feelings and to find a policy which did so. It is not unfair to say there were elements in the South African bodies that did not view with favour the *de facto* status which the Society, as the oldest body in South Africa, enjoyed. This status was strengthened by the professional regard in which incorporated accountants were held and by a decision of the Supreme Court in regard to the designation. Their attention having been called to a person not a member of the Society using the designation 'Incorporated Accountant (South Africa)', the members of the Cape Town Committee in their individual capacity joined together and applied for an interdict to restrain the person concerned from using that designation. The court followed the Warrington judgment (England) of 1907 and granted the interdict.

About that time visits were paid to South Africa, first by the President, G. S. Pitt, and later by Sir James Martin, who went to South Africa in his capacity as President of the London Chamber of Commerce (to which he was elected in 1925) to

[1] G. E. Noyce, *The Accountancy Profession in South Africa.*

attend the Congress of Chambers of Commerce of the British
Empire. There were no formal negotiations with the South
African bodies, but the visitors made friendly and personal con-
tacts with members of the profession in the principal cities in
support of the long-established position of the Incorporated
Society in South Africa.

Following the withdrawal of the 1923 Bill, the four South
African bodies co-operated more closely. Previously they had
formed a General Examining Board to conduct examinations
on a common basis and now they promoted a short Bill, which
was passed by the Union Parliament as 'The Chartered Accountants Designation Act, 1927 (S. Africa)': this Act authorized their
members to use the designation 'Chartered Accountant (South
Africa)' or 'C.A. (S.A.)'. Reaction among United Kingdom
bodies was not altogether favourable. The South African
Societies then prepared common or similar by-laws which
provided for service under articles and examinations as a basis
for admission, with power to recognize for membership the
qualifications of other bodies obtained after articled service. The
Incorporated Society's three committees formed an Advisory
Committee for South Africa. An arrangement was evolved
whereby a candidate who wished to qualify as an incorporated
accountant would be articled simultaneously under the rules
of a South African Society and of the Incorporated Society; he
was required to pass the examinations of the General Examining
Board and thereafter the final examination of the Society (in
South Africa), omitting the legal subjects and taking papers
set in London, modified to South African practice. The candidates' scripts were adjudicated by the examiners in London and
the results were determined by the London Council. This
arrangement, amended in detail, subsisted up to the time of
Integration.

International Congresses

Accountancy as an organized profession received some impetus
in an international setting during the period 1920-30.

In response to a cordial invitation, the profession in the
United Kingdom was represented at the twentieth convention
(1924) of the American Institute of Accountants in the city of

St. Louis, U.S.A., by Mr. George R. Freeman, C.B.E., who became President of the English Institute in 1925–6; by R. G. Simpson, M.C., C.A., who in 1951–2 was elected the first President after the formation of the Institute of Chartered Accountants of Scotland; and by Mr. A. A. Garrett, the Secretary of the Society.

There had been an international motif at the Accountants' Congress held at St. Louis in 1904, which was organized by the profession in America. The idea was revived some twenty years later, on the initiative of Emanuel van Dien, Amsterdam, and the Netherlands Institute of Accountants: and the Second International Congress on Accounting was held in Amsterdam in 1926, the Secretary of which was G. W. Frese. The newly completed Colonial Institute in Amsterdam was a fine setting for the meetings, and the proceedings were facilitated by Emanuel van Dien's fluency in four or five European languages. There were delegations from the accountancy bodies of the United Kingdom and Ireland; that from the Institute being headed by Sir Arthur Whinney and that from the Society by Thomas Keens, Vice-President (the President being absent in South Africa). Sir William Plender contributed a paper on 'The Accountant's Certificate in relation to the accountant's responsibility'; and C. Hewetson Nelson and F. Ogden Whiteley (Society) submitted papers on 'Standard costs' and 'Accounts of local authorities' respectively—parts of a programme which, appropriately designed to give opportunities for all delegations, was perhaps a little overweighted. Notably the hosts successfully created the atmosphere for an international congress at a time when emotions left by the war had not completely disappeared; and the excellent organization afforded pleasure to all the visitors.

Colonel R. H. Montgomery, New York, extended an invitation for the next congress to be held in New York in 1929, and this was accepted. Liaison was to be maintained by the secretariat of the Amsterdam Congress until the American organization for the next congress was established—a procedure which has been followed subsequently.

The Society's delegation to the New York Congress was again led by Thomas Keens, who had become President. The guests were welcomed by Colonel R. H. Montgomery, the President of the Congress, which, in his address, he described as 'a grand free-for-all checking-up party'. In a more serious and somewhat philosophic vein he invited the congress to reflect that 'when others do not keep their feet upon the ground we must do so. The public relies upon us, and has a right to rely upon us, not so much for unreasoning conservatism as for intelligent accuracy.'

A heat wave visited New York for the week of the congress, the programme of which was carried out with American enthusiasm and generous hospitality. Although some of the visitors found the heat and humidity rather trying, the occasion was for them a memorable experience.

Prior to the congress, the Society's delegation were entertained in Canada by the Canadian Chartered Accountants and by members of the Society; after the proceedings in New York were concluded, they were guests of the American Institute of Accountants in Washington, D.C., a short visit of great interest.

VIII. TAXATION: COMPANIES

Income Tax, Supertax, Excess Profits Duty

WHAT of the work of the profession in the period from the virtual end of the First World War to 1930? The general situation may be viewed in part by a brief glance at reports of official committees and of a Royal Commission and legislation in regard to taxation and companies. It would be a mistake, however, to think of the work of the profession as arising from legislation only, important as legislation was and is.

The Income Tax Act, 1918, usefully consolidated the legislation of nearly eighty years: but during the next decade taxation became increasingly a flexible instrument of government with considerable complications, particularly in the years immediately succeeding the war. The raising of revenue—the main purpose—granting reliefs, removing inequities, stopping gaps, the termination of emergency taxes, and introducing new ones could scarcely avoid complications. Further, in proposing or amending taxation, the Government had also to consider the effects of taxation upon the state of the country's economy at any given time and the use of taxation as a part of social policy.

A Royal Commission on Income Tax, before which evidence on behalf of the Society was given by W. G. Rayner, past President, published its report in 1920.[1] It recommended the retention of taxation at the source and the abolition of three years' average as the basis for assessment of business profits, and of differentiation in the rate of tax on earned and unearned incomes. There would be substituted an earned income allowance and an increased exemption limit or abatement for all single persons and married couples, children's allowances would be irrespective of total income and the first £225 of assessable income would be taxed at half-rate. Administrative changes suggested were the six-year period for additional assessments (no limit in cases of fraud), but only one year for rectification in favour of a taxpayer; and on appeals before Commissioners of

[1] Cmd. 615, 1920.

Taxes a chartered or incorporated accountant should be appointed as consultant for each division. Drastic proposals for the production of original books of account for examination by assessing authorities seemed likely to meet with strenuous opposition.

*   *   *

As often in the course of the subsequent forty years, the Government were greatly concerned about the size and character of the floating debt, and ideas were advanced that it might be reduced by means of some kind of capital levy. A report (1920) of a Select Committee on the Increase of Wealth (War),[1] which considered a tax on capital or war wealth practicable but difficult administratively, aroused much protest on the part of financial and commercial interests. The tax was not accepted by the Government.

*   *   *

The Budget and the Finance Act of 1920 gave effect to the recommendations of the Royal Commission for adjustment of the burden of income tax by reducing 'sudden jumps', and for affording relief to lower incomes. The methods then adopted have in the main remained in force to the present time. Procedure was authorized to deal equitably with double taxation within the Empire. But the liability to supertax was to commence at £2,000 instead of at £2,500, with an increase in rates; this figure has persisted with uncomfortable familiarity, till, after modest relief in 1957, favourable change was made in 1961 for earned income. The standard rate of income tax continued at 6s., and the excess profits duty was raised from 40 to 60 per cent., when there was expectation of its abolition. Were a warwealth levy to be brought into operation, if advised by the Select Committee then sitting, the extra 20 per cent. would be dropped. The Government, however, refrained from so controversial a step. A corporation profits tax of 1s. in the pound on profits of companies was imposed for the first time, but in that form lasted for a few years only. Other recommendations of the Royal Commission, including the abolition of the three years' average, were the subject of a Revenue Bill introduced

[1] *House of Commons Paper* 102, 1920.

later in the 1921 session: the Bill, however, was withdrawn and the recommendations were left to be dealt with at a later date. Incidentally in the 1920 Budget, postage on inland letters became 2d. instead of 1½d., and receipt stamps 2d. instead of 1d.

By the Finance Act, 1926, assessment on the profits of the previous year was substituted for the three years' average as from 1 April 1927. Schedule E assessments remained on the actual year and were not changed to the preceding year. The weary course of the excess profits duty, which became a regular bugbear, continued until 30 September 1926, when the duty was finally abolished (save as to assessments made or claims preferred before that date). Considerable repayments had been made and a large amount of uncollectable arrears written off by the Government. (In the three months to 30 June 1925 receipts from excess profits duty were £2,560,000, while the repayments were £2,640,000. £123 million was still in assessment and unpaid and much of that sum was not likely to be paid.)

*　　　　*　　　　*

The progressive development of private companies, frequently carrying on businesses previously conducted as partnerships, gave emphasis to the question of undistributed profits and supertax; and this was the subject of an important section of the Finance Act, 1922. The partners of a firm were liable for income tax and supertax on the profits of the firm whether distributed to the partners or not. In a private company, the directors had been liable for income tax and supertax on their remuneration and dividends received from the company; similarly shareholders on dividends only: thus undistributed profits suffered income tax but not supertax. The purpose of section 21 in the 1922 Act was indicated in the preamble to the section: 'With a view to preventing the avoidance of the payment of supertax through the withholding from distribution of income of a company, which would otherwise be distributed.' This preamble was inserted in the House after considerable pressure and after some difficulty: without the preamble the section might have been oppressive. Powers were given to the Special Commissioners to direct assessment to supertax of the whole income of a private company where it appeared that the company had not, after the end of its financial year, distributed a reasonable part of its income to the members, regard being had to the requirements of the company for current needs and for future development. Part of the procedure was set forth in a schedule: where the Special Commissioners called for information and accounts, the directors might, among other details, furnish a certificate by the auditor that (a) he was satisfied that the information in a declaration by the directors was sufficient for him to form an opinion whether the proposed distribution was a reasonable part of the income (b) a prima facie case was made out that the proposed distribution was reasonable. An appeal from a determination by the Special Commissioners could be made either by the company or by the Inland Revenue to the Board of Referees. The qualifications of the auditor in the schedule—'member of an incorporated society of accountants'—perpetuated the unsatisfactory definition of an accountant in the Revenue Act, 1903, and invited some critical professional comment.

*   *   *

By 1925–6, after successive reductions, the standard rate of income tax was 4s.: this was the lowest rate between 1916 (when it was raised to a peak of 5s.) and 1959 (7s. 9d.).

The references made here to income tax and other forms of direct taxation are necessarily perfunctory, for the subject is almost inexhaustible. It is no wonder that directors of companies and business and professional men turned increasingly to qualified accountants for advice and assistance in sustaining the administrative and financial burdens of direct taxation. Dealing with clients and arriving at correct assessments—including solutions of arguable points—with Inland Revenue officials called for specialized and up-to-date knowledge on the part of accountants as well as qualities of character and tact. To younger members of the Society and students preparing for their examinations, the imperative knowledge of taxation required was a formidable problem, after a considerable period of absence on active service when so many changes and complications had been introduced. But they rose to the occasion; and indeed the accountancy profession has continuously realized the enormous importance of taxation as a branch of its work—both in respect of the obligations of business and taxpayers and the administration of taxation by the Board of Inland Revenue.

In the early twenties special questions of income-tax administration were dealt with by the Chancellor of the Exchequer: these were of more than passing interest.

In June 1921, in the House of Commons, the following question regarding the production of taxpayers' books was put to the Chancellor of the Exchequer:

Whether instructions had at any time been given to H.M. inspectors or surveyors of taxes to demand production from any taxpayer of books for inspection; if in certain cases this course had been adopted; and if by order of his department, under what authority?

The Financial Secretary to the Treasury replied:

The answer to the first part of the question is in the negative. As regards the second part, cases arise from time to time in which inspection of a taxpayer's books is desirable to resolve doubts or settle questions outstanding, but such an inspection is in no case made without the taxpayer's concurrence.

The second aspect was also dealt with by question and answer in the House (1923), when the Financial Secretary to the Treasury circulated a statement of the practice followed by the Inland Revenue in dealing with voluntary disclosure by taxpayers of previous fraud or evasion of taxation: the procedure was relevant to instructions given to practising accountants to deal with 'back duty', or cases in which such circumstances became known to them.

Lastly, in the hope of introducing simplification, a review of income-tax forms was made by a committee appointed by the Chancellor of the Exchequer under the Hon. Mr. Justice Rowlatt, the judge who at that time usually took revenue cases. Several bodies submitted memoranda, including the bodies of Chartered Accountants and the Society: three or four representatives of the Society were invited to meet informally the chairman and a member of the committee. The discussion was at a well-informed level: the conversations took place in the chairman's dignified room at Somerset House and left a pleasant impression by the charm of Mr. Justice Rowlatt and of Sir Richard Hopkins, chairman of the Board of Inland Revenue, and of Sir

Edward Harrison, Chief Inspector of Taxes, who was also present. The report of the committee (1924)[1] seemed to be a little disappointing by reason of the limited recommendations made. In fact in opening the report the committee said they were unable to recommend any extensive or fundamental re-casting of the forms. The committee rightly stated, however, that submissions made from various quarters tended to view the problem from their own angle, while the committee had to consider the administration of the system as a whole and the multitude of taxpayers whose circumstances varied infinitely. The report specifically referred to the consolidation of the two forms used for schedule D and for schedule E suggested by the Society—'the most important consolidation advocated before us'. Some 250,000 people had recently been transferred from schedule D to schedule E and the committee thought that—contrary to the view of the Society—a combined form would present many with quite irrelevant questions: they favoured specialization rather than consolidation of forms; but the admitted difficulty was to ensure that each taxpayer received the form appropriate to his case and not the wrong one, as sometimes happened. Generally speaking, simplification was not such an easy matter as many were inclined to believe.

*   *   *

In 1931 the Council recommended a course which, although no doubt it was already followed by most practising members, was of much public importance. The following resolution was adopted by the Council and was published in the *Incorporated Accountants' Journal* and elsewhere for general information: 'The Council of the Society recommends all members to observe the common practice adopted by incorporated accountants of keeping the monies of clients in a separate banking account or banking accounts exclusively used for the purpose.'

National Debt: The Gold Standard

A general but penetrating inquiry into national debt and taxa-tion was made by the committee under Lord Colwyn, 1924–7.[2] A joint memorandum was submitted on behalf of the accoun-tancy bodies, and Sir James Martin was a witness on behalf of the

[1] Cmd. 2019, 1924.   [2] Cmd. 2800, 1927.

Association of British Chambers of Commerce. The evidence referred to the general scramble for higher wages, salaries, and prices, and to the prosperity of certain industries dependent on the home market; they were able to pass higher costs to prices, with unfavourable reaction on competitive trades in the export markets of the world. High taxation, although inevitable, had adversely affected the supply of working capital and of capital for industry. It seemed prudent to make a reduction of the national debt gradually by applying part of any budgetary surpluses to this purpose and part to reduction of taxation: this policy was preferable to embarking on new expenditure, however expedient: the process of funding was desirable to deal with excessive floating debt. Sir James, in his verbal evidence, pointed out that a capital levy for the purpose of repayment of national debt would seriously dislocate trade and finance, in which stability was the first consideration, and would increase unemployment (which at that time was serious): it would undoubtedly lead to deflation. In addition to the internal situation and the swollen national debt, there was tremendous difficulty and not a little confusion, at any rate to ordinary observers, from such burning questions as the American debt settlement (1923) and inter-Allied indebtedness, as well as from the more formidable reparations problem. The American debt settlement was strongly opposed by the Prime Minister (Rt. Hon. A. Bonar Law, M.P.) but was accepted, albeit reluctantly, by the Cabinet.[1]

Sir Josiah Stamp, who was a member of the Colwyn Committee, was increasingly regarded as an authority on these incessant financial and economic problems. Prominence was given to them by the occurrence, particularly on the Continent, of acute inflation. Writing on the subject of 'money measure' in 1926, Sir Josiah made a comment of more than transitory significance: 'I do not hesitate to say that the greatest evil of our time is the instability of the money unit as a measure of real values.' And what a tale has unfolded since!

Advised by the Cunliffe Committee in 1918, the Government, through the Bank of England, directed monetary policy towards attaining a stable currency. In February 1925, the

[1] Sir Henry Clay, *Lord Norman.*

Chamberlain Committee, to whom the problem of the return to the Gold Standard had been referred, concluded 'there was no alternative comparable with a return to the former gold parity of the sovereign'.[1] This conclusion was doubtless shared in financial and political quarters, and it was accepted by the Government. The Chancellor of the Exchequer announced at the end of April that the Bank of England would sell gold for export at the coinage price of £3. 17s. 10½d. per oz., and the Restoration of the Gold Standard was formally effected by the Gold Standard Act, 1925.[2] 'The Pound looks the Dollar in the face' was the caption of a newspaper placard: no doubt people felt some pride in the achievement; but alas, its deflationary effects in terms of industrial troubles and unemployment had to be reckoned with. This policy and the impossibly high demand for reparations from Germany found a fearless critic in John Maynard Keynes, whose facile and often caustic pen set forth his criticisms in articles and in his books.

The Companies Act, 1929

Since the Companies (Consolidation) Act, 1908, the area of the operation of companies had greatly extended, notably by way of private companies and, latterly, of holding companies: so had the corresponding area of professional work, although, through the development of holding companies, perhaps with some concentration. The time had come for a comprehensive review to be made of company law and practice: a new act after the lapse of some twenty years since the 1908 Act was clearly needed. There had been a Companies Act of 1917 of some minor consequence and the work of Lord Wrenbury's Committee of 1918 had been limited in scope and had not been followed by legislation.

Accordingly, in January 1925 the President of the Board of Trade appointed a committee to consider what amendments were desirable in the Companies Acts, 1908 to 1917. The chairman was Wilfrid Greene, K.C., a distinguished member of the Bar, who was afterwards Lord Greene, Master of the Rolls, and who commanded high personal and professional regard. The other members included William Cash, F.C.A., Sir James

---

[1] Ibid.   [2] Sir Ralph Hawtrey, *The Gold Standard*.

Martin, F.S.A.A., and Sir William McLintock, K.B.E., C.V.O., C.A. Memoranda were submitted respectively by the Scottish Chartered Accountants, the English Institute, and the Society, and verbal evidence was given by representatives (A. B. Bryden, C.A., Walter Reid, C.A., S. J. Pears, F.C.A., G. S. Pitt, F.S.A.A.). The committee's report[1] published in June 1926 formed the basis of the Companies Act, 1929.

Its general background was indicated in the statement that the great majority of companies were honestly and conscientiously managed: and that cases of fraud or improper dealing which had attracted considerable publicity created an exaggerated idea of evils in the public mind. (There had been some bad floatations, a notorious case in the courts, and some fraudulent trading by private companies which gave a disproportionate impression relative to the general high degree of honest management.) The report stated that cases in which auditors fell below the level of their duty were few and far between. Therefore, a certain amount of elasticity was essential and it was undesirable to impose undue restrictions upon the activities of honest men. Consideration was given to the questions of the accounts of holding companies, and of how to give shareholders reasonable information without presenting them with bulky details of subsidiary companies, which would be more confusing than clarifying; also how to prevent abuses arising from inter-company transactions.

In the *City Equitable* case, 1924,[2] the court said that the auditor honestly and carefully discharged what he believed to be his duty. But he had relied on a certificate from stockbrokers, which proved to be fraudulent, and had not inspected the securities. He did not suffer liability since one of the articles (then fairly common) exempted directors and officers from liability for loss except if due to wilful default. The committee discussed whether the certificate of securities, which an auditor should be entitled to accept, should be fixed by statute, but considered that a change in the law was not required: the particular certificate which a careful auditor should accept must be left to him, and any default would be covered by the general law of negligence. The protection given to auditors by a 'wilful

[1] Cmd. 2657, 1926.   [2] [1925] 1 Ch. 407. C.A.

default' clause was unwarranted, and became forbidden by the terms of the 1929 Act, subject to the court having power to grant relief in special circumstances.

A heading 'Secret Reserves' was included in the memoranda of the Institute and the Society: the view was expressed that in certain cases they were desirable, provided they were included in balance-sheet items and were not used for manipulation of profits or for unjustifiable dealings in shares.

Since the committee thought that in general the law as it stood with regard to the powers of auditors was satisfactory, little change was made by the Act. But the position of an auditor was somewhat strengthened, and he was specifically empowered to attend the general meeting of the company and could make a statement or give explanations: a company was prohibited from being the auditor, and this provision maintained a professional position of individual or firm's responsibility and independence. Except in the case of private companies, partners and employees of directors or other officers of the company were ineligible for appointment as auditors: but the Act was completely silent on the professional qualifications of auditors, and a proposal that auditors when signing reports should state their professional qualifications did not find its way to the statute book. (Certainly there was the difficulty of a suitable description in the case of firms whose partners were not all members of one body.)

Up to the 1929 Act, there was no statutory obligation on a company to keep proper accounts: afterwards directors were bound so to do, to lay a profit and loss account and balance sheet before the company annually in general meeting, and, unless the company were a private company, to send balance sheet and directors' and auditors' reports to members. Nothing was said in the Act about the contents of the profit and loss account, and that represented the view of the professional witnesses before the Greene Committee; in fact some disliked statutory prescription to issue a profit and loss account or of what a balance sheet should disclose. However, following the recommendations made and to bring statutory obligation into line with the best professional practice, and for more substantial reasons, the Act prescribed that the balance sheet must contain a summary of the share capital, and an indication of the general nature of the liabilities and assets and how the values of the fixed assets had been arrived at; separate items were required for goodwill and preliminary expenses, and for the aggregate of any loans to directors; a note was necessary if a liability was secured (but not of the relevant asset). Investments in, and loans to or from, subsidiary companies (as defined) were to be stated separately and, sufficiently, in the aggregate. The Greene Committee was not prepared to make consolidated balance sheets compulsory or to deprive private companies, being subsidiaries of a parent company, of their privileges, such as exemption from filing accounts.

The Act afforded to creditors two valuable safeguards: first by extending from three to six months the period, before the commencement of a winding up, which rendered invalid a floating charge, unless the company was solvent when the charge was created: and secondly, by modified procedure to give creditors effective control in a voluntary winding up if the company were insolvent.

The Act of 1929 was accepted as a balanced piece of legislation and represented the general level of professional opinion in accountancy, so far as accounts and audit were concerned. A few years later, a distressing event (p. 186) induced some people in the profession to wonder whether the Act should have gone farther in prescribing the form and contents of balance sheets and profit and loss accounts.

IX. THE DEPARTMENTAL COMMITTEE
ON REGISTRATION

Parliamentary Proceedings on Municipal Bills

FOR some ten years after the First World War, the Society jointly with the English Institute was engaged in intense parliamentary activity. The audit clauses in municipal and certain private Bills followed the precedents approved by Parliament in 1914, when the Chairman of the Local Legislation Committee had pronounced that the standard of auditors' qualifications was that of the Institute and the Society (p. 85). The opening shot in the contentious period 1920 to 1930 was on the third reading of the Coventry Corporation Bill (1920) in the House of Commons. Two members of the Labour Party moved the recommittal of the Bill and addressed the House in favour of widening the audit clause by authorizing the corporation to appoint one or more accountants to act as auditor or auditors, if possible with the approval of the Ministry of Health—an obligation which the Ministry declined. Speaking with care and firmness in opposition to the motion, Sir William Middlebrook, M.P., Chairman of the Local Legislation Committee, said that if the bodies outside the two mentioned in the Bill would, on any future Bills, 'submit their evidence and let us know what their standard of qualification is, there is no bar against them in favour of the chartered and incorporated societies'. That the other bodies had not done, up to that date. The Chairman of Ways and Means also intervened to point out that it would be an undesirable practice for the House to review the proceedings of Private Bill Committees which heard evidence and acted in a judicial capacity. After these statements the motion to recommit was withdrawn. The position was the same in regard to the Wallasey Bill and was similar in the case of the Salford Bill: in that session the three Bills were passed with provisions for the appointment of members of the Institute or of the Society.

In subsequent sessions, petitions were lodged by other bodies

against municipal Bills: at first the petitions—which came before the Local Legislation Committee—were either withdrawn
or did not succeed, and, in one instance, the opposition completely collapsed on the evidence. The Institute and Society
were not called upon to submit evidence, but their counsel,
W. E. Tyldesley Jones, K.C., and F. J. Wrottesley, K.C. (afterwards Lord Justice Wrottesley), addressed the committee and
cross-examined witnesses giving evidence on behalf of petitioners. By 1929 considerable improvement had been effected in
the standards of one of the petitioning bodies, the representatives of which gave evidence on the Chester Corporation Bill.
Matters came to a head on this Bill. The position had been
reached that the Local Legislation Committee from session to
session had, with much patience, heard these contests between
the accountancy bodies: they may have felt that they were not
entirely a suitable body to be called on constantly to adjudicate
on the claims made. Moreover, promoters of Bills were put to
considerable expense and inconvenience: they wished to maintain a high standard of audit, and, generally speaking, did not
desire any change in the standard form of audit clauses. These
clauses were important to the accountancy bodies as determining by Parliament the general standard for auditors' qualifications—apart from the immediate but essential issue of the
audit of the accounts of municipal corporations and the public interest involved. The Chairman of the Committee, Sir
Thomas Robinson, M.P., announced that the committee had
decided not to amend the audit clause (which followed precedent): he added a statement that sound and reliable accounting was of paramount importance to industry, commerce, and
the investing public, and the committee considered the time
had arrived for establishing a register of properly qualified persons on the lines of the law and medical service, and suggested
that the accounting world should seriously consider the matter
of the register, the training and qualifications required, and that
all qualified persons should have the opportunity of giving
public service. Nobody could tell who would be on the committee in the next Parliament but they would have some difficulty in dealing with a clause like the clause in the Chester Bill,
unless something was done by the accounting world.

Next year, on the Cardiff Bill, evidence was again given by the petitioners. By that time the Departmental Committee on Registration had been appointed (p. 165). Counsel on behalf of the Institute and the Society submitted that the issue was about to be considered elsewhere and no formal opposition was offered. The committee decided to include in the audit clause the name of the London Association of Accountants Ltd., thereby rendering its members eligible for appointment as auditor of the Cardiff Corporation. By this decision the long line of precedents—about 74 and extending over forty years—came to an end. Regard may willingly be paid to the tenacity of the petitioners and the ability with which their case and evidence—mainly given by Mr. J. C. Latham, their Secretary—were submitted.

Even at this interval, however, retrospect upon these proceedings (1920–30), does not modify the view then taken by the Institute and the Society and the propriety of their frequent action in Parliament. No doubt there were considerations of prestige perhaps tinged with some emotion: but the issues concerned parliamentary recognition of the public practice of accountancy, the character of the training and qualifications of its practitioners, discipline exercised by the councils and generally the factors which constituted accountancy as a profession. Moreover, forty years ago the stage of development reached by the Institute and by the Society called for defence of the recognition they had received in Acts of Parliament and in other important precedents. Extension by the addition of standards of others, different and more flexible and, as the Institute and Society thought, without doubt less mature, might have had unfavourable reactions upon them. The frequent murmuring of chartered and incorporated accountants in a small or moderate way of practice at the ease with which less qualified or unqualified persons could practise imposed a duty upon the Councils to defend their position: and they also felt a responsibility towards the large number of young men and women—many ex-service men—who since 1919 had complied with the requirements of the two bodies by examination and professional service.

Naturally, the Institute and Society did not receive the

decision on the Cardiff Bill with approbation, but they were not
disgruntled. In the preceding ten years each body had developed
increasing strength within itself: parliamentary precedents remained important, but perhaps had become less paramount.
Further, the penultimate decision in the Local Legislation Committee (1929) led to an impartial investigation into the profession by a Departmental Committee (p. 165); and later there was
an Act of Parliament which settled the question of municipal
audits (p. 184).

The record of this phase of the Society's activities cannot pass
without reference to the cordial working of the Hon. George
Colville, Secretary of the English Institute, in co-operation with
the Society's secretariat, and of the parliamentary agents and
the respective solicitors in the onerous and continuous work of
preparation of briefs and vigilance in the actual proceedings.

*   *   *

Action took place soon after Sir Thomas Robinson's statement of 1929: but a few years earlier there had been two or
three discussions which call for comment.

In April 1923, at the request of Sir James Martin, a meeting
of representatives of the Scottish, English, and Irish Chartered
Accountants and of the Society was held in London to discuss
the desirability of registration. William Cash, President of the
English Institute, was host and was asked to take the chair.
There were before the meeting the general principles of registration, the attacks—hitherto unsuccessful—made in Parliament
upon the audit clauses in municipal Bills and the likelihood that
these attacks would be renewed—as in fact they were. If a satisfactory measure of registration could be accomplished, that
particular problem and others would have a chance of being
solved. It was a cordial and friendly meeting and there seemed
some inclination to explore the prospects. To achieve success—
assuming agreement were reached on its terms—it was clear
that the suggested Bill must be a Government measure.
Sir William (Lord) Plender, who was present, was asked to
consult the Board of Trade. In the following June the representatives were in Edinburgh as guests at a dinner given by the
Edinburgh Society, and again met. A report that the Board of
Trade was not disposed to sponsor a Registration Bill was

received: also, some doubts had presented themselves since the earlier meeting, as well as realization of difficulties and the disadvantages of a too-embracing register. Clearly, the circumstances and the views entertained did not favour any attempt to secure registration. Accordingly, in terms which implied no rebuff on the initiative taken, a resolution was adopted unanimously, that for the time being the introduction of legislation was not considered desirable and that the conference stand adjourned.

*   *   *

The presidential address of Sir Nicholas Waterhouse, K.B.E., at the autumnal meeting of the English Institute in October 1928, was an unpremeditated prologue to the Departmental Committee on Registration of 1930 (the appointment of the committee had not of course been mooted in 1928). Sir Nicholas was definitely against registration and submitted his considerations in a fair and balanced statement. He presented the reputation and status enjoyed by the chartered accountants of England and Wales, Scotland and Ireland, and, in a liberal spirit, referred to the work of the Society, whose activities 'are actuated by aims and ideals similar to our own' and whose members 'have taken a large share in bringing the accountancy profession to the honourable status which it has reached to-day'. Yet in spite of that—he implied with some personal surprise—there were still a number of members of the Institute and of the Society who continued to favour some form of registration under which all practising accountants, qualified and unqualified, who could put up an argument for inclusion as suitable persons would be labelled 'Registered Accountants'. Whatever might be the beneficial effect of such a scheme by imposing restrictions on the activities of certain individuals and bodies, how could the advantages outweigh the balance on the other side?

Within the Society itself, however, year after year, the representatives of the District Societies at the annual conferences brought forward the question of registration, which almost became an article of faith among them. They were people who knew the difficulties of public practice, particularly in the provinces, and believed that registration would bring both professional and public advantages—a view which, it was suggested from time to time, was shared by a considerable number of their fellow practitioners who were members of the Institute.

Impressed by the authority of Sir Thomas Robinson's statement (1929) and somewhat concerned at the situation in the Local Legislation Committee, the Society's Council formally reaffirmed its belief in registration as being in the interests of the public and the profession, and considered that a Bill ought to be promoted in Parliament.

There was a feeling that the Society should not wait upon events and should take a somewhat independent line; and some publicity was given to the statement of the Council. In the circumstances the initiative thus taken by the Society may have been right: but some might think—and probably the Institute did so think—that it savoured of rather much haste. The state of affairs as between the chartered accountants and the Society for a period—happily a short one—subsequent to Sir Thomas Robinson's statement on registration (March 1929) was rather difficult. Fortunately there was sufficient wisdom and tolerance to prevent matters reaching an impasse, in spite of some scarcely auspicious moves on both sides.

Consultations between the Scottish Chartered Accountants, the Institute, and the Society ensued. The Institute suggested that the President of the Board of Trade be asked to appoint a Departmental Committee on Registration. The Society would probably have preferred steps to prepare a Bill: but it was clear that the Scottish Chartered Accountants and the Institute did not favour registration, and the Society's representatives were rather troubled by an approach which appeared to them as *chose jugée*. This point of view was appreciated by the chartered accountants present at joint consultations: a draft memorandum under discussion was accordingly amended, which became an agreed statement of request for submission to the Board of Trade.

The Departmental Committee under Viscount Goschen

A deputation waited upon the President of the Board, William Graham, M.P., who on 7 February 1930 appointed a Departmental Committee. The Chairman was Viscount Goschen, G.C.S.I., G.C.I.E., and the other members were men of affairs drawn from a wide field of public activities whose impartiality commanded respect. The terms of reference were: 'To consider and report whether it is desirable to restrict the practice of the profession of Accountancy to persons whose names would be inscribed in a Register established by law, and if so to report on the method by which such register should be established and controlled.'

*   *   *

Memoranda of evidence were put in by the accountancy and other bodies, some Government departments, and individual practising accountants. The Society's memorandum comprised information about its examinations, membership, and the disciplinary powers of the Council, a statement of classes of candidates then covered by the by-laws for non-articled clerks, and a copy of the 1911 Bill, slightly amended to bring it up to date; particulars were included of some specific cases in which members of the public had suffered from unqualified accountants (the Society was the only body that offered such information). It was reported that of 5,225 members of the Society (1 January 1930), 2,386 were in practice, 2,839 were non-practising; 87 per cent. of the total had passed the Society's final examination, 4 per cent. the examinations of approved bodies, and the remaining 9 per cent. included original and early members and members of other bodies of standing in the United Kingdom and the British dominions elected to the Society. No person had been elected since 1912 unless he had passed the Society's examinations or the examinations of another approved body of accountants. The memorandum represented that any person could commence practice as an accountant without compliance with any standard of qualification or of discipline and conduct—sometimes under the guise of a mercantile agency, an income-tax agency, &c.

*   *   *

The first verbal evidence was given by Sir William (Lord) Plender, then President of the Institute, William Cash, past President, and the Hon. George Colville, Secretary.

Sir William, referring to the 1911 Bill (p. 74), which was

blocked in the House of Commons, said it became evident that amendments which would have been necessary to get the Bill passed (had it gone forward) were such that registration on a basis adequate to safeguard the public and acceptable to the profession would not have been forthcoming. Since 1911 there had been a large growth in the membership of the Institute and in the status of chartered accountants; and other bodies had grown too. The position in 1930 was different from 1911; and even in 1911 opposition to registration as a monopoly would have been considerable. Inquiries had been made recently among leading accountants, and Sir William was of opinion they were not in favour of registration. He thought that registration would lead to a levelling down (he quoted two members of the Society's Council who had spoken in that sense) and to a possible assumption of equality in professional skill; and there was no real public demand for registration—certainly an absence of demand from such bodies as the Bankers' Association, the Federation of British Industries, and Lloyd's. A reference to the status enjoyed by chartered accountants included particulars of numerous appointments to Government committees and formidable statistics showing that auditors of public companies were in the main chartered accountants. Opposition was to be expected from the municipal treasurers, railway accountants, and (by reason of their incidental interest in certain accountancy work) the Chartered Institute of Secretaries, banks, insurance companies, solicitors, and from companies and charities authorized to appoint lay auditors. Again a great deal of work was done by persons not members of the Institute or Society—not large work—and they probably did it well enough to satisfy clients. Even if registration were limited to chartered accountants in practice, incorporated accountants in practice, and other practising accountants, there would be some 25,000 to 30,000 persons included; and among so large a number he foresaw great difficulty in maintaining high standards of conduct. Asked if, in the absence of registration, the risks to the public might not become greater in future, Sir William said he did not think so; the public already realized what accountancy meant and were fully cognizant of people who were competent to do accountancy work. A resolution had been passed by the Institute's

Council that in its opinion there was no public demand for registration and that it would not be in the public interest. If, however, if were enforced by legislation, the Council asked that members of the Institute, a body incorporated by royal charter, should be excluded from such legislation, and that it should continue as a separate entity, with the rights and privileges assigned by the royal charter. In concluding his evidence, Sir William reinforced the contents of this resolution and asked that if registration were recommended the chartered bodies should be left outside and—with some emphasis—that their members should continue to use the description of, and practise as, chartered accountants.

When William Cash, past President of the Institute, went into the witness chair, he agreed that the chartered bodies would rather not have registration: he was then asked about the definition (Revenue Act, 1903; Income Tax Act, 1918): 'Accountant means a person who has been admitted a member of an incorporated society of accountants.' The Hon. George Colville, Secretary of the Institute, intervened to say that some of the newer bodies came into existence on the strength of that definition; he produced the advertisement of one of such bodies claiming that by the provision its members were entitled to plead before Commissioners of Income Tax. William Cash was a very experienced parliamentary witness and he answered with much delicacy questions, on the one hand, relative to articles for five years and premiums and, on the other, concerning the growth of smaller-class work, carried out by persons of limited experience, who entertained the hope of registration. On grounds of public policy, he suggested that registration, with restricted conditions in the future, might inflict some hardship on comparatively poor men, who might have some qualification to carry on, in a limited sense, the profession of accountancy, as they were then able so to do.

Representatives of the Scottish Chartered Accountants, R. D. Raine, C.A., and L. B. Bell, C.A., Edinburgh, Peter Rintoul, C.A., Glasgow, and John Reid, C.A., Aberdeen, gave their evidence after Sir James Martin (p. 168). They pointed to the difficulty of defining accountancy for the purpose of registration, and represented that the profession was in a satisfactory position in Scotland and had no desire for registration. The section of the public interested in accountancy matters was content with the present situation and had been led by experience and tradition (from 1854 when the Edinburgh Society was founded) to discriminate between the qualified and the unqualified. The Scottish Chartered Accountants did not consider registration was desirable.

In opening his evidence on behalf of the Society, Sir James Martin asked the chairman's permission to make a statement on events which had occurred quite recently. He said, first, that any legislation which excluded the Institute—as the Institute had requested—would not meet with the voluntary acceptance of the Society. Secondly, the Local Legislation Committee had that year added to the standard form of audit clause in municipal Bills the name of another body of accountants. Out of courtesy to the Departmental Committee, the Institute and the Society had not offered opposition or evidence; but he thought, with respect, that the Local Legislation Committee had pre-judged the very issue referred to the Departmental Committee. With the chartered accountants opposed to registration and, conversely, with the expectation of requests from other quarters for registration on quite unacceptable lines, the position of the Society was somewhat isolated. But Sir James gave his evidence with much skill, backed by his lifelong conviction about statutory registration for the profession of accountancy. He envisaged the setting up of a register (a) to comprise initially the name of every accountant who proved that he was in bona fide public practice, and (b) to which thereafter admission would be open only to those persons having prescribed experience and qualification by examination. (It may be wondered if Sir James had quite realized that setting the minimum standard for (b) would involve difficulties immensely greater in 1930 than at the time of the 1911 Bill.) The chairman asked Sir James whether the small business man made inquiry about any accountant he proposed should audit his accounts and whether there was public demand for registration. Sir James said it was astonishing the way people rushed into things without inquiry; and that the public were mainly interested in a few subjects worked up by the press. He was emphatic as to the undesirability of accountants starting in practice without qualification and without being under any control or discipline: hence the need for registration. Questions were then directed to the inclusion of accountants not in practice as well as accountants in practice. The representative of the Board of Trade pointed out that in the terms of reference, 'practice' did not mean 'practice' as distinct from 'not in practice' in the sense indicated by Sir James; and another member of the committee drew attention to the fact that those town clerks who were solicitors held practising certificates. Sir James thought it would be impossible to place restrictions on the appointment of persons, whether qualified or not, to whole-time positions as employees of business firms and companies: he considered the problem was incapable of solution on those lines. Then there was the question of auditors of companies, about whose qualifications there was nothing in the (recent) Companies Act, 1929. Sir James, who was a member of the Greene Committee on Companies, said that that committee decided to leave the matter alone because of the immense trouble there was in Parliament about the qualifications of auditors. 'We did not consider the public interest suffered', and Sir James assented to the chairman's observation that companies took care to have properly qualified men. But he was of opinion that statutory registration limited to auditors of companies would be useless for the purpose which the Society had in view.

Henry Morgan, President of the Society, followed Sir James. The public could be misled by unsatisfactory persons holding themselves out as practising accountants—a view illustrated by a specific case—but there were reputable persons in smaller places who practised, although they did not hold a professional qualification. He believed the Society's draft Bill would cover that situation and that many persons registered at first would fall away, which would facilitate the exercise of disciplinary control. A member of the committee propounded what seemed to him a practical possibility. At the formation of the register all persons in practice holding a qualification of standing would be included in section A of the register; others in practice not complying with the standard would be included in section B. Future admissions to be to section A only: persons in section B to be given facilities to qualify for section A by enlarged experience, examinations, &c. Section B in time would disappear. At first Henry Morgan was sceptical and preferred the Society's Bill: but after an exchange of views he lent himself more favourably to the suggestions, although they offered what would be a rather long-term prospect.

C. Hewetson Nelson, chairman of the Board of Examiners, gave evidence in regard to the Society's examinations; and Mr. R. Wilson Bartlett represented strongly the position in cities and towns away from London, where unqualified practising accountants were more in evidence than was sometimes thought, to the detriment of the public and qualified practitioners.

*   *   *

The evidence of the London Association of Accountants Ltd. was in favour of registration but on more expansive lines than the proposals of the Society. The representatives submitted that the decision of the Local Legislation Committee to include the name of the Association in the Cardiff Corporation Bill (given almost concurrently with the commencement of the sittings of the Departmental Committee) had removed a professional stigma from its members. Naturally, the representatives of the Association attached great weight to that decision and made the most of their newly won success.

From a standpoint somewhat different from that of the bodies which had already given evidence, the Institute of Municipal Treasurers and Accountants favoured registration; but subject to the distinct condition that members of that Institute who were city, borough, and county treasurers or chief financial officers of other local authorities should be eligible to be included in the register in the same way as practising accountants. On the general question, they had become aware of the need for registration by observation in areas throughout the country, particularly of the variety of persons, often without any qualifications and sometimes quite incompetent, who managed to get themselves elected as borough auditors under the Municipal Corporations Act. The proceedings on municipal Bills also pointed to establishing a properly constituted register.

Continuing, the Departmental Committee heard or received

the views of no less than ten bodies of accountants, in addition to those of the seven bodies (including three of Scottish Chartered Accountants) already mentioned. It is astonishing how so many bodies came into existence—in fact four of them had each a membership of but 300 or less. The number of these bodies added confusion to a difficult situation. The aggregate membership of the seventeen bodies which submitted evidence was no less than 26,400.

Then there were practising accountants (nine in all) who came before the committee and who were not members of any body. They had been accountants' clerks and turned their experience to public practice, which they carried on in a proper professional manner. One of them spoke scathingly of the up-and-coming so-called practising accountants, and gave a touch of humour to rather serious evidence by saying 'They stick up cards in public houses and circularize and advertise in the press!' That kind of thing was indeed degrading and it was resented by the more sensitive among reputable practising accountants.

★   ★   ★

Memoranda or evidence were submitted by nine non-accountancy organizations; mainly their attitude was neutral, with some slight bias in favour by the Chambers of Commerce, against on the part of the Federation of British Industries, while the National Chamber of Trade was doubtful. The last body indicated that the small trader was content with a less highly qualified and less expensive service than was implied by registration, which savoured of monopoly.

Information, not very extensive, had been obtained by the Law Society from the Provincial Law Societies. There was some, but not substantial, evidence of unsatisfactory work by unqualified accountants. The committee were reminded that solicitors managed trusts and kept trust accounts; and that they were perfectly competent to handle these affairs.

The Co-operative Union was interested in co-operative auditors, who were on the staff of the independent audit department of the Co-operative Wholesale Society: they audited the accounts of some of the co-operative societies and were included in the list of public auditors authorized by the Treasury for the purpose. Its witness entertained the idea of registration being a 'national' matter rather than one for control by the professional bodies.

The views of some of the Government departments given publicly to the committee had special interest. The Chief Inspector of Taxes spoke for the Board of Inland Revenue. Beginning with the definition of an accountant as 'a member of an incorporated body of accountants' in the Income Tax Act, 1918, and in other Acts dealing with the revenue, the Chief Inspector said the definition had arisen from the disinclination of commissioners to refuse access to taxpayers' agents, who frequently were accountants. It had not been of much value since new bodies of accountants could always be formed; but on the other hand it had not given rise to any serious difficulty. (The point was of course that the statutory definition coupled with facilities under the Companies Act had unwittingly encouraged the formation of new bodies.) When inspectors had figures and accounts submitted by accountants, they made more searching inquiries if they were not satisfied with the qualifications or competence of the accountants than if the accountants were properly qualified persons. Small traders suffered more from the incompleteness of their own accounts than from the incompetence of their agents. He agreed that a register would be of some assistance to inspectors, but they would have to continue to exercise their judgement, particularly during the inevitable and long transitional period after the register was set up. The evidence of the Chief Inspector was essentially fair and factual and he was mindful of the varying standards amongst those who acted for taxpayers: but the evidence did not lend any weight to registration as being necessary or desirable.

The other witness from the Civil Service was the Chief Registrar of Friendly Societies, who was responsible for making recommendations for appointments to the Treasury List of Public Auditors under the Industrial & Provident and Friendly Societies Acts. In exercising this responsibility, he had regard to the amount of public audit work in different areas and to the number of public auditors which the work required. In order to maintain a standard, regulations—then current—permitted applications for new appointments to be limited to chartered and incorporated accountants. An arrangement made with the

Society of Incorporated Accountants enabled the younger generation of potential co-operative auditors who could prove experience acceptable to the Society to sit for the Society's examinations. Thus those who qualified in that way rendered themselves eligible for appointment. He favoured a register of accountants, which would relieve him of an onerous part of his duties when making recommendations for appointments and for the professional qualifications required.

The Treasury did not give verbal evidence but submitted a memorandum. The memorandum comprised a list of official audits for which the Treasury made appointments: the audits were mainly carried out by the Comptroller and Auditor-General or by other Government departments or by individual civil servants. The Treasury saw no disadvantage in a register, provided that initially and in the future it was restricted to persons with a reasonable standard of attainment and efficiency. The terms 'accountant' and 'principal accountant' had been used in statutes and official documents from time anterior to the formation of the professional bodies. Therefore a special description of persons registered would be necessary. There was a question whether senior civil servants engaged on accountancy work should be admitted to the proposed register *ex officio*: civil servants who held qualifications from the principal bodies should not be debarred from registration, although in the membership lists they were described as 'not in practice'. Finally, the facilities given by the Society for civil servants of suitable standing and with adequate experience in accountancy to be admitted to the Society's examinations were of considerable value to the Government service; and it was hoped that nothing would be done to prejudice their continuance.

The foregoing summary indicates that the Departmental Committee had received very comprehensive evidence—from the more senior bodies, the newer ones, unattached practising accountants, important non-accountancy organizations, and two or three Government departments. All points of view had been presented and were received by the Departmental Committee and its distinguished Chairman, Viscount Goschen, with impartiality and open-mindedness.

★   ★   ★

While the proceedings of the committee were in progress, the annual meetings of the principal accountancy bodies took place. Each President had a duty to report to his members the character and direction of the evidence given on behalf of his body. There can be no doubt that the respective councils were supported by the members generally in the policies pursued: these policies were made plain in the speeches delivered, which, read thirty years later, seem a little contentious. It is true that at the Institute's meeting one or two individuals were inclined to be critical; but they were persuaded to accept the policy of the Council by the arguments of the President and by the general tenor of opinion.

In the interval before the publication of the committee's report, and as the number of witnesses increased and the evidence lengthened, leading members of the Society became increasingly sceptical of the committee reporting in favour of registration—and they were probably not alone in that view.

Report of the Committee

The report of the Departmental Committee[1] was published on 31 July 1930.[2] The substance of the report was presented in an interesting way and it included a comprehensive table giving the names, dates of foundation, and membership of the seventeen bodies which had submitted evidence.

The second part of the report was a readable summary of different sections of the evidence, and the third part set forth the opinions and conclusions of the committee. The evidence was reviewed with relevant arguments and assessed in relation to the terms of reference. If many of the arguments taken piecemeal were unimpeachable—although not all—they seemed somewhat lacking in strength relative to the situation *as a whole* as it was then.

First there was the difficulty (an admitted difficulty) of defining accountancy for the purpose of the restriction of practice: none of the definitions submitted, the committee thought, satisfactorily covered the whole field. A great diversity of work

[1] Cmd. 3645, 1930.
[2] The following paragraphs do not follow the order of the contents of the report, nor do they purport to be other than a bare outline thereof.

was comprised in accountancy, from what was little more than book-keeping to advising on financial reconstructions and floatations. And there were solicitors and banks who carried out income-tax work and administered trusts; and other persons not accountants did work which fell within the general scope or accountancy, including a variety of clerks, who assisted traders in their spare time, and income-tax experts. Discussing the possibility of a register, the committee stated that as things were anyone could hold himself out to the public as an accountant, and unqualified persons offered their services to the public and secured employment particularly in connexion with income-tax work; and there were people who had been expelled from the accountancy bodies. But the meaning of 'unqualified' was coloured by the requirements for membership of the particular body represented by the witness. So far as the public were concerned, the proper test was whether a person was competent to carry out the particular work he offered to do and led the public to believe he was able to do, e.g. a clerk might be competent to assist a small trader with his accounts but not to conduct general practice. The committee then envisaged the situation if a register were set up. Initially it would comprise all persons then in practice, and thereafter entry would be subject to tests. It would be only after the lapse of a generation that the public would have assurance that every person whose name was on the register was really qualified for practice as a public accountant. Still the public would have an immediate guarantee as to future entrants and of discipline over all accountants registered. After the completion of the original register, no doubt future candidates would be required to show a high standard of education and qualification—and this high standard would be necessary to ensure that all persons accepted possessed the necessary competence to practise in the higher branches of the profession. In view of the divergent nature of the work of accountants, the controlling authority might then find itself under considerable pressure to reduce the standard. A high standard could involve considerable hardship: first, on men who intended to undertake the less important accountancy work only and who would have to go to trouble and expense to pass difficult examinations in subjects they might never require in practice; and secondly,

many of the public would be compelled to employ persons of
unnecessarily high skill to carry out work at present done
efficiently by persons not so highly qualified. On the other
hand, a low standard would recognize as competent to practise
in the higher branches of the profession men who had inadequate qualifications. Again, a clerk who in his spare time assisted
a trader with his accounts was doing useful work and it would
not be in the public interest to prevent his doing so. The
Chamber of Trade had expressed fear that the setting up of a
monopoly would result in an increase in fees. (The aspect of the
less important kinds of accountancy work was certainly material
to the question of the public interest; but it seems to have been
given rather much emphasis by the committee; and the depressing reaction of the existing situation upon qualified practitioners
who carried on the smaller practices in a proper professional
manner was hardly given due weight.) It was from firmer
ground that attention was directed to the fact that such demand
as there was for registration came from sections within the
profession and not from other quarters; that there was little
evidence of the public or taxpayers having suffered from the
incompetence or lack of integrity of unqualified accountants;
and that outside authoritative organizations were mainly
neutral or indifferent.

*   *   *

If one may take a flight of fancy, it is possible to imagine the
situation which confronted the committee after the members
had reviewed all the evidence.

One approach might have been: Here is a profession of importance to the public and to the country which is occupied
with the affairs of companies, industry, finance, and the proper
assessment of income tax and other direct taxation. Its organization as a whole—if unquestionably good in sections—is extremely untidy; the standards of respective sections are high,
moderate, or very doubtful; and in fact anyone with or without qualifications can, in the present state of the law, start
practice as an accountant. Moreover, new bodies of accountants are being formed continually, no doubt in the hope of
securing benefits of possible registration for their members.
Then there is this perennial pother before the Local Legislation

Committee about the standard of auditors' qualifications for municipal audits. In this situation, ought something to be done? If nothing is done, will the situation deteriorate further and will it become increasingly difficult to do anything about it as time goes on? Can we prepare a rational and workable scheme to cover all the disparate elements which will give the public some guarantee for the future and introduce a level of high and regular standards? And if we can, is such a scheme likely to be acceptable to Parliament or will Parliament scent monopoly; and will it be proof against attack by all the interests which have been brought to our notice? Will such a scheme accomplish the maintenance of a high standard or lead to some levelling down ; and will it be in the interests of the profession and more particularly of the public?

It would have required more conviction and faith than the evidence is likely to have produced to have enabled the committee to come to a clear conclusion in the affirmative.

The second approach might have been: We have received evidence from no less than seventeen bodies of accountants, much of it conflicting in substance and certainly in emphasis. The chartered bodies, which are the oldest and the members of which represent some 45 per cent. of the total membership of all the seventeen bodies, are emphatically opposed to registration, and in fact ask to be excluded from any scheme which might be recommended. Of the other nine 'non-accountancy' professional and business bodies which have submitted evidence, some are doubtful, some very slightly favourable, the members of others are quite satisfied with the present accountancy service they receive, and most are neutral or indifferent to registration. The Civil Service is neutral—slightly favourable here, slightly unfavourable there. The Treasury drew attention to senior civil servants who conducted official audits and to accountants in the departments who had professional qualifications: it was suggested that they should not be debarred from the register. The scheme of registration indicated by the Society is rational and is not to be ignored; but in face of the situation disclosed to us it would meet with much opposition, and the scheme would be difficult to initiate and to administer. It is material that a definition of 'public or practising accountant' completely satisfactory to us has not been submitted and in fact the difficulty was emphasized by some of the witnesses. Again, there is no evidence of demand for registration on the part of the public. There are instances of incompetence on the part of some of those who are not members of the more senior bodies and who practise as accountants, some under other guises: but there is not a great deal of specific evidence that the public is seriously prejudiced through the incompetence or lack of integrity of a number of practising accountants. At the higher levels of accountancy practice (e.g. the audits of public companies) and on the part of large concerns, it seems clear that clients are satisfied. In the middle range competent business men are able to discriminate in the selection of their professional accountants. The small trader is apparently content with such service as he receives, often from accountants not members of the senior or of any bodies; or it is good enough, even if it is part-time work by clerks with accountancy or book-keeping experience: and he is undoubtedly apprehensive lest under registration he would have to pay higher fees than he does at present for an unnecessarily high standard of service. And, finally, among the witnesses favouring registration, some do not contemplate registration limited to those who carry on public practice as ordinarily understood, or claim specific and important exceptions to such restriction.

It seemed that the committee took the second of these approaches, and its penultimate view was: 'We can only conclude on the evidence before us that, for the most part, the general public is not influenced or misled by the fact that an individual describes himself as an "accountant" but bases its selection of an accountant principally on personal knowledge or local reputation.' Not surprisingly, the final conclusion was: '*On the evidence before us we are unanimously of the opinion that it is not desirable to restrict the practice of the profession of accountancy to persons whose names would be inscribed in a register established by law.*'

An addendum to the committee's main conclusion discussed the possibility that only persons whose names were on a register should be permitted to carry out audits required by statute— e.g. of companies, municipalities, industrial and provident societies. The suggestion seemed to offer some attractions, but, after consideration, the committee were unable to recommend it. To fix a standard for such a limited but important register and to apply it to applicants would have been extremely difficult and would probably have involved considerable and disputable discrimination. Moreover, the committee were not prepared to recommend what the Greene Committee on companies had deliberately omitted, nor were they willing to contemplate auditors with statutory qualifications for the 90,000 private companies then on the companies register.

*   *   *

The Profession and the Report

How was the report received? The editor of the *Incorporated Accountants' Journal*, who for over forty years had been a consistent advocate of registration, accepted the report as fair judgement and without major criticism, although he felt that the committee in one or two places were getting on to rather dangerous ground. He was conscious and acknowledged that the profession itself was deeply divided on the question.

Appreciating past ruffled feelings which it desired to assuage, *The Accountant* in restrained language commented favourably on the report and on the fact that the registration question had now been considered authoritatively. Particularly it referred to the committee's view that the general public were not influenced or misled by the fact that an individual described himself as an 'accountant'.

The *Certified Accountants' Journal* paid respect to the authority and competence of the committee and its proceedings even if it was disappointed with the findings: its main ground for criticism—from its own point of view—was in regard to a good deal of the evidence, unfavourable to registration, submitted to the committee.

One opinion on the report—outside the profession—was given by *The Economist*. It regretted that the committee had returned a purely negative answer and had marshalled all the difficulties—initiating the register and the test of qualification— and found no demand from the public. It was not impressed by the findings and believed a register was necessary both for the public and the profession. But the heading of the note was 'No Register for Auditors'; its contents referred not only to the increase in public companies but to the almost inevitable tendency of legislation to put onerous duties upon auditors—perhaps a slightly more restricted concept than the implications of registration as presented to the committee.

Among the members of the Society's Council were those, including the President (Henry Morgan), who, although they had believed in registration, were glad that the problem had been investigated and the report issued. Some quietus was now given to the continuous representations of the District Societies, who had greatly underestimated the difficulties and the volume of critical opinion. Further, the registration question had been a cause of rift between the Institute and the Society, which to many interested was a matter of serious regret; and, from that point of view, it was well that the matter had, for the time being, been settled. In the immediate future registration could not to be regarded as practical politics: but on the part of the Council and members there was unabated faith in the Society's general policy and prospects, and in the place which the Society occupied in the profession.

In the profession itself, the report was received with relief, indifference, or disappointment according to individual standpoints. Certainly the evidence and the report refuted the belief of those who had thought that the case for registration had only to be investigated impartially to be proved. Any scheme likely to be effective would probably not have been accepted by Parliament; and a scheme attempting to meet the varying points of view would have been of little use. Authority was given to the report by the status and personnel of the Departmental Committee and by reason of the exhaustive inquiry made and the unanimity of the committee in reaching its conclusions.

The Jubilee of the Institute of Chartered Accountants in England and Wales

This part of the history may end on a happier note. In 1930 the President and Secretary of the Society and Sir James Martin were received with much cordiality by Sir William (Lord)

Plender, Bart., G.B.E., then President of the Institute, as guests at the Jubilee Dinner held in Guildhall, London. The Council of the Society extended its sincere congratulations to the Institute and it recognized warmly the great contribution which the Institute had made to the profession of accountancy. With the registration problem disposed of, the outlook was much improved.

1931–1939

X. THE GREAT DEPRESSION

Its Onset and Outcome

THE period 1931 to 1939 opened in the midst of severe
economic crisis and ended in the cataclysm of war. An unprecedented world-wide slump had been touched off by the collapse of the stock markets in the U.S.A. in 1929, which
followed a period of intense speculation. Signs of the impending
collapse had already become apparent to the visitors to the
International Congress on Accounting in New York during
that year. But the end of the speculative boom was only one of
many intractable causes of the slump: contributory were the
confused international financial situation and a tremendous
fall in the prices of primary products with lamentable effect
on export trade everywhere; over-production and under-con-
sumption were conspicuous. Competitive moves were made
by all countries in an attempt to protect themselves and their
economies: restrictions on imports, quotas, and exchange controls were imposed, and many people eventually came to think
that these steps aggravated the situation as a whole. At home,
prolonged deflation followed the return (1925) to the Gold
Standard at pre-1914 parity; and by the early 1930's unemployment reached disastrous dimensions, particularly in the areas of
heavy industry. Unemployment was even worse in America
and Germany. There were intense political repercussions in
several countries—in the United Kingdom accentuated by
drastic Government economies in expenditure. Important
banks in Austria and Germany failed in 1931: European
countries began to repatriate rapidly short-term funds which
they held in London, and the country was forced off the Gold
Standard. Yet on the day when this happened the ordinary
customer visiting his bank in London could not notice that

anything so serious was actually happening. There were no banking failures in the United Kingdom (except a minor one, which arose from unsound banking principles and which does not affect the broad statement). Widespread bank defaults, however, occurred in the U.S.A., which abandoned the Gold Standard (1933):[1] for a time this upset the foreign exchanges on the international money markets. In 1933 a World Economic Conference assembled in London to seek and to recommend policies that might remedy the economic disaster which had overtaken the world. The conference came to the point of believing that the immediate key to the situation was the stabilization of the value of the dollar at a suitable rate in terms of gold. But President Franklin Roosevelt, who was wrestling with the serious problems of his own country, was unable to agree. The Economic Conference settled nothing—it was a failure.

However, the forces of recovery gradually became active, aided by Government measures, which included a reduction in interest rates—stimulating movement in the building trade[2]— and possibly by the Ottawa Agreement and other agreements affecting foreign trade. Unemployment dropped and there was some improvement in the situation by 1937, although unemployment was still at a seriously high level. A set-back then occurred, soon to be moderated by developing war production in manufacturing industries. During this period belief in the 'rationalization' of industry manifested itself increasingly: in effect, the concentration of industry in larger undertakings and the closing of smaller and uneconomic units. This tendency resulted in a degree of concentration of professional work and adversely affected some firms.

These circumstances were hardly propitious for the accountancy profession, which flourishes with economic prosperity. Yet it did not suffer in a major degree: notwithstanding the jests of after-dinner speakers that accountancy thrives in good times and bad, it is true that in periods of depression clients need advice and help in solving their problems as they do in periods of expansion and prosperity. Among the junior members of the Society there was some unemployment, but not a lot. The number of men who had registered with the Society's

[1] W. Arthur Lewis, *Economic Survey 1919-39*.   [2] Ibid.

Appointments Department was large enough to be noticeable. For some reason or another the position for a year or two seemed to become intensified in August and September; and the holiday months in the Society's office were apt to be overcast by calls from members seeking jobs. But the more general effect was probably in some stagnation of rates of salaries—an indication of the widespread economic situation, and more immediately an outcome of stationary or reduced fees paid to firms, slackness in new business, and the comparative lack of vacancies in commerce and industry. A member of Council expressed concern at the large number of replies he received in response to an advertisement for a qualified man for his staff. An investigation was made: it disclosed that while a proportion of the men who had sought the services of the Appointments Department were out of employment, the majority were those desiring to improve their positions at better salaries than they were earning. In any case, the number on the appointments register was not a large percentage of membership. The question was also raised whether the Society was accepting too many candidates in the prevailing circumstances. A practising Fellow could take three articled clerks and a practising Associate two. Actually the total quota that was permissible for all the practising members was not by any means filled; and by-law candidates were employed on an economic footing. There was no ground for regulative action, which, unless imperative, was clearly undesirable. Fortunately, unemployment was not at any time a serious factor in the Society. Speaking in Belfast in 1937, the President (Mr. Walter Holman) said he did not think there was any question of overcrowding in the profession as the demand for accountants was still equal to the supply. The position was more satisfactory than it was in some occupations.

The Municipal Corporations (Audit) Act, 1933

The fact that the Goschen Committee (1930) had been unable to recommend registration meant that the Local Legislation Committee of the House of Commons and municipal corporations were left with the question of the qualifications to be prescribed in Bills which provided for professional audit, although a new precedent had been set by the Cardiff Bill decision of 1930 (p. 161). It was probable that this situation had engaged the attention of the (then) Ministry of Health, particularly as some extensive reform of local government was contemplated by the National Government elected in 1931. In the session of 1933, Mr. Maurice Petherick, M.P., secured a high place in the ballot for private members' Bills and, with the blessing of the Government, he introduced the Municipal Corporations (Audit) Bill. The Bill withstood the hazards attendant on a private member's Bill, including some speeches in the House rather off the mark: but informed guidance was given by the sponsor of the Bill and by the Parliamentary Secretary to the Ministry, and the Bill was eventually passed. Its provisions were subsequently included in the Local Government Act, 1933. That Act provided that in every borough, unless an alternative method of audit was in force or adopted, there should be elective auditors and the mayor's auditor. But the council might, by resolution passed by two-thirds of the members voting and duly confirmed, adopt as an alternative either (a) district audit of the Ministry of Health, or (b) professional audit. Where professional audit was adopted, no person was qualified for appointment as auditor unless he was a member of one or more of the following professional bodies:

the Institute of Chartered Accountants in England and Wales;
the Society of Incorporated Accountants and Auditors;
the Society of Accountants in Edinburgh;
the Institute of Accountants and Actuaries in Glasgow;
the Society of Accountants in Aberdeen;
the London Association of Certified Accountants Ltd.;
the Corporation of Accountants Ltd.

Embodied in the Local Government Act, 1933, the provisions resolved a long controversy and established a standard of auditors' qualifications, approved by Parliament. The Local Legislation Committee was relieved of possible controversy and the municipal corporations of audit provisions in any Bills they might promote.

An incidental corollary of the Act was not altogether favourable to the profession. By general Act, all urban district councils were already subject to district audit: from time to time the larger urban district councils received the status of municipal corporations. District audit having already been in operation, change to professional audit, although it could be called for, was unlikely.

The Accounts of Companies

The affairs of the Royal Mail Steam Packet Company (incorporated by royal charter) and the accounts of the company for 1926 and 1927 became in 1931 a cause of much anxiety and distress to the whole profession. (The company had suffered considerably from the depressed state of shipping.) The auditor, a man of singular integrity and highly regarded, was rightly cleared of a serious allegation after a trial which lasted nine days. The allegation against the auditor was that he aided and abetted the chairman in regard to the annual report of the company for 1926 which, it was said, was false in a material particular and concealed the true position with intent to deceive: similarly in respect of the report for 1927. The charge arose from an item in the published profit and loss account: 'Balance for the year, including dividends on shares in allied and other companies, adjustment of taxation reserves *less* depreciation of fleet, etc.' The omnibus item included a transfer of an undisclosed amount from a previous provision no longer required, while the operations in each of the two years resulted in a loss, not otherwise indicated. The issue concerned the words and their implication 'including adjustment of taxation reserves', which had been inserted at the instance of the auditor. Little exception was taken to the balance sheets. (There were other allegations in the case against the chairman of the company, but with these the auditor was in no way concerned.) At the trial, expert evidence was given by Lord Plender, the President of the Institute (H. L. H. Hill), the President of the Society (Henry Morgan), and Sir William McLintock, who discharged their onerous duty with confidence. Practising accountants generally had not the slightest doubt about the complete baselessness of a criminal charge; and the exoneration of the auditor was received with much satisfaction. It now seems that an accounting technique had become fairly common practice without appreciation of its possible implications—but it did not so appear at the time. The company, being incorporated by royal charter, was not subject to the Companies Act, yet the considerations involved also concerned other companies; neither the Companies (Consolidation) Act, 1908, nor the Companies Act, 1929, prescribed the contents of a profit and loss account, although the 1929 Act provided that a profit and loss account must be submitted to the shareholders.

In the *Royal Mail* case Mr. Justice (Lord) Wright made some observations on secret reserves, which commanded much subsequent attention:

It was said by a very learned Judge on one occasion, by way of observation and not by judgment, that a company, that is to say the shareholders, could not complain if the position of the finances of the company was better than the accounts disclosed. That has been quoted from time to time as a justification for this method of keeping reserves secret. But there may be very great evils if those who have the control and management of the companies, and who control and manage companies for the benefit of the shareholders who entrust their monies to companies, have very large portions of the company's assets left in the secret disposition of the managing authority. It may work very well in many cases: no doubt it does. It is a practice which is being followed, no doubt, by many concerns of the highest standing. On the other hand, it may be the subject of almost intolerable abuse. Such a system may be used to cover up negligences, irregularities, and almost breaches of faith. It is said to be a matter of domestic concern between the company and the shareholders, but if the shareholders do not know and cannot know what the position is, how can they form any view about it at all?

*　　　*　　　*

Following the case, the Council of the Society appointed a special committee to consider whether in regard to company accounts and audit any amendment of the law was deemed necessary, and/or what, if any, alterations of a voluntary character might be considered desirable in the compilation of company accounts and their certification by professional auditors. The fact that the Council appointed this committee was indicative of a feeling that some opinion should be expressed on behalf of the Society. The position was delicate and there was considerable discussion in the committee as to how far any recommendations should go, since the questions were highly technical and concerned the whole profession; and at least one purpose was to increase public confidence. The report of the committee, having been adopted by the Council, was submitted to the Board of Trade and was given some publicity. *Inter alia*, it made the following recommendations:

(a) That the profit and loss account should show the true balance of profit or loss for the period covered by the account.

(b) That in the profit and loss account any debits or credits which are abnormal in character or extraneous in their nature to the ordinary transactions of the company, together with any reserves from a previous period no longer required, should be stated separately.

Some modification in the case of banking and similar institutions was recognized. Further, recommendation was made for the treatment of profits and losses of subsidiary companies in the accounts of a holding company, for which the provisions of the 1929 Act were considered inadequate; the purpose was to show the results of the holding company's business as a whole. The committee were of opinion that effective action must be by way of legislation and suggested a Departmental Committee to consider these matters; but this suggestion the Board of Trade were then unable to accept, having regard to the comparatively recent Companies Act, 1929.

A somewhat different approach was made by the Council of the Institute, which took counsel's opinion: the opinion was circulated among all the Institute's members. Counsel were not prepared to lay down general principles for guidance arising from the circumstances in the *Royal Mail* case. Some members of the Institute thought that the opinion did not help them very much; but at the annual meeting of the Institute, the President made an able statement which he emphasized was personal only and which, while it refrained from offering official guidance, considerably clarified the situation. An extract from that speech by H. L. H. Hill may be quoted:

In my view the dangers arising from publishing more informative accounts have been overstated and the legitimate claims of shareholders have not received adequate recognition. . . . I feel that we can do nothing better calculated to maintain and increase the confidence we now enjoy than to use our influence to make the profit and loss account increasingly valuable as some guide to earning capacity.

★ ★ ★

The question was considered at length at the International Congress in London (1933) (p. 192), at which there were three papers on 'The auditor's responsibility in relation to balance sheets and profit and loss accounts' from the British, American, and German points of view respectively. The discussion was at a high level and was mainly directed to the profit and loss account, secret reserves, and subsidiaries. Henry Morgan presented and extended the case set forth in the Society's report (p. 188), including the need for legislation, which he expounded with much cogency. He was supported by several speakers. It was known already that considerable variation of opinion existed in the profession, and this was reflected in the papers and in the discussion. No doubt some thought the Society's report committed it too far, yet was somewhat imprecise in the the use of the terms 'true balance', 'abnormal', or 'extraneous' (items). Certainly many who spoke were against immediate legislation and believed that the powers and moral authority of the auditor were sufficient to deal with the issues. There was not necessarily impropriety in the creation of secret reserves, which might be for the benefit of the business. It was not possible to be dogmatic; each case must be considered on its merits and judgement exercised, according to the circumstances, but so that the published accounts were not misleading.

Without straining too far the nuances of opinions expressed with delicacy at the congress, it is possible to represent the position broadly by the following quotations. In his paper Henry Morgan said:

I think that most accountants today would agree that if any feature of the profit and loss account involved anything of an improper or misleading character, it would be the auditor's duty to draw attention to it in his report. What we should regard as being improper or misleading, however, presents a problem of no little difficulty, having regard to current law and practice especially in regard to holding and subsidiary companies. There is no doubt that the great majority of shareholders regard the balance shown by the profit and loss account as representing the actual result for the period covered by the account, and it follows that, unless it is clearly shown in what respects and to what extent the balance shown differs from the actual earnings, the profit and loss account is apt to be misleading to the majority of shareholders.

Lord Plender gave his views in a brief speech:

First, the auditor's position as regards transfers to or from profit and loss to inner provisions or reserves. If directors in the honest exercise of their judgement set aside a sum or sums for unmatured but possible contingencies ... which they think are necessary in the best interests of a company, few if any auditors would question the desirability, if not the obligation, to see that the profits were stated after referring to such provisions having been made. It does not follow, however, that an auditor in reporting on the accounts would feel it to be his duty to state in his report the actual amount so set aside, if the directors thought that in the company's best interests the amount should not be disclosed, and they themselves refrained from doing so. Nor, if such sum (or accumulations of such transfers) were included in an omnibus item on the debit side of the balance sheet and the fact was clearly stated that it was so included, would an auditor necessarily consider it to be his duty to mention the amount in his report if the directors, acting to the best of their judgement ... refrained from stating the amount? I think not. . . .

But when profits of a year are supplemented or losses lessened or turned into apparent profits by transfers from contingency provisions . . . no longer required—and become, in effect, therefore, free reserves—or current revenue charges are debited thereto, then it may be said that different considerations arise, and it would require very cogent reasons for the amounts not to be disclosed. But general principles . . . cannot in all conceivable conditions be regarded as sacrosanct and I would not care to dogmatise on the subject. . . .

. . . Auditors may have their views [but] they are not the managers of a company's affairs; the directors are, and appointed by the shareholders for the purpose, to whom they are accountable.

*   *   *

A responsible but not invulnerable view of these matters outside the profession is of interest. At the annual general meeting in 1932 of a large and well-known concern, the chairman was reported as saying:[1]

I think the man in the street reads balance sheets and profit and loss accounts with intelligence so that when he sees on various lines of his balance sheet, statements like 'provision for contingencies', 'credit balances and reserves', he knows that something has been withheld from the figure of profits shown and that there are reserves of which he has no specific knowledge. Further he is wise enough not to ask for precise details of those reserves because he knows that it is not always expedient to give such detailed information. If the shareholder gets a certificate from auditors of repute which says 'Assets are correctly shown on this balance sheet and the liabilities are not greater than they appear on this balance sheet', he should be reasonably satisfied and I believe he is.

Henry Morgan, when President of the Society, was instrumental at meetings of the Society and otherwise in drawing public attention to the question of reform in company accounts and prospectuses. He gave facts and figures of a number of unsatisfactory floatations in 1928-9, of companies which after a few years came to grief. The floatations and the losses sustained justified his strictures; these failures had doubtless been accentuated by the general depression from 1930.

The *Royal Mail* case and the circumstances at that time showed clearly that there was need for more information in published accounts of companies—and for relevant and recent facts in the prospectuses of companies. In the immediately succeeding years companies' accounts received much consideration at meetings and conferences and in the professional periodicals. Voluntarily and without legislation until the Companies Act, 1948, companies and the profession co-operated and much improvement was effected.

[1] *The Economist*, 18 June 1932.

XI. PROFESSIONAL EDUCATION AND RESEARCH

Fourth and Fifth International Congresses

THE Fourth International Congress on Accounting assembled in London in July 1933, and was sponsored by the bodies of accountants recognized by the Parliament of the United Kingdom and by the Institute of Chartered Accountants in Ireland. Lord Plender, G.B.E., was President, Sir James Martin Vice-President, with the Hon. George Colville as Secretary and Mr. R. Wynne Bankes, C.B.E. (Institute) and Mr. A. A. Garrett (Society) as Assistant Secretaries. Among other representatives, H. L. H. Hill, the President of the Institute, and Mr. E. Casselton Elliott, the President of the Society, served on the Congress Committee and were active in the proceedings of the congress and in entertaining guests. A conspectus of the deliberations was indicated by Lord Plender in his address of welcome. 'In the complexities of modern business there are hardly any directions in which our experience and advice may not be of value in connection with financial policy, the form and presentation of accounts or in relation to effective methods of record control and organization.' Auditors' responsibilities, holding companies and combinations, depreciation, and statutory undertakings were prominent among discussions on nine topics; and Sir Josiah Stamp, G.B.E., gave a paper on international finance. Incidentally, he wrote the concluding section of this intricate subject between church and lunch on a Sunday and returned the proof of the first sections immediately. By kind permission of the Dean and Chapter, a service was held in Westminster Abbey: the address was given by His Grace the Archbishop of York (Dr. William Temple), who spoke to the text 'Seek ye first the Kingdom of God and his righteousness'. He said that trust and trustworthiness developed one another in the world, and that those who were gathered in the Abbey were in a quite peculiar degree the custodians of that sacred principle of trust and trustworthiness. The Congress

Dinner in Guildhall was honoured by the presence of His Royal Highness Prince George (the late Duke of Kent). In addition to a delightful garden party to the visitors given by Lord and Lady Plender at their country home at Sundridge, Kent, a friendly and informal arrangement was introduced by the members of the committee individually having private dinner parties at their homes and elsewhere at which they entertained visiting delegates.

It is pleasing to recall that the Congress Committee adjusted in a friendly way the delicacies that the organization of an international congress cannot fail to present.

★   ★   ★

A very interesting affair was the fiftieth anniversary celebration of the American Institute of Accountants in New York in 1937. Representatives of the British and Irish accountancy bodies were warmly welcomed by their American hosts, led by Colonel R. H. Montgomery, President, who was well known for his services to the profession in the U.S.A. and at international gatherings.

★   ★   ★

Berlin was the scene of the Fifth International Congress in September 1938, when tension between Britain and Germany had come to a serious pass: so much so that in the week preceding the congress Mr. R. Wynne Bankes (Institute) flew to Berlin to ascertain the situation and whether the congress was to be postponed: he found that the hosts were expecting the visitors, some of whom had already arrived, and that postponement had not even been thought of. The British delegates met in London and discussed the disturbing circumstances. They felt some British responsibility and decided to attend, the delegation to be limited to officially nominated representatives. It was led by (Sir) Charles Palmour, President of the Institute, who was supported by Mr. Walter Holman, the President of the Society, the Presidents of other bodies in the United Kingdom and Ireland, and some other delegates. The principal sponsors of the congress were members of the *Institut der Wirtschaftprüfer*, and there seemed to be some Government inspiration. It was well organized and the proceedings, both business and social, passed off without incident, although visitors could not fail to be aware of Nazi influence in the congress, notwithstanding friendly attitudes on the part of individual members of the profession in Germany. On the last day of the congress, the Rt. Hon. Neville Chamberlain, Prime Minister, was on his mission to Hitler at Godesberg: rumours, some sinister, were rife in Berlin, and it was with relief that delegates returned to their own country.

Courses at Cambridge and Oxford: Research Committee Established

It has always been a doctrine in the profession that obtaining a qualification and the relevant studies are but the prelude to continuous although less formalized study throughout a professional career. This need has been met by meetings of the district societies, the periodical conferences of the professional bodies, international congresses, and the professional periodicals; and, in addition, on the part of individuals, by the study of new textbooks, Acts of Parliament, and Government publications as necessary. Perhaps, however, the most effective factor is the mutual exchange of experience for which the meetings and conferences have provided opportunities. In any case the time available for these studies to people busily engaged each day is necessarily limited. It is obvious that with the progress of the profession, with new legislation and more complicated taxation, this element in professional life becomes of increasing moment.

In 1934 an idea was born which provided the Society—and indeed the profession—with a further invaluable facility for these purposes. By a happy inspiration, Mr. Bertram Nelson—then a junior member of the Council—suggested that the Society should arrange a short residential course for younger members of the Society—if possible at a college at Oxford or Cambridge, out of term time. Through the goodwill of the Master and Fellows, a course was held at Gonville and Caius College, Cambridge, during a week in July 1934. This privilege was greatly appreciated by the Council, particularly as at that time colleges were hesitant to be burdened with out-of-term activities of this kind—a practice which since the war has become more generally accepted. Rooms, the junior combination room, buttery, sports ground, and hall were placed at the disposal of the Society, and dinner and other daily meals in hall were arranged. The Organizing Committee invited some half a dozen members and one or two visitors to give lectures in the college hall as the basis of the course, and texts or summaries were provided in college for perusal by those attending. The feature of the course was the division of people—about 150 in all—into groups of about fifteen each, under the guidance of a senior member, who was the group chairman; and the group met in his room for discussion after each lecture. The system was subsequently developed so that the lecturer, whose paper was printed and circulated in advance, introduced his subject in a comparatively short speech: after the discussions in groups (which the lecturer visited) the groups nominated spokesmen, who addressed the whole assembly; a reply was then given by the lecturer. This organization enabled a good programme to be fulfilled within the few days available without undue pressure, and with the maximum concentration of views. The members of the first course were invited by the Dean to the Sunday morning service at King's College Chapel. At subsequent courses the service was in the chapel of the college in which the course was held, and several distinguished preachers have been guests of the Society. Members much enjoyed the informal social side of the course; and cricket, tennis, and golf matches were arranged; on that first occasion, some three or four people had the unexpected opportunity of a visit to Newmarket. Mr. and Mrs. E. Cassleton Elliott kindly entertained the whole course at a garden party at their home at Harpenden. The final event was a guest-night dinner in hall, when the Master of Caius, who was then Vice-Chancellor of the University, and other dons were present. The secretariat received help from the bursar and domestic bursar of the college on all occasions and enjoyed the advantage of their experience and imagination. About twelve women members of the Society attended the 1934 course and were accommodated at Newnham. The Secretary was informed that, having been paid much gallant attention, they had passed a resolution recommending that the attendance of women members at future courses should be limited to twelve!

Before the war further courses were held at Caius College, Cambridge, and at New College, Oxford (Presidents, Mr. R. Wilson Bartlett and Mr. Walter Holman). At New College, the Warden, the Rt. Hon. H. A. L. Fisher, O.M., F.R.S., presided at guest-night dinner—in accordance with the custom of the college. Robed in his doctor's gown and standing at high table in the ancient hall, artistically lit, he gave a brilliant speech in which he showed how quickly his mind had disposed itself to the assembled company of accountants.

The experiment by the Society of these short residential courses proved to be an unqualified success; and after the war similar arrangements were organized by other bodies in the profession at home and in the British Commonwealth and became an established feature of professional education.

A singularly worth-while activity, outside the immediate work of the Society, was developed in the 1930's by an invitation from the Paymaster Captain in charge of the Accountant Officers' Technical Course, Royal Navy, at Portsmouth, to some members of the Society to give lectures at the course. The idea was that these officers—seconded to the course for a few months —should be able to acquire some basic knowledge of accounting as applied to commercial and administrative purposes, of published accounts, and of financial and investment procedure. These were very pleasant occasions when the visitors addressed the officers and were entertained in the distinguished Mess at the Royal Naval Barracks.

*   *   *

The quickening of interest in professional education was reflected in the establishment of the Incorporated Accountants' Research Committee (1935). Its formation was on the suggestion of one or two younger members of the Society and the proposal was approved by the Council, who invited Richard A. Witty to be the first chairman. The members forming the nucleus of the committee sought the participation of other members of the Society who might be interested: the committee was not one of the formal committees of Council although two or three Council members served thereon. Perhaps some of the more conservatively minded members of Council, whilst giving their consent to the idea, were a little reserved about the new departure. But the committee got down to work, and in the United Kingdom and Ireland—and probably in the British dominions—it was the first Research Committee in the accountancy profession. (Cordial acknowledgement is due to the research work which had already been undertaken by the American Institute of Accountants.) A programme was organized, but, as might be expected, the translation of its general purpose into precise projects was not altogether straight-forward; this demanded both thought and tenacity, of which the committee did not fail. Before the war, the committee issued its first research publication *Standard Practice in Auditing*: Mr. W. J. Back was mainly responsible for this work, which included a memorandum on Machine Accounting by Mr. R. N. Barnett. Two other members collected material for a project on the *Design of Accounts*, and criticisms were requested upon draft forms published in *Accountancy* (p. 235). The work of the English Institute's Taxation and Financial Relations Committee was different: it engaged in official research, resulting in statements having the authority of the Council.

The Society's Fiftieth Year: Sir James Martin

The first half of 1935 was a period of great rejoicing in the country and in the Society. King George V and Queen Mary and their subjects celebrated the twenty-fifth year of the King's reign. Beautiful late spring days in London were a fine setting for memorable demonstrations of loyalty and affection in all parts of London. Some official seats in the Mall were allotted to the Council of the Society to view the Silver Jubilee Procession; this was made particularly interesting by being split at intervals into a series of small cavalcades in which the great men of the country took part: notably there were the Prime Minister's procession and the Speaker's procession, for which the Speaker's state coach drawn by Whitbread's horses was used. These cavalcades preceded Their Majesties, who followed in an open horse carriage. On other days the King and Queen drove informally to different parts of London, to be welcomed with great enthusiasm. King George's Jubilee Trust was established and the Society contributed three hundred guineas. That year Sir Stephen Killik, F.S.A.A., was Lord Mayor, and on Lord

Mayor's Day (1934) the historic coach halted at Incorporated Accountants' Hall for presentation by the President of honorary membership to Sir Stephen. It fell to him to meet Their Majesties at Temple Bar in May 1935, and to offer the Sword of the City to the King before the royal procession proceeded to St. Paul's for the Service of Thanksgiving. Sir Stephen was created K.C.V.O., and later G.B.E.

By fortunate coincidence 1935 was the fiftieth anniversary of the Society. At the unanimous invitation of the Council, Sir James Martin and C. Hewetson Nelson, Liverpool, became President and Vice-President. To permit of this arrangement, Mr. E. Cassleton Elliott, who was chairman of the Reception Committee, shortened his period of office as President and Mr. R. Wilson Bartlett requested that his nomination to the presidency be deferred: this was a generous decision on their part, which their colleagues accepted with felicity. Unique in the history of the Society was the entertainment of the members at the Mansion House, London, by a Lord Mayor (Sir Stephen Killik) who was one of their number: his daughter, Mrs. Stanley Greenland, was Lady Mayoress. Later in the week he was the principal guest at the Society's dinner in Guildhall, which had been made available by the courtesy of the Corporation of London: Sir James Martin—a dignified but somewhat frail figure—presided and read a gracious message from the King: and the toast of the Society was proposed by Sir Boyd (Lord) Merriman, President of the Probate, Divorce, and Admiralty Division of the High Court, previously Solicitor-General. At a morning meeting at Incorporated Accountants' Hall, the Vice-President reviewed events in the Society's history and messages of congratulation were read. The London members gave hospitality to the visiting members at an afternoon reception, at which there was a small exhibition of old works on accountancy and of Ackerman's coloured prints: the Hall was floodlit at night. A de luxe edition of the brochure on the Hall, printed by the Curwen Press, was presented to guests. The proceedings of the week concluded with a Ball at the Dorchester. Harold Stabler, who enjoyed considerable repute as a designer and silversmith at that period, had been commissioned to execute a new President's badge incorporating the Society's arms. The badge

THE LORD MAYOR'S COACH STOPS AT THE HALL, 9 NOVEMBER 1934
Sir Stephen Killik, G.B.E., K.C.V.O., F.S.A.A., Lord Mayor

FIRST COURSE AT GONVILLE AND CAIUS COLLEGE, CAMBRIDGE, 1934

* E. Cassleton Elliott, President

was presented to the Society by Sir James Martin and was worn for the first time during the celebrations. Harold Stabler also designed a chairman's badge for the London District Society and for some of the other District Societies. An old silver soup tureen (used for flowers) and two antique tankards were gifts from the past Presidents; and two antique chairs were presented by Arthur Collins. The Society's staff were remembered by the institution of a welcome staff pension scheme—a feature that was less common in 1935 than in the 1950's. In 1929, at the time of the opening of the Hall, a panel setting forth the names of the President and Hall Committee had been placed on the inner staircase wall; and a similar panel to commemorate the events of 1935 was added in that year.[1]

★   ★   ★

But 1935 was also a year of sadness for the Society, as in August of that year Sir James Martin died while on holiday. The memorial service was at St. Mary Abbots, Kensington, where Sir James, who was a devout churchman, was a member of the congregation. The sense of loss was felt profoundly, particularly in the Council. During the sixteen years since he retired from being Secretary, he had always been at hand to advise and counsel—sometimes perhaps to warn: in his activities in the City and when called to serve on Government committees, he carried with him always his obligation to the Society. In the Society itself Sir James achieved in a remarkable degree the function of adviser—the capacity to co-operate yet to be detached, to avoid undue influence but to help the Council: indeed the authority and responsibilities of the President for the time being were cardinal with him. During his fifty years' connexion with the Society some particular purposes had met with success; in others, circumstances had been too strong. But he had never been daunted by frustration and found the enduring strength of the Society in its increasing standards, its main policy, and in its members. Short-term disappointments might well lead to more lasting satisfaction. Sensitive and forthcoming as he was in maintaining relations with other bodies, he thought the Society should avoid looking over its shoulder: rather he

[1] See Appendix IV.

found in the Society's own work, initiative, and organization the key to progress. With that attitude and his wider outlook on the profession, and by reason of his personal qualities, he was always listened to with respect at the Institute. In a personal conversation in the 1930's, when thinking of the future, he said he would not live to see an arrangement with the Institute; the time was not ripe, but he believed it would come some day.

The members of the Society, on the initiative of the Council, subscribed £3,600 to the Sir James Martin Memorial Fund: this sum was handed to the trustees of the Incorporated Accountants' Benevolent Fund, of which he had been Honorary Secretary and subsequently President. Although for over fifteen years he had taken no part in the administration of the Society's examinations, Sir James always had a soft corner in his heart for the task which confronted young articled clerks in order to pass the intermediate examination. The Council decided, therefore, to offer special encouragement to articled clerks of outstanding merit by establishing two annual James Martin Memorial Exhibitions, awarded on the results of the intermediate examination and after interview of two or three eligible candidates by the Board of Examiners.

Other Activities

The fiftieth anniversary of the Institute of Municipal Treasurers and Accountants (Incorporated) in December 1935 was the occasion of cordial congratulations from the Society. A considerable number of its members were also incorporated accountants, and by a well-established and welcome convention, without *ad hoc* right of nomination, two municipal treasurers were always on the Council of the Society. The friendly relations between the two bodies over the course of their concurrent history have enabled a few differences of view to be resolved or accepted, and only on rare occasions have serious questions arisen. Perhaps the feeling of the I.M.T.A. and of individual principal municipal treasurers that their status was virtually similar to that of accountants in public practice was rather stronger than the view generally entertained by the Society: but members in that capacity were eligible to be elected to Fellowship and a permissible facility enabled them to declare themselves to be 'practising Fellows' and as such to retain articled clerks. A pleasant feature was the personal participation of the municipal members in the Society's activities. With goodwill, the I.M.T.A. received a Royal Charter in 1959.

★   ★   ★

In 1938 William Strachan retired from the editorship of the *Incorporated Accountants' Journal*, with which he had been associated since its inception. Leo T. Little, B.Sc. (Econ.), had been appointed Deputy Secretary of the Society in 1937: and he now undertook the duties of Editor of the *Journal*, which then became *Accountancy*. Little brought much imagination to his task, and the periodical was presented in new format and type, with a daffodil cover, printed in blue ink—an attractive production but it may now seem a little extravagant in terms of 1960 costs and postage. The contents were expanded and included articles by a number of new contributors, so that *Accountancy* became increasingly a monthly publication of general professional interest, besides reporting the work of the Society and of the profession.

★   ★   ★

After the opening of the Hall in 1929 and the formation of the London District Society, activities in London increased. During the presidency of Henry Morgan, by permission of the Corporation, a dinner was given by the Society in Guildhall (1932). A notable speech was made by Lord Macmillan, a Scottish Advocate who had become a Lord of Appeal in Ordinary, and who presided over the committee, 1929 to 1931, appointed to inquire into the relations of finance and industry. John Maynard (Lord) Keynes, whose writings and work had great influence in determining present and future economic policy, was on the Macmillan Committee. Among the committee's findings[1] were recommendations that central banks should endeavour to raise prices—which had fallen disastrously —and that the Bank of England should increase its normal stock of gold and foreign exchange: the report drew attention to the desirability of greater co-operation between financial interests and industry, and to the difficulty of small undertakings in obtaining access to the capital market: this finding became

[1] Cmd. 3897, 1931.

described as the 'Macmillan Gap'. Projecting the Macmillan report forward to 1960, the first objective has become a need for stability in prices, the second is an almost daily preoccupation with 'the authorities', and the third has been met by new institutions, or new activities of existing institutions, and undoubtedly by a change in outlook; another problem, however—that of meeting death duties from closely held shares—has become of serious consequence.

At a similar function in Guildhall in the spring of 1939, Mr. Walter Holman (London) presided, and the Society was honoured by the presence of His Royal Highness the Duke of Kent: a memorable function for the assembled seven hundred members and guests. On this occasion, as on many others, Mr. Holman gave a succinct and polished speech, much enjoyed by the company. Unhappily, His Royal Highness and his private secretary were killed in an aeroplane accident during the subsequent war when flying on duty. Mr. Holman sustained for many years the duties of chairman of the Examination and Membership Committee, and the tendency to restraint in that committee's membership policy was amply justified in subsequent years and by the course of events.

In a more intimate setting, Mr. R. Wilson Bartlett, Newport, Mon., who was President from 1935 to 1937, gave a number of private luncheons at Incorporated Accountants' Hall to distinguished guests: and he presented a panel placed at the east end of the large hall on which were inscribed the names of Presidents of the Society. In Council and committees, Mr. Wilson Bartlett was always vigilant in presenting the point of view of members away from London as a constituent element in the Society's policy as a whole. For many years he was chairman of the Disciplinary Committee.

The comparatively late emergence (1930) of the London District Society accentuated the value of an organization for members in London, where it is probably more difficult to maintain continuous interest than it is elsewhere. Evidence of the progress made is to be found in the report of a luncheon given by the London District Society at the Savoy in October 1936, in honour of Sir Stephen Killik, K.C.V.O., G.B.E., F.S.A.A., a former Lord Mayor: a distinguished company, including the chairman of the London County Council and the Earl of Limerick, and heads of City institutions, assembled as guests of the London members, of whom, in that year, Mr. Edward Baldry was chairman. Sir Stephen Killik had relinquished accountancy for the Stock Exchange; and in the course of speeches reference was made to the desirability of an annual certificate by a qualified accountant as to the affairs and accounting records of Stock Exchange firms, similar to the certificate required by Lloyd's in respect of the accounts of underwriters.

Two other special occasions should be mentioned. At the invitation of the members in Northern Ireland, a conference was held in Belfast in 1937, and opened by the Vice-Chancellor of Queen's University. The members were entertained by the Lord Mayor of Belfast (Sir Crawford McCullagh, Bart.) and by the Prime Minister of Northern Ireland (Lord Craigavon). The main topic at the business meetings was 'Accountancy in relation to Irish commerce and industry', introduced by Mr. D. Tilfourd Boyd; he gave the conference an account of the background of the work of the profession in Ireland, which disclosed considerable research. The last major social event before war broke out was a conference in Nottingham (1939) over which Mr. Percy Toothill (Sheffield) presided, and during Fred Prior's chairmanship of the District Society. The members enjoyed facilities at University College (now the University of Nottingham), and the proceedings were particularly remembered for the personal popularity of Mr. and Mrs. Toothill and Mr. and Mrs. Prior.

*   *   *

The Statute of Westminster, 1931, formally recognized the British dominions as free and independent countries: this status with concomitant feelings and emotions inevitably, although gradually, affected in a quite friendly way the relations between British accountancy bodies and those in the Commonwealth. In the period 1931 to 1939, however, the Society's overseas affairs were not concerned with any major questions of policy. District Societies were established in Bengal and Bombay, the Commonwealth Institute of Accountants celebrated its fiftieth anniversary in Melbourne, and the arrangements previously made in South Africa to control the Society's membership and examinations worked satisfactorily. Just before the outbreak of war a further but unsuccessful attempt was made to obtain a Registration Bill in South Africa.

A number of British firms of accountants had offices and partners in Paris, and in 1936 the French Government introduced regulations to exercise some control over *Commissaires aux Comptes* (auditors of public companies): the regulations had some slight nationalistic tendency. British accountants practising in France were required to lodge particulars of their professional credentials with the appropriate Government department. At the request of members of the Society in Paris, the Council authorized the issue of special memoranda of their qualifications and membership which, with much formality, were required to be under seal, notarially attested, and finally tied up with red tape and sealing-wax. The position of the members in Paris thus became regularized.

The modern Unit Trust—an expanding medium of investment—first made its appearance in the early 1930's. In the public interest it was desirable that some survey should be made of such activities as then existed. In 1936 a Departmental Committee to consider Fixed Trusts was set up; its chairman was Sir Alan Garrett Anderson, G.B.E., a well-known figure in City shipping affairs. The committee found it necessary to include flexible as well as fixed trusts in its deliberations. Evidence was given for the Society by Henry Morgan and Mr. R. Wilson Bartlett. The report[1] made certain recommendations; but the problem was eventually dealt with under the Prevention of Fraud (Investment) Act, 1939 (amended in 1957), and Board of Trade Regulations. A Unit Trust may offer units to the public only if the Board of Trade has been satisfied as to the powers and terms in the trust deed: managers—usually a limited company—and the trustees must be quite independent of each other.

In order to accelerate availability of information on the Stock Exchange, and to the press and investors, the Stock Exchange Committee in 1938 requested companies whose securities were quoted to furnish preliminary figures when announcing final dividends in advance of the publication of annual reports.

[1] Cmd. 5259, 1936.

Before communicating with the companies the Committee invited the views of the English Institute, the Society and the Chartered Secretaries on the form of the announcements.

Income-tax legislation had been consolidated by the Income Tax Act, 1918, to which were added subsequent Finance Acts. There was also a great amount of case law. Consideration was given to the possibility of codification by a committee appointed by the Chancellor of the Exchequer, which reported in 1936. The subject was tremendously complicated and difficult, and the learned report[1] has remained on record without attempt to deal with complete codification by legislation. The Edinburgh Chartered Accountants, with much intensive work, reviewed the contents and prepared a statement of their views thereon.

★   ★   ★

Notable among public attainments of members of the Society may be mentioned the peerage conferred upon Sir Josiah Stamp G.B.E. (Hon. Member), who had also become G.C.B.; the election to the Senate of the Union of South Africa of the Hon. W. J. O'Brien; the election of Sir Thomas Keens, D.L., previously M.P., as chairman of the Bedfordshire County Council—he also received the honour of Knight Bachelor; and the appointment of Henry Morgan as chairman of the Council of the London Chamber of Commerce. Sir Charles Wilson, John Potter, Sir Adam Maitland and Mr. Alexander Critchley had been, or were, members of Parliament.

International Tension

King George V died in 1936, beloved by all his subjects at home and in the British dominions. After a painful phase in the succession and the abdication of Edward VIII, George VI (Duke of York) ascended the Throne and was crowned in Westminster Abbey in 1937. The President of the Society, Mr. R. Wilson Bartlett, received a command to be present.

Slowly the nation had climbed out of the depression and unemployment of 1930 to 1934, deplorable accounts of which had been brought to London by members who were professionally engaged in or near parts of the country especially

[1] Cmds. 5131, 5132, 1936.

affected. But although economic affairs improved, the years from 1934 onwards could hardly be described as prosperous; and deterioration in the European international situation from 1936 to 1939 disturbed the mind and, towards the end, the activities of the nation. Immediately before the signing of the Munich Pact of 1938, war seemed imminent, reservists were called up, and gas masks made their appearance; the Secretary of the Society was in communication with the command of the Officers Emergency Reserve of the army, which recruited officers having special qualifications. Events in Germany soon demonstrated that the relief afforded by the Munich Pact was illusory and the situation rapidly became worse. Compulsory military service of six months commenced in May 1939 (the first conscription in peace-time), the Royal Air Force and the Territorial Army were expanded, and there was some switch to the manufacture of munitions. The Chancellor of the Exchequer had already (1937) imposed a national defence contribution on business profits, and in April 1938, the standard rate of income tax was raised to 5s. 6d. in the £. A supplement to *Accountancy* afforded members advice on the national defence contribution. A similar supplement, comprising counsel's opinion, had been issued on the Companies Act, 1929 and this practice was followed periodically when new questions arose from legislation.

On the civil side the Ministry of Labour communicated with the accountancy bodies and requested them to co-operate with the Ministry in setting up a register of qualified accountants who, in the event of war, would volunteer for service in Government departments or elsewhere as required: meantime, a first Schedule of Reserved Occupations covered accountancy and some 3,450 questionnaires to form the register were completed by members of the Society. Mr. Walter Holman, then President, represented the Society in these matters and throughout the war gave unremitting service in dealing with the ever-present question of personnel.

Depressingly, the probability of war increased and on 3 September 1939, after the invasion of Poland, the nation learnt with grim fortitude that, after a tense sitting of Parliament, the Government had declared war on Germany.

1939–1945

XII. ACCOUNTANCY AND THE NATION

The Outbreak of War and Its Course

ON the outbreak of war in September 1939 the nation girded its loins with determination and gravity: it was under no illusions. A complete absence of jingoism and of wishful optimism reflected the prospect of unknown burdens and of suffering; and there was the certainty of air warfare on the battlefields, at sea, and at home. That mood was made the more realistic by the black-out at night, immediately imposed, and by the wail of sirens operated experimentally: and it was intensified as windows in homes and offices and in factories were obscured at nightfall. Men of the armed forces, whether regulars, territorials, conscripts, or reservists, not already at their stations hastened to report for duty. Unprecedented scenes of the evacuation to the country of large numbers of children were witnessed in London and other cities: and, at an early date, severe rationing of petrol was put into effect, on a basis of essential journeys only. An immediate responsibility arose to protect Incorporated Accountants' Hall: sand-bags—as far as procurable—were stacked against outside walls, an air-raid shelter was constructed in the basement, and, as soon as practicable, the stained glass windows on the first floor were removed and sent to the country for safe storage.

Parliament passed the Emergency Powers (Defence) Act, 1939, conferring on the Government extensive powers to prosecute the war, and voted a credit of £500 million. The transport of armies and air force to France and elsewhere was carried out with efficiency and safety and there was some activity at sea. But, unexpectedly, apart from minor engagements, there was little fighting in France in the remaining months of 1939 and early 1940: in fact there seemed to be an

incongruous state of military quietude. Then in the spring of
1940 the storm burst: the German armies rapidly overran Holland and Belgium and their tanks poured through the eastern
defences of France. Fighting a great rearguard action, incessantly
bombed, the British armies were pushed to the coast, and by
'a miracle of deliverance' were for the most part evacuated from
Dunkirk. At about the same time Norway was occupied by the
German forces.

Political upheaval followed. The Rt. Hon. Winston S.
Churchill was called to lead the country, and one of his first
and distressing duties was to warn Parliament 'to prepare itself
for hard and heavy tidings': but a few days later (4 June 1940),
after the Dunkirk evacuation, he created confidence, gave inspiration, and added a masterpiece to the English language by
his memorable speech and declaration:

... we shall go on to the end, we shall fight in France, we shall fight
on the seas and oceans, we shall fight with growing confidence and
growing strength in the air, we shall defend our island whatever the
cost may be, we shall fight on the beaches, we shall fight on the
landing grounds, we shall fight in the fields and on the streets, we
shall fight in the hills: we shall never surrender. ...[1]

and the country knew that he meant it.

Except for General de Gaulle and the Free French Forces,
France made an armistice with Germany and the 'Vichy'
Government under Marshal Petain was installed. Gall and
wormwood though it was, His Majesty's Government felt
compelled to give orders for action by the Royal Navy against
the French Mediterranean Fleet, which it was feared might
otherwise fall into enemy hands.

For a time the British Commonwealth faced the war alone
and with its armies denuded of equipment: the whole industrial
machine in the United Kingdom, particularly the production of
aircraft, was not only accelerated but was expanded with fierce
intensity. Simultaneously, steps were taken to prepare against
the possibility of invasion contemplated by the Germans, which,
however, was not attempted. That epic of courage, skill, and

---

[1] *Into Battle.*

genius—the Battle of Britain—in August and September 1940 denied mastery of the skies to the enemy and put heart into the country. Severe bombing of London followed shortly, and, at various times, cities all over the country likewise suffered, mainly by night attacks. There was a great fire in the City of London (December 1940); the chamber of the House of Commons was destroyed (1941); yet neither the Government and Parliament, nor the Law Courts moved from London; Their Majesties remained in residence at Buckingham Palace, which did not escape enemy action. With the growing strength of the air arm and in anti-aircraft artillery and technique, attacks on Germany increased and defence of the United Kingdom became more effective: there were long intervals when the country was free of air attack, affording much relief.

During and after 1940 the war spread all over the globe. There were the accession of Italy to the enemy, the invasion of Russia by Germany, the tragedy of the United States Fleet at Pearl Harbour. The United Kingdom and the British dominions were joined by the U.S.A. and Russia in the struggle. Great battles moved to and fro in North Africa, and Egypt was saved by the battle of El Alamein. The Japanese ran amuck in the Far East and over the South Seas: Malaya, Hong Kong, and Burma fell, Australia was threatened. So the war continued with many vicissitudes: the country received good news and bad with calm resolve—and there was indeed bad news from time to time. But positive hope came from many successful air operations, brilliant naval actions (the Battle of the River Plate, the destruction of the *Scharnhorst* and of the great battleship *Bismarck*), the conquest of North Africa and the surrender of Italy, and from American, Australian, and New Zealand successes in the South Seas, after earlier frustrated efforts. Morale was sustained by the high purposes of the war and by never-failing belief in the outcome of the struggle. This belief was strengthened by the journeys of the Prime Minister to North Africa, and by his meetings with President Roosevelt and afterwards with Roosevelt and Stalin. At the same time these were years of preparation in the United Kingdom, the dominions, and the U.S.A. from which evolved the great scheme of the invasion of occupied France on D-Day 1944.

The Profession and the War Effort

From September 1939 the broad purposes of Parliament and the Government were first the military defeat of the enemy, secondly the defence of the country, and thirdly the maintenance of the life of the nation.

In addition to the decisions of the Government on high policy and for action in emergencies, it was necessary to organize the whole active population according to their several physical and special capabilities, to obtain and to utilize to the best advantage all material resources, to ensure the highest level of production and manufacture, and to take measures for the necessary finance. This organization called for tight control and a continuous determination of priorities. High and increasing demand was impinging on comparatively restricted numbers and limited and uncertain material resources. In May 1940, in circumstances of unparalleled gravity, the Government obtained yet wider authority to control all persons and property in the country. The Society's annual meeting was held that month, and at the opening of the proceedings a resolution was adopted unanimously pledging full support to the Government: the resolution went on:

Professional societies, like trade unions, have matured in the atmosphere of liberty of which the free association of nations in the British Commonwealth is the ultimate expression. The Society welcomes the temporary sacrifice of this liberty with the confidence that only by this means can it be preserved and ultimately restored. The Society hopes that it may be privileged to be used without stint as one of the instruments of the national will to succeed in the present struggle to preserve liberty in all its forms.

When determined, the execution of policies and decisions was effected by necessary legislation, by Statutory Rules and Orders made by Ministers, and administratively through the respective departments. Existing departments were expanded and some new Ministries were formed, namely Food, Aircraft Production, Economic Warfare, Information, Production (the last in addition to the existing Ministry of Supply), and Raw Materials.

*   *   *

Calling-up for the armed forces and the regulation of civilian personnel were administered by a much enlarged Ministry of Labour and National Service. Wherever possible, the departments obtained the co-operation of representative bodies—particularly of professional bodies—to secure the services of people with professional and technical qualifications. The group covered a varied and wide field, and accountancy and the services of qualified accountants had their due and indeed important place in the Schedule of Reserved Occupations. The schedule was on a basis of persons as defined by age and prescribed occupations being reserved for work of national importance in lieu of military service. Already at the outbreak of war a joint committee of representatives of the Scottish and English chartered accountants, of incorporated accountants, and of certified accountants had been formed to act in conjunction with the Ministry of Labour. Resort was made immediately to the register of qualified accountants who had volunteered to accept suitable whole-time appointments. The secretaries, equipped with gas masks, journeyed to an office on the outskirts of London for meetings with officials of the Ministry of Labour for the purpose of recommendations to fill urgent vacancies for accountants in the various departments and elsewhere. In order to avoid overlapping, and to secure some uniformity of administration, it had been agreed that such appointments should be made only through the register: but so urgent was the situation in some departments that insistent requests came to the secretaries for direct help in finding suitable men, which they had firmly to refer to the Ministry. Nevertheless, this central register was operated expeditiously and with the minimum of procedure so that vacancies notified were filled with little delay.

Control of the supply of raw materials was one of the major functions of the Ministry of Supply. To ensure that the scheme should work effectively and smoothly the Minister desired to appoint a few firms of accountants—one for each main control. At his instance, an Accountants' Advisory Selection Committee, representative of the accountancy bodies, was set up to make recommendations for appointment. The chairman was Sir Nicholas Waterhouse, F.C.A., and the Society's members were Mr. Percy Toothill (President) and Sir Thomas Keens. The delicate task was carried out with harmonious co-operation and the services of the firms appointed were required for several years. About the same time, Mr. E. Cassleton Elliott, past President, was appointed Controller of Costings at the Ministry of Supply.

*   *   *

For a good part of the war the main preoccupation of the accountancy bodies was the question of personnel. Many partners and staff (admitted and unadmitted) were called up for His Majesty's forces or volunteered: the call from the Government departments made a further draft on firms, and the firms themselves were to be faced with new problems in their practices and an increased burden of work caused by heavy taxation and other emergency responsibilities on behalf of clients. At the level of firms, all these changes and attenuation of staffs caused much dislocation, borne stoically but not without some piecemeal criticism. In the early stages there was perhaps a feeling that diversion of staffs could have been reduced by firms being entrusted with services on behalf of the departments—thus preserving the value of trained teams—or by part-time work. This view was presented by Mr. Percy Toothill (President) in his speech at the Society's annual general meeting in May 1940. The services of members in their professional and practising capacity were, however, increasingly utilized, directly or indirectly, by the departments in several ways as the war proceeded, notably in the administration of controls. Concurrently there were personal obligations to be fulfilled—Home Guard, Civil Defence, or Fire-guard duties at night and at week-ends.

In the Schedule of Reserved Occupations changes in age were made at one or two intervals: by 1941 qualified accountants and audit assistants having ten years' experience with practising accountants were reserved at thirty. A proclamation in 1942 declared that all men up to forty-five were liable for military service. This caused some concern in the profession; but the authorities, while not suggesting block modification, indicated recognition of the specific position of accountants and procedure by way of individual deferment. Applications for the deferment of partners and staff were made to the Joint Committee, which, at meetings in London and aided by representatives from the District Societies, made recommendations thereon—within round limits advised by the Ministry of Labour. Renewals of expired deferments were approved in appropriate cases. Representatives of the District Societies who attended did not fail to make known their views as to the pressure upon them from the Ministries and the Inland Revenue, and the continued inadequacy in the numbers of trained personnel. The committee enjoyed the complete confidence of the Ministry: it worked strictly within the limits prescribed from time to time, and its recommendations were always accepted without question. The committee had the advantage of the assiduous and harmonious work of the chairman, (Sir) Charles Palmour (Institute), and of the vice-chairman, Mr. Walter Holman (Society). The situation became more acute as women were called up, and the committee were charged with affording information to Manpower Boards to obtain deferment of women engaged in accountants' offices. The procedure was somewhat different, since the criteria were age and 'mobility': many of the young women affected had been engaged as substitutes and meantime had received some elementary training—and there was of course the considerable category of secretaries and typists. A further movement out of the profession was thus suffered.

★　　　★　　　★

The whole question of securing the most favourable use of the services of trained personnel in the Civil Service was the subject of the Sixteenth Report of the Select Committee on National Expenditure,[1] October 1942. The committee considered the situation which had arisen from the scarcity of qualified persons available. Sir James Rae, Under-Secretary of the Treasury, had been requested to co-ordinate departmental reviews: for this purpose the accountancy bodies were invited to nominate professional assessors to consult with senior officials immediately concerned, and afterwards to be associated with reports to the heads of four departments—not to the Treasury. Those nominated were:

Sir Nicholas Waterhouse, F.C.A. (to the War Office);

[1] *House of Commons Paper* 120, 1941-2.

Mr. (Sir) Russell Kettle, F.C.A. (to the Ministry of Aircraft
Production);

E. Furnival Jones, F.C.A., F.S.A.A. (to the Ministry of
Supply);

Mr. Edward Baldry, F.S.A.A. (to the Admiralty).

Sir James Rae asked them to consider the elimination of non-
essential functions, the inevitable relaxation of peace-time
standards, the avoidance of overlapping functions between the
departments, and the careful division of labour. By these means,
demands on qualified professional services would be kept at
a minimum, and work not requiring qualified people could be
devolved on others. In suitable cases the employment of firms
of professional consultants on a fee basis would be a useful
alternative to direct recruitment. The reviews made disclosed
that the departments were fully aware of the need for economy
in the use of professional staff, that no case of real extravagance
had come to light, and that effect was given to the utilization of
professional firms.

War Finance and Taxation: P.A.Y.E.

When, in the first part of 1939, the prospect of war became
more likely, the first tentative Schedule of Reserved Occupations had indicated that a national emergency would impose
special responsibilities on the profession. The extended and increasing powers of the Government after September 1939 were
exercised by way of control and regulation of finance, business,
supplies, and other civil affairs in which accountability was
implicit; and there was the inevitability of heavy taxation. As
early as in the September issue, 1939 (before the outbreak of
war), *Accountancy* said: 'The full list of emergency measures is
a long one, but it is short compared with what war itself would
bring. Full-blooded control of our economic life has not yet
arrived.' It certainly came in increasing measure during the war
and—although with gradual relaxations—was prolonged when
the war was over. The profession became deeply involved.

The earliest and immediate steps were that bank rate was
increased from 2 to 4 per cent.—reduced again to 2 per cent.
in two months, the level at which it then remained for twelve

years: minimum prices were fixed for gilt-edged securities, to prevent their being thrown on the market: foreign exchange was stringently controlled: foreign securities held by residents were ordered to be registered, and in due course were compulsorily acquired by the Government. These purchases went to augment the comparatively limited resources of foreign currency—notably dollars—which were essential for purchases of material made in the U.S.A.: American legislation at that time prohibited the sale of war supplies except on a 'cash and carry' basis, until the 'Lend-Lease' arrangement negotiated with President Roosevelt gave imperative relief. Continuous additions were made to the initial Defence (Finance) Regulations. The Courts (Emergency Powers) Act, 1939, passed shortly after the outbreak of war, placed restrictions on the recovery of debts, the exercise of remedies, the rights of mortgagees, and on bankruptcy and winding-up. By another measure, a ban was placed on capital issues—including free bonus shares—to prevent competition with the Government for the available supply of capital; power was given to the Capital Issues Committee to grant relief in exceptional circumstances: later, restrictions were placed on increases in dividends.

*   *   *

No time could be lost in facing the almost terrifying problem of financing the war, and the Chancellor of the Exchequer introduced a supplementary Budget at the end of September 1939. This and subsequent war Budgets, as well as the continuous administration of taxation, had critical and additional implications for the profession, involving more work, study, and knowledge—and accompanied by severe attentuation of staffs (p. 212). This was matched by a corresponding burden on the staff of the Board of Inland Revenue. The September 1939 Budget, which subsequently seemed but a prologue to the exercise of taxation realities, was based on estimated expenditure of £1,933 million (at the outbreak of war on the basis of the previous estimate the amount was £951 million) and revenue of £995 million (previous estimate £943 million), leaving £938 million to be borrowed. The standard rate of income tax was fixed at 7s. 6d. (7s. effective 1939/40), with some changes in allowances; surtax and estate duty were increased.

But the most momentous change was the imposition of an excess profits tax of 60 per cent. on profits in excess of a standard, replacing the pre-war limited armaments profits duty: the national defence contribution of 5 per cent. companies, 4 per cent. other businesses, remained chargeable if it exceeded excess profits tax.

To sketch a panorama of war-time Budgets—which included a further supplementary Budget in 1940—would be a long and serious task. There are, however, a few features that ought to be mentioned. Forging, as they did, weapons in the nation's armoury of finance during the years of struggle, they are indications of the sacrifices made by all classes in the community and of the contribution of business and industry—and indeed of the serious taxation situation, to which the working of the profession had to adapt itself. Two Budgets in 1940 (April and July) brought the standard rate of income tax to 8s. 6d., increased excess profits tax to 100 per cent., raised the rates of surtax and estate duties, and imposed a purchase tax; the purchase tax was first at a flat rate, then revised to discriminate against luxuries and semi-luxuries, and was operated at the wholesale level, requiring the registration of wholesalers. For the purpose of estate duty, section 55 (Finance Act, 1940) placed the valuation of shares in certain private limited companies on the basis of net assets. The section was complicated and many thought oppressive in its effects. Some relief was eventually afforded in the Finance Act, 1954, but difficulties remained. Schedule E income tax on salaries and wages was directed to be deducted at source —a heavy addition to the administrative side of business, industry, and public services. It was the drastic provisions of the 1941 Budget, continued, and, in the case of indirect taxation, extended in subsequent war Budgets, which left no room for doubt in the mind of every individual and in all business concerns of the Government's inflexible purpose in war finance. Increases in the standard rate of income tax to 10s. in the £ and in the reduced rate to 6s. 6d. were accompanied by reductions in allowances to one-tenth for earned income (maximum £150), personal allowance £80 single, £140 married, allowance for each child £50: total exemption limit was lowered to £110. These prescriptions remained throughout the war and no doubt the tax burden represented the maximum which was tolerable and practicable for both individuals and businesses and the optimum in total yield. Yet as the net spread to smaller incomes it was not sufficiently realized that although the proclaimed standard rate of income tax was 10s. in the £, the effective rate for a large number of people was far less, e.g. for a married man with two children having £400 p.a. earned income, income tax was £39 giving an effective rate of 1s. 11½d.

For quite respectable reasons but also as a 'tranquillizer', it was at this point that the now notorious 'post-war credits' were introduced; each taxpayer was furnished annually, on payment of tax, with a non-negotiable certificate of the additional tax paid (maximum £65 p.a.) arising from the reduction in allowances imposed by the 1941 Budget. Although the conditions of subsequent encashment were not precisely defined, the scheme was unquestionably devised with bona fide if very optimistic intention. The slow maturity of the credits after the war—on the basis of age—was occasioned by the fear of stimulating an active or potential inflationary situation; by 1959 a large sum was still outstanding, when some comfort was given to taxpayers concerned. John Maynard (Lord) Keynes had suggested to the Government a form of direct compulsory saving; and he wrote a book in popular form, *How to pay for the War*. The Government, however, were not prepared to impose direct compulsory saving, but introduced the post-war credits, which, if different in form from direct compulsory saving, had similar effect. Concurrently a tremendous national savings drive was organized on a voluntary basis; its ubiquitous activities were promoted in offices, factories, and households, and extended to every remote hamlet and farmhouse: the needs of the country and the merits of national savings certificates and defence bonds, made available easily, met with a splendid response.

The purpose of war-time taxation and saving was not only financial but to remove high consumption demand on the restricted supply of goods of all kinds, and thus to put restraint upon inflationary forces and to maintain supplies for the war. Broadly, war-time Budgets provided that about one-half of the country's expenditure was met from taxation, and the other half was raised by borrowing and foreign disinvestment. Borrowing was covered by large loans from the market at a low rate of interest and by the proceeds of the national savings drive. By 1944/5, 53 per cent. of total expenditure of the Government was met from revenue—a higher percentage than in any previous war year. Twelve million persons were liable for P.A.Y.E., of whom 7½ million were weekly wage-earners.

*   *   *

The pressure on food supplies and the losses of shipping at sea gave great importance to agriculture: large areas of grassland were ploughed and changed to growing corn. After a long period of pre-war depression, farming—as was to be welcomed —became a more prosperous and essential industry with growth of profits, of which the schedule B, rental, basis was an inadequate measure. Thus in the April 1941 Budget, farms of which the assessable rent was £300 or over were transferred to schedule D, business profits basis, and in the following year the lower limit was made £100. More adequate book-keeping for small farmers no doubt seemed a trial to them, but opinion in the profession probably considered that, even allowing for the special hazards and physical labour of farming, there was a good case for transfer to schedule D. Moreover, with such measures as guaranteed prices and subsidies, and their negotiation with the Ministry of Agriculture by the National Farmers' Union, there was need for more information as to farming operations. Co-operation between the National Farmers' Union and the profession facilitated these matters, particularly the furnishing of necessary accounting information to the N.F.U. A reasonable view of this situation might be that the great majority of farms in the country were comparatively small— under 100 acres—and that the difficulties of the farmers with clerical work were not to be underestimated.

*   *   *

The assessment, administration, and effects of the excess profits tax were found to be complicated, and as time went on experience of its operation threw up anomalies, hardships, and some gaps. Each Finance Act accordingly introduced modifications or new features. The tax commenced at 60 per cent.: after it was increased to 100 per cent. the Government gave an assurance, converted into a statutory right, that 20 per cent. would be treated as a credit for the purpose of post-war rehabilitation and reconstruction, subject to such conditions as should be determined later by Parliament. Meantime, as expansion proceeded, many technical questions arose—exceptional depreciation of buildings, plant, machinery and equipment, and increases in capital employed—all of which received legislative attention. By 1944 a large number of small businesses had come within the scope of excess profits tax, and in the Finance Act of that year some modest relief was afforded by an increase in the minimum standard and percentage of capital by a round £1,000 per business; this gave benefit to about 30,000 businesses and lightened the amount of taxation work. On the other hand, in 1944 the Finance Act of 1941 was strengthened to defeat avoidance of tax by 'transactions', having avoidance as a main purpose, which had resulted in a higher standard. The application of excess profits tax legislation to business and industry was an increasing care of practising members of the profession, and of their clients, and of industrial accountants.

★ ★ ★

The system as first introduced of deducting at source schedule E tax from salaries and wages was not satisfactory, since it left the taxpayer continuously in arrears. The Inland Revenue staff worked on this problem and evolved an almost revolutionary scheme, which became 'Pay-as-you-earn' or P.A.Y.E. In challenging and incongruous circumstances, the system was operated from April 1944: its initiation involved a degree of 'tax forgiveness'. To bring such a scheme into force under the conditions prevailing was a tribute to the inventiveness of the Inland Revenue and to the co-operation of employers in making it effective, although early operation of P.A.Y.E. was not free from difficulties. A past President of the Society observed that in the absence of such a scheme it would have been impossible to have secured proper assessment and payment of tax on the enormous number of individual weekly and monthly earnings. Publicity was afforded by officials of the Inland Revenue giving talks to meetings of members of the profession—which were very largely attended—and of employers.

Concentration, Contracts, and Costing

It was not only in dealing with direct taxation that the profession carried extended responsibilities. In 1940 there was some 'concentration of industry': production in certain lines was concentrated in 'nucleus' concerns, releasing less necessary productive capacity and factories and providing much-needed extra and dispersed storage space. At first, and not unnaturally, concentration caused some disquiet amongst the concerns affected. The rationing of food and clothing at the point of retail sale, restrictions on restaurants, and the application of the Limitation of Supplies Orders occasioned new work. After consultation between the Board of Trade and a committee of representatives of the accountancy bodies, a form of certificate for operating limitation of supplies was evolved: the problem was to have a form of certificate which at once would give assurance to the authorities and was such that a practising accountant could reasonably be expected to sign it. The suspension of bankruptcy was effected by the Liabilities (War-Time Adjustment) Act, and some practising members of the Society were appointed Liabilities Adjustment Officers. In another direction several practising accountants were appointed as controllers of concerns of enemy proprietorship or having enemy connexions—supervised by the Board of Trade. In some cases these concerns provided goods having war-time importance to His Majesty's Government

'Security' was one of the instruments of war exercised by the Government; and to avoid risks the Ministry of Information set up a voluntary system by which companies submitted to the Ministry in draft their proposed annual reports and accounts. This control was fairly and sympathetically applied and companies were particularly careful in preparing the drafts to avoid any information which might conceivably compromise security. The shortage and rationing of paper demanded considerable ingenuity on the part of secretaries and printers in setting out reports and accounts within the area of paper allowed.

From 1940 it became clear that war damage by enemy action was to become one of the major war problems. Parliament passed legislation (War Damage Act, 1941) which afforded financial protection by Part I, War Damage to premises, and Part II, War Damage to chattels and business goods; funds were built up by war damage contributions based on schedule A and by premiums paid through insurance companies.

*　　　*　　　*

Comparatively early in the war the Government set up a Central Price Regulation Committee; the chairman was Mr. Raymond Evershed, K.C., now Lord Evershed, Master of the Rolls, and Mr. (Sir) Richard Yeabsley, F.C.A., F.S.A.A., was responsible for the costing operations involved. Throughout the country there were Local Price Regulation Committees, on several of which accountants served.

'To take the profit out of war' was not only concerned with moral considerations but was a vital factor in the functioning of the nation's war-time economy: the application of the principle with its wide ramifications—to some of which allusion has already been made—involved restraints as well as intensified activities; and for managements, adjustments and indeed discomforts. Accountability and independent certification at a thousand-and-one points were called for by Government departments; the Government, through the excess profits tax at 100 per cent. and income tax, laid a heavy hand on profits, to provide resources necessary for the unparalleled outgoings of the Exchequer. But if 'to take the profit out of war' was essential, it was even more important to restrain excessive profits, which by reason of the imperative demands and the comparative shortage of supplies and labour, could scarcely be avoided. In the pressure of war-time production, excess profits tax was hardly calculated to encourage economy in the expanding, changing, and often improvised manufacturing industries. It was far better to prevent excessive profits arising. And so there was built up a great system of costing, the more necessary since frequently—and for sound technical reasons and the urgency of demands—contracts had to be placed on a cost plus percentage basis: and there was the further objective of the most favourable use of materials and labour, calling for both physical and accounting control. Food and clothing for the civil population were included at many levels. These functions were discharged by the enlarged costing departments of the Ministries, by industrial accountants, and by practising firms, whose accounts of costs of clients were accepted by the Ministries, subject to the right of review.

Naturally the profession as such was directly engaged in the civil side of the stupendous war effort; but there was also the gallant service of its members who were with His Majesty's forces—most of them served in a military capacity and some were called on for their professional services and experience, exercised from time to time almost in the midst of fighting. Several distinguished themselves in battle and received high awards.

XIII. THE DOMESTIC AFFAIRS OF THE SOCIETY DURING THE WAR

Concessions to War Candidates: Examinations Continued

WHAT of the domestic affairs of the Society? First a small Emergency Committee of the Council was appointed to which full powers were delegated. It dealt with some urgent matters at the beginning of the war; but, notwithstanding the vicissitudes of London, the Council met regularly throughout the period of 1939 to 1945.

The Emergency Committee decided that the examinations should continue to be held half-yearly. The big cities, vulnerable to enemy action, were not places for examinations; and, following early inquiry, the Council was fortunate in receiving the co-operation of the respective Headmasters of Sedbergh, Yorks., and of Taunton, Somerset, and of the Principal of Southport Technical College. Residential accommodation was kindly provided by the housemasters or was arranged at hotels, and some members of Council who attended and the Society's staff were assisted by masters and by members in the neighbourhoods. The candidates invariably included men in uniform who had obtained leave to attend. These half-yearly activities provided pleasant interludes for the Society's staff, made the more agreeable by the welcome afforded them and some war-time hospitality. Occasionally, in leisure hours, some youthful exuberance on the part of assembled candidates called for a little official restraint!

★   ★   ★

An early question arose about the maintenance of practices where sole practitioners had volunteered or had already been called up for military or other national service: the position was similar even if a partner were left to conduct the practice but in circumstances in which association with some other firm was necessary. It was of course best that any arrangements with other practitioners should be made privately. But to meet this urgent problem the Council prepared a memorandum for guidance to those interested—particularly for the preservation of goodwill. It was indicated that if a member so affected had serious difficulty in making an arrangement *pro tem.* the Society's office or a District Society would be glad to suggest the name of other members who might be willing to co-operate. These temporary arrangements seem to have worked satisfactorily and no complaints arose subsequently.

The Council modified immediately the regulations for admission to the examinations—on the one hand to give assurance and facilities to candidates about to be, or who had been called up; and, on the other, to maintain a standard of training which was implicit in the Society's qualification, a responsibility owed to the men themselves and to the Society. At a time of great uncertainty it was not possible to prescribe by hard-and-fast rules, although the by-laws remained in force. Accordingly the Council passed resolutions giving discretion to the Examination and Membership Committee to consider all examination applications on their merits from both articled clerks and by-law candidates, so that (*a*) no candidate should be unnecessarily prejudiced by undertaking whole-time national service, (*b*) the committee should be satisfied that the candidate had had a reasonable period of professional training. There was added a reminder to principals that as articles of clerkship were a contract, the period required, upon a clerk returning from His Majesty's forces, was primarily a matter for arrangement between principal and articled clerk. The structure of these resolutions was congruous with the system of 'deferment of calling-up' administered by the Ministry of Labour and National Service, applicable to men undergoing study and whole-time training with a view to a not distant examination. Candidates affected could apply for accelerated admission to the intermediate or final examination, and deferment was generally approved in these cases. Occasionally the Ministry referred cases to quasi-judicial tribunals; over each of them a barrister presided, assisted by two lay assessors. No appeal to a tribunal was permitted to a candidate, although in a referred case he was asked to attend, accompanied if need be by the Secretary of the Society; but legal representation was excluded. The Ministry, however, very fairly referred to a tribunal any case

THE HALL, SHOWING WAR DAMAGE: JULY 1944

in which their attention was called to an anomalous decision: a series of precedents was gradually built up by the tribunals. Whatever may be said in criticism of administrative tribunals, the informality and sympathetic attitude of those appointed to hear these special appeals left a favourable impression of fairness and impartiality.

Overseas the examinations were held, but at infrequent intervals: the dispatch of questions from London was subject to postal censorship. This was carried out immediately on personal application, so that the risk of the questions being compromised was eliminated. Fortunately, neither questions to overseas centres nor candidates' scripts in return were completely lost in transit. A great work was undertaken by the joint war organization of the British Red Cross Society and St. John in conjunction with the International Red Cross by the dispatch of textbooks to several prisoner-of-war camps. The organization was established at the Bodleian, Oxford, and was in charge of Ethel Herdman, M.A. (Oxon.), and J. Grafton Milne, D.Litt., the Librarian of Corpus Christi College, who invited gifts of books from professional and scientific bodies. The use of books donated by the accountancy bodies, in conjunction with improvised classes arranged by those qualified men who were in the camps, not only promoted useful study but relieved interminable tedium and boredom. Courageously, Ethel Herdman proposed that through the agency of the Red Cross arrangements should be made to conduct professional examinations in the camps. At first this counsel of goodwill and perfection seemed—quite fairly—to the Society's Examination Committee to be impracticable. But with pleasant and winning insistence Miss Herdman gave assurances that the difficulties could be surmounted: they were, and the committee later agreed to her representations. One or two of the Society's examinations were conducted in this way (as were examinations similarly conducted for the Institute and the Scottish C.A.s) without incident or question, with much advantage to students who were unfortunate enough to be prisoners-of-war.

★　　　★　　　★

Many of the events described in the foregoing pages took place during the presidency of Mr. Percy Toothill, Sheffield, who was elected by the Council in May 1939: he had but a few months of peace-time activity and then addressed himself with unfailing zeal—notwithstanding uncomfortable travelling—to the host of problems which confronted the Society. He enjoyed much personal popularity throughout the Society and particularly among his immediate colleagues. He was succeeded in 1942 by Richard A. Witty, London, who brought to the office a unique tradition, by reason of his early training under Sir James Martin and his active interest in the Society from that time onwards.

Proposed Co-ordination of the Profession

Richard Witty in his outlook on accountancy was moved by two main considerations—an unquenchable faith in the Society and its policy and a belief that some further development in the organization of the profession was desirable. Keeping his own counsel, he entertained a satisfactory view of the various co-operative efforts among the accountancy bodies for war-time purposes. He got into touch with (Sir) Charles Palmour, then President of the Institute, to inquire whether at that favourable juncture some approach could be made to the further orientation of the profession. Mutual regard between the two Presidents created the right atmosphere, and Richard Witty with good judgement made it clear that he hoped the initiative would come from the Institute. Preliminary conversations between a few senior members of the Institute and of the Society took place, and a favourable if tentative suggestion emerged to proceed with discussions. The basis was that all bodies concerned should retain their own independent existence, and the purpose should be 'co-ordination of the profession' to include, but to extend beyond, legislation to provide for the licensing of accountants in public practice. At these preliminary conversations it was interesting that, on the one hand, senior members of the Institute who had opposed registration in 1930 were agreeable to the proposed exploratory conversations, while Witty himself acknowledged the strength of the Institute's case against registration in the situation of 1930. At the invitation of the Institute, a Joint Committee was formed in 1942 representative of the Scottish Chartered Accountants, the English

Institute, the Society, the Association, and the Irish Institute (for Northern Ireland). The chairman was Charles Palmour and the Society's representatives were Richard Witty (also vice-chairman), Mr. E. Cassleton Elliott, Mr. Walter Holman, and Mr. Bertram Nelson.

Attempts at registration had a bad history; the word itself recalled past frustration, and for that reason, and as indicating a wider purpose, the subject became known as 'co-ordination of the profession'. The committee's work was directed to the preparation of a draft Public Accountants Bill for the co-ordination of the profession of accountancy in the United Kingdom. It continued its labours during the war, not without some set-backs, but the final stages were not reached until the late 1940's. Meantime, Sir William Jowitt, K.C., M.P., Minister without Portfolio in charge of post-war reconstruction (afterwards Lord Chancellor), had made known his interest in 'a system whereby the accountancy profession was given a much higher power to look after its own members'.

Incorporated Accountants' Hall: War Damage

Against the vast panorama of the war and the multitudinous activities of the profession, the fortunes of Incorporated Accountants' Hall were a diminutive factor; but they loomed large to those who were carrying on the Society's work, and are inevitably a part of this record. In December 1940 a landmine struck a mortal blow to the Middle Temple Library, immediately to the east; and the severe blast caused damage to the roof, windows, and parts of the interior of the Society's Hall: work by the staff and by a firm of builders made a satisfactory transformation and in a month or two all rooms became usable. In 1941 there was a valiant and successful fight with a fire which consumed the neighbouring building barely thirty feet from the north wall. By 1944 it was hoped that damage to the Hall was at an end; but it was not to be. In July 1944, during the short-lived attack by flying-bombs, one exploded violently in the night between the Hall and Electra House (to the west) causing great damage to each. Regular fire-watching parties of the staff took duty at night and fortunately no one at the Hall was injured on that or any other occasion. Next day, the Rt. Hon.

(Earl) Clement Attlee, M.P., Deputy Prime Minister, Admiral Lord Mountevans—in charge of London bomb damage—and Captain (Sir) Charles Norton, M.C., Chief Air Raid Precautions Warden of Westminster, made a call at the Hall; and their practical interest was appreciated. Meantime, Mr. Walter Holman, past President, and his partner, A. Stuart Allen, came to the Hall to find the staff assembled in the public garden in front, and imparted some welcome morale. With the assistance of James Fay, chief clerk, they secured the goodwill of a neighbouring firm of incorporated accountants, who kindly provided some temporary accommodation for two years. Considerable and urgent demolition reduced the risk of dangerous collapse at the Hall and then parts of the ground floor and basement were reoccupied. Some temporary work proceeded until, without warning, all the labour employed was withdrawn and in the gable roof a wide open gap was left covered with a tarpaulin only, which flapped badly on a windy day; rainwater soon came into the Hall. However, after a few months some first-aid works were carried out and additional rooms became available for work. Curiously the books in the library, which were thrown into piles by the blast, suffered little damage, and records stored in the first-floor strong-room were saved from damp and water just in time, after the jammed door was opened by Chubb's. Security reasons imposed restriction on any public announcement of the damage until October 1944. All the protective operations had been directed with much courage by Sergeant H. Harling, the hall-keeper, who with Mrs. Harling lived on the premises, sometimes in very trying circumstances, throughout the war. Acknowledgement must be made of the continuous co-operation of the staff of Electra House, immediately adjacent to the Hall. Much help was given by the English Institute, the Law Society, and the Chartered Auctioneers' Institute by providing the Society with accommodation for meetings and library facilities.

*   *   *

Here tribute should be paid to some prominent members of the Society who died during the war period. Edward Whittaker, Southampton, had been a founder member of the Council, on which he served for over fifty years. Arthur E.

Piggott, Manchester, who had been a member of Council, was Secretary of the Manchester District Society for over fifty years. Great loss to the nation and the Society was suffered by the death of Lord Stamp, an honorary member, when his home was bombed and his wife and eldest son were also killed: there was an impressive memorial service in Westminster Abbey. Henry Morgan, President 1929 to 1932, and President of the Association of British Chambers of Commerce from 1942 to 1944, died in 1944; and Emanuel van Dien, honorary member, Amsterdam, during the occupation of Holland.

*   *   *

Amid the troubles of the war, the thoughtfulness of members of the profession in the British Dominions and in the United States of America was manifested by generous invitations to take care of children of members living in the United Kingdom, if transport and other circumstances permitted. After the war, during the period of austerity, food parcels were liberally sent to the accountancy bodies at home, some of which were used for the comfort of beneficiaries of the benevolent funds.

XIV. PREPARATIONS FOR PEACE

Accountancy and Management

VICTORY seemed now to be assured, and from late 1943 the thoughts of the profession and the Council were directed to after-the-war problems. An approach was made by the Society to the question of the finance of small businesses, and the Board of Trade were furnished with a memorandum: this memorandum presented one among many discussions on the subject of the 'Macmillan gap'. The outcome of the various discussions was the formation—no doubt with Government inspiration—of the Industrial and Commercial Finance Corporation Ltd., backed by the support of bankers: there was, however, neither Government financial participation nor a public issue of shares. The corporation has proved a useful addition to financial institutions; and other finance houses and merchant bankers are known to have interested themselves in this kind of business. Judgement and experience were enlisted in discerning the sound and well-managed concerns with reasonably good prospects, and in declining requests, encompassed with hope and optimism rather than satisfactory past performance. The situation was one with which practising accountants were familiar.

*　　　*　　　*

The redeployment of a large part of the personnel and effort of the profession for the purposes of war production gave impetus to accountancy in relation to management, and particularly to the status of qualified accountants not in practice holding important positions in industry. These circumstances appealed to Richard Witty's imagination, and the theme was taken up by him at meetings of District Societies, and in two of his presidential speeches at annual meetings. A welcome development was the election to the Council in 1946 of Mr. Leonard Hawkins, F.S.A.A., then Comptroller of the London Passenger Transport Board, the first industrial accountant to be so elected. Later, the Council agreed to consider for election to Fellowship applications by Associates holding positions of exceptional importance as industrial accountants and comptrollers, which could, in the opinion of the Council, be regarded as comparable in standing to public practice. The policy was applied with care and caution but with acceptability: the number of Fellows thus elected over a period of years was necessarily limited.

*　　*　　*

By 1944 the Council felt the time had come to give more concrete interpretation to the general resolutions passed on the outbreak of war covering examination candidates who had rendered full-time war service. After mutual discussions among the accountancy bodies and with the Ministry of Labour, it was agreed that each body, within the scope of its by-laws, would grant parallel concessions—a helpful principle was thus established. In his speech at the annual meeting in May, the President announced that (in broad terms) articled clerks could qualify on completing three years of professional service, by-law candidates on five years' service, with provision in certain cases for exemption from the intermediate examination. The effect was that war candidates could sit for the final examination within a reasonable interval after demobilization. Certain concessions were also approved applicable to demobilized men and women who took up accountancy as a career for the first time. The details to cover the various cases were set forth in formal modifications of the normal by-laws.

The Cohen Committee on Companies

A big chapter was opened in 1943 when the President of the Board of Trade set up the Departmental Committee on Companies, under the distinguished chairman the Hon. Mr. Justice (now Lord) Cohen. The only member of the accountancy profession on the committee was Mr. (Sir) Russell Kettle, F.C.A. Normally, a revision of the existing Companies Act at the end of about twenty years would seem to be necessary; but the course of events and the development of ideas and practice in regard to companies since the 1929 Act gave particular significance to the appointment of the committee. The disastrous boom floatations in the pre-1929 years, followed by the great depression, had produced a chastened frame of mind. The enlarged structure of companies, especially of holding companies and their controlled subsidiaries, was not merely the by-product of financial technique: it arose from the fashionable doctrine of rationalization. But probably the most persistent feature had been the increased demand for publicity in the affairs of companies on the part of shareholders and particularly by the financial press. Continuous discussion in the profession and elsewhere and the influence of public and financial opinion had led, by a voluntary process, to the accounts of companies affording more information than in the past, and beyond the minimum requirements of the Companies Act. Again there were such questions as the contents of the profit and loss account, secret reserves, the position of subsidiaries, and the accounts of holding companies. Thus there seemed to be gaps in the Act which merited consideration. Moreover, opinion generally had moved to a wider conception of public responsibility on the part of companies without impairing the initiative of directors and managements. The Society's Council prepared a memorandum for the Cohen Committee, and verbal evidence was given by its representatives and by those of other accountancy bodies.

Post-War Fiscal Policy

Besides separate efforts, some useful work was done jointly by the professional accountancy bodies. At the request of the Chancellor of the Exchequer, a memorandum on post-war fiscal policy was prepared and submitted to the Board of Inland Revenue. (Other memoranda were drawn up independently by the Federation of British Industries and the Association of British Chambers of Commerce.) The main text of the memorandum from the profession was the disparity between commercial methods of computing profits and the methods adopted under existing law and practice for taxation purposes. The structure of the income-tax law was then nearly a century old, modified by allowances for depreciation (1878) and obsolescence (1918). And the methods of computing income were illogical and full of anomalies, which when tax was only a few pence in the £ were comparatively unimportant; but when taxes were of modern dimensions they were likely to be fatal to maintenance and development in many undertakings. Depreciation, it was claimed, should be deducted in arriving at profits, whether such depreciation arose from wear and tear, obsolescence, effluxion of time (leases), or depletion (wasting assets). The discussion of the issues was naturally influenced by the prospective position of industry after the war, when the replacement of overworked plant and obsolete buildings, and the adaptation of war-built factories and equipment to peace-time purposes would become a major problem. The representatives of the profession therefore addressed themselves to further questions—whether maintenance and development of industry would be encouraged by a closer relation of taxation assessments to commercial profits, by a differential rate of tax on profits retained for capital extensions, and by some form of allowance directly expenditure was incurred for necessary extensions and renewals of fixed assets. The question of a differential rate was presented by balanced argument rather than by precise recommendation, and was concerned with contemporary circumstances: but the passage of time and experience have undoubtedly altered the views entertained in 1944. The usefulness of this considerable work found expression in the Income Tax Act, 1945, which was greatly influenced by the prior independent discussions and was well received.

The Universities and the Accountancy Profession

Some younger minds in the profession, thinking of the future, reflected on the question of professional education. Regulations of the professional bodies determined in precise terms the character and length of practical training and prescribed the examinations to be passed as conditions for obtaining a qualification in accountancy. The councils were indeed interested in the mental equipment and promotion of professional knowledge of students, first by much care in the preparation of the syllabuses of the examinations, and secondly through the work of the District and Students' Societies: and there was the regular publication of up-to-date information by the professional journals. The more specific studies of articled clerks and other examination candidates, however, were left to the students themselves, guided by their principals. Mainly, students took courses, both postal and oral, with admirable private coaching organizations, which had given valued service, or attended classes in accountancy provided in educational institutions. The pattern seemed to be somewhat untidy and the system, such as it was, might be thought to be rather *laissez-faire*. However reasonable that view might be, the answer respecting the past at any rate, was that the precise requirements of training and the examinations, even with the uncharted system of studies, had produced men of high qualifications who had won repute and public regard for the profession. But was existing procedure sufficient? (In Scotland the Scottish Chartered Accountants had their own officially sponsored tutorial classes.) The practical question was whether, through the universities and officially supported by the accountancy bodies, systematic courses of study at university level could be provided for students for the profession. Those who were zealous in initiating these proposals were moved by the ideal of extending and broadening knowledge and of implanting in students for the profession similar ideals and purpose: it was desired to give emphasis to accountancy as a learned profession. Following contacts made with some of the universities, an invitation was received for representatives of the profession to meet a committee of the Council of Vice-Chancellors of the Universities in England and Wales. It was decided to form a joint committee to explore possibilities, and the committee were fortunate in having as chairman Sir Arnold McNair, K.C., LL.D., Vice-Chancellor of Liverpool University (afterwards he became Lord McNair and Presiding Judge of the International Court of Justice at The Hague). The committee approached the question with the prospect of expansion in university education after the war and that undergraduates would be assisted by State or local authority scholarships. Many of the ablest boys and girls in the country would increasingly go up to the universities and the profession ought to be able to attract a number of them after they had taken their degrees. The representatives of the profession had to keep in mind the paramount importance of practical training, whilst the universities indicated that academic standards must be maintained and were averse to purely vocational courses. Thus proposals emerged whereby university courses in the departments of economics or commerce— whether for B.A., B.Com., or B.Sc. (Economics) degrees—

would be modified to comprise accountancy and legal subjects, approved by the profession; that whole-time attendance at the university for nine terms (2¾ years) should be during the currency of articles for five years; and that practical training in the office must be for a minimum of three years, part before commencing the course, and the rest in vacations and after completing the degree: the total period would cover 5¾ years. The degree would be accepted in lieu of the professional intermediate examination and all must pass the final examination. The scheme was accepted by the councils, the committee continued its work, and the professional bodies made grants to the universities. (For good reasons Oxford and Cambridge did not come into the Scheme.) The arrangement attracted some undergraduates; but it has been disappointing that the number who have qualified through the Universities Scheme has been comparatively small. In 1957 Mr. W. E. Parker, C.B.E., F.C.A., in a review of Training for the Profession, suggested that university subjects should be chosen for their own sake irrespective of a career in accountancy. Graduates in any subjects could serve articles for three years. Hence the combined course offered little advantage in time spent; and principals probably selected graduates for their adaptability and judgement rather than for theoretical knowledge. Characteristic of articles served in the ordinary way is the continuous integration of studies and work. Mr. Parker believed that, guided by his principal, an articled clerk advantageously developed 'a method of approach, an attitude of mind, a process of thought and a mode of practical application'. It seems that principals and candidates preferred the usual methods of training.

Continuation of Research

After being in abeyance for a time, the work of the Research Committee was gradually resumed and Mr. Bertram Nelson succeeded Richard A. Witty as chairman. Mr. F. Sewell Bray and Mr. H. Basil Sheasby concentrated on *Design of Accounts* (p. 197). A number of accounting forms had previously been drafted, or furnished to the committee: the forms were edited and others prepared, including a model form of company accounts, and some new ideas were incorporated in a set of executorship and trust accounts. Including these, there were twenty-five sets covering a variety of industries and businesses. In a concise and illuminating chapter the authors set forth their views on 'design' and 'the interpretation of accounts': indeed they suggested as an ideal the inclusion in published revenue accounts of operational items, going a good deal further than was then current practice: they enjoined both clarity and comprehensiveness, and avoidance of omnibus items. The President of the Society contributed a Foreword, in which he referred to recent discussions on the inadequacy of published accounts and the use of accountancy data for management purposes as a basis of operational action: *Design of Accounts* was a response to these topical purposes. An interesting corollary was a review of the work by F. R. M. de Paula, F.C.A., published in *Accountancy*: he had had experience of practice and in industry as well as having been sometime Professor of Accounting in London University. Accountants in their work, he thought, were individualists in a high degree. In consequence, for a long period, no provision had been made for the building up of an accepted technique and body of scientific knowledge. He therefore warmly welcomed the development marked by the establishment of the Society's Research Committee in 1935 and by the Institute's Taxation and Financial Relations Committee in 1942. The Institute's Committee had published recommendations on accounting principles, numbers I to VI, and these by the Institute's courtesy were included as an appendix in *Design of Accounts*.

Having overcome war-time difficulties in arranging paper, printing, and binding, the Oxford University Press published the first edition on behalf of the Incorporated Accountants' Research Committee in July 1944. Its issue and other details were arranged amid the confusion caused by the bombing of Incorporated Accountants' Hall. The first edition sold rapidly and a second impression was produced and was soon taken up: second and third editions (revised) appeared in 1947 and 1949.

*   *   *

An important step and one useful to the whole profession was taken by the English Institute in 1942 by the formation of its Taxation and Financial Relations Committee. The Committee consisted of some members of its Council and other members from all parts of the country; and later became known as the Taxation and Research Committee. Its work has included preparation of material for the consideration of the Institute's Council, (a) as the basis of evidence to various Government committees, and (b) for the purpose of authoritative statements made from time to time upon the actual work of members of the profession. Commencing in 1942, a series of Recommendations on Accounting Principles was published, primarily for the information of members of the Institute. (Up to 1960 there were twenty-two Recommendations, including some earlier ones cancelled but incorporated in later issues.) The Recommendations have been accepted in the profession and elsewhere as of high authority. In addition, the Institute issued Memoranda on Company Law, Management Accounting, Mechanized Accounting, and other subjects. The Recommendations and Memoranda, together with the Royal Charter, By-laws of the Institute, and pronouncements on professional conduct, were eventually made available to members of the Institute in loose-leaf form, with a suitable binder, described as 'Members' Handbook'. The Recommendations and Memoranda have the commendable quality of being succinct.

VE Day + 1, 9 May 1945

The years of consultation and planning between the Allied Governments and the leaders of armies, navies, and air forces, the intensive training of the armed forces, and the great output of industry culminated in the heart-stirring landings in France on D-Day, 6 June 1944. There followed the battles in northern France, the drive eastward and through the Low Countries, the heroism and check at Arnhem, and then the advance into Germany. It was fortunate that the recapture of the Channel Ports and northern coast of France put out of action the launching sites for flying-bombs and missiles which had been mainly directed by the Germans against London in the summer of 1944. An ugly threat was removed: but some missiles continued to be launched from Holland.

At home thoughts of 'after the war' were stimulated by the

Government's three White Papers of 1944 on future social and economic policy, foreshadowing later legislation. These statements of policy gave much encouragement both in the armed forces and among the civilian population now accustomed to an accepted régime of austerity. National Insurance[1] and Pensions were to be available to every adult on a contributory basis; also a National Health Service[2] (sequels of the Beveridge Report of late 1942). To eliminate any recurrence of the disastrous circumstances of the 1930's, full employment[3] was to be a prior objective of the Government's financial and industrial measures: the policy was begotten of the writings and views of John Maynard (Lord) Keynes on the relationship of money, credit, production, saving, investment, and consumption, not, however, without cautionary hints about latent inflation and the great need to increase exports: the question had practical implications for both demobilization and the prospective large-scale redeployment of industry. The order of demobilization would be determined on the combined principle of age and length of service, with some priority to men immediately needed for reconstruction work, but national service would continue for men from eighteen to twenty-seven years of age. Complementary to these several proposals was the Butler Education Act of 1944—the first great educational reform since the Balfour Act of 1902. All children would enjoy secondary 'modern' or 'technical' education; those above the average could move to grammar schools and reach the sixth-form; for the more gifted, Government and local authority grants would be available to enable them to go up to a university; and generally there would be an extension of university education.

*   *   *

These events induced urgency in all the accountancy bodies who were making preparations to give assistance to serving members and students when they returned to the profession after demobilization. For some, the question of re-employment might be a problem, and for all there would be need for courses of instruction to re-attune their minds to professional work, and particularly to revive their knowledge.

[1] Cmds. 6550, 6551.   [2] Cmd. 6502.   [3] Cmd. 6527.

Considerable changes and developments in the current work of the profession had occurred during their absence on active service. The Government had announced that there would be a scheme of grants to ex-service men and women for training and education: and consultations with the Ministry of Labour took place to discuss how, and within what limits, the grants for students and for members could most usefully be applied. Thus, organization was created and was available to deal with these matters when demobilization began to be effective.

Throughout the war the more vital parts of the Society's routine work were being kept in being. The President met annually the representatives of the Branches and District Societies at the annual conference in London and made some visits as circumstances permitted. *Accountancy* was published each month without fail, although precise punctuality was sometimes frustrated through the exigencies of printing and transport. At first the editing was in the hands of Leo T. Little until his war-time appointment with the Ministry of Aircraft Production: from then until 1946 its appearance was made possible by the practical interest of Richard A. Witty, the consultative advice of Mr. W. Manning Dacey, a financial journalist (now Economic Adviser to Lloyds Bank), and the unfailing sub-editorial work of Miss A. H. Page, the Society's Librarian. The Society's regular staff was reduced to seven and unhappily James Fay, the chief clerk, had a breakdown in health which necessitated his retirement in 1945. He received a presentation from the Council with their best wishes; the London Students' Society, which he had served with much devotion as secretary for over twenty-five years, recorded high appreciation of his work. For a few years from 1944 the administration had the help as Assistant Secretary of Brigadier O. H. Tidbury, M.C., p.s.c., who had recently retired from the army.

*   *   *

By 1945 France had been liberated; the British, Commonwealth, and American armies, under the supreme command of General Dwight Eisenhower (U.S.A.), advanced on Germany eastward, the Russians westward; air raids on Great Britain ceased; hopes were high. After the capitulation of the German forces to Field-Marshal Montgomery in Germany and to Field-Marshal Alexander in Italy, and the occupation by the American army of other parts of Germany, Hitler committed suicide, and Germany surrendered unconditionally on 7 May 1945.

The Society's annual meeting had been fixed for 9 May, which it happened became VE Day (Victory in Europe)+1, and was a public holiday. However, the Council met in the morning, and after lunch—which Brigadier Tidbury had somehow managed to arrange—the meeting was held by kind permission at the Auctioneers' and Estate Agents' Institute. Prompted by the sense of relief and thankfulness, the members joined in the national anthem and Richard A. Witty gave his presidential address. The attendance was rather thin and no doubt many members found the victory celebrations in the streets of London an historic occasion not to be missed. In his address, the President referred to the fact that 1945 was the Diamond Jubilee of the Society; and it was a matter of great satisfaction that the year coincided with the completion in Europe of the great undertaking of the Allied nations. He paid a moving tribute to the members and students who had fallen in the war; and anticipated a warm welcome on their return for those who were prisoners-of-war—with whom he had been in touch—and for others serving with His Majesty's forces. In good heart the Society turned its activities to restoring its organization and to assisting returning members and students.

Meantime the Allies had to complete their victory by the defeat of Japan, which was accomplished in August 1945.

COUNCIL AND STAFF, VE DAY+1, 9 MAY 1945

* Richard A. Witry, President

† F. Woolley, Vice-President

1945–1949

XV. THE FIRST YEARS OF PEACE

A Period of Austerity

ON VE Day King George VI and Queen Elizabeth and the great Prime Minister appeared on the balcony of Buckingham Palace and received a tremendous welcome from the thousands of people gathered in the Mall: at night the lights went up in a war-scarred London: it was a thrilling experience. After a short interval, a general election resulted in a House of Commons with a large Labour majority. The King sent for the Rt. Hon. Clement Attlee, M.P., who became Prime Minister and formed a Labour Government. Immediately a conference took place at Potsdam attended by the heads of the Allied Governments to determine policy towards the defeated countries—in continuation of what had been agreed at the Yalta meeting before the end of the war. The Allies had to decide on the governance of the occupied countries, then in a state of complete physical and moral chaos; and they had on their hands the appalling problem of refugees, the defeated populations, and prisoners-of-war: for all countries, victorious and defeated alike, the question of food supplies was paramount. If the defeat of Japan in August 1945 brought all hostilities to a close, it ushered in the atomic age with vast potentialities for good and evil. After the great upheaval in the world, the end of fighting was the beginning of a period of troublesome and intense international politics. A forum for these international affairs was the newly established United Nations, which also organized humanitarian efforts of relief in devastated countries through the United Nations Relief and Rehabilitation Association (U.N.R.R.A.).

At home early expectation of better things faded in some disappointment: a prolonged period of austerity ensued during

which the rationing of food, clothing, and petrol was imperative—mitigated by the generosity of many Commonwealth
countries which restricted their own food consumption—
and there were shortages of fuel, heat, lighting, and of housing
and accommodation. But fortunately the widespread fear of
unemployment was defeated by the gradual realization of full
employment, to which Government policy and industrial
activity were wisely directed. An enormous programme of re-
building, restoration, and new construction lay ahead—which
was subject to control and licensing. The cessation of American
Lend-Lease after the defeat of Japan, save for commitments
already made, precipitated a critical situation—the urgent need
of supplies and the absence of immediate dollar resources to
pay for them. At the Bretton Woods Conference (U.S.A.
1944) the delegates had drawn up a scheme to establish an
International Monetary Fund and an International Bank for
Reconstruction and Development to provide finance for an
impoverished world. In the situation of the autumn of 1945,
the British Government negotiated with the American Government an immediate dollar loan, which was arranged in
December 1945: the amount was £1,100 million in dollars
($3,750 million), and could be drawn up to the end of 1951.[1]
Terms of repayment and conditions were agreed, including
the acceptance of the Bretton Woods scheme and of the
avoidance of discrimination in dollar-sterling operations. By
July 1947 convertibility was formally restored, only to be
suspended in the following month: alas, sterling was unable to
stand up to the pressure upon it! By August 1947 no less than
$3,350 million of the maximum loan of $3,750 million had
been drawn, largely in the purchase of urgent requirements.[1]
It was a serious object lesson in international finance.

Government Finance and Taxation

The Chancellor of the Exchequer continued and intensified the
war-time policy of cheap money with a 2 per cent. bank rate.
Soon after the war large loans were issued—some in exchange
for existing obligations—with a fairly long date for repayment:
afterwards the nationalization stocks were added to the list of

[1] *Annual Register.*

Government securities. The low rate of interest offered was favourable to the Exchequer; but some financial writers viewed certain of these operations rather critically, by reason of the large amounts thought to have been taken up initially by Government departments, and considered them contributory to inflation. However that may be, the losses suffered some years later by holders of gilt-edged securities, due to the erosion of the value of money and a variety of other causes, have not only been serious to persons, trusts, and institutions but have profoundly affected the once accepted status of Trustee Investments and the investment policy of trustees and institutions.

Taxation was maintained at high rates; and indeed it was a decade after the war before appreciable relief was given. The war-time standard rate of income tax of 10s. in the £ was slightly reduced in the years after 1945 to 9s. and 9s. 6d.: it was not until 1959 that it was dropped to 7s. 9d. Progressively, however, some relief was afforded by more favourable allowances (including one for old age) and by greater graduation of reduced rates at the lower ranges of taxable income: on the other hand, the comparatively low maximum of the earned income allowance remained for a long time, with, it was claimed by many, disincentive effect, especially with the addition of surtax. Surtax *rates*, increased in 1947/8, were never reduced, but for 1956/7 certain personal allowances were deductible from assessable income (the excess over £2,000): in 1961/2 earned income relief was extended to surtax assessments. Modifications in estate duty (1946 and 1949) were comparatively in favour of the lowest ranges of estates, but involved for large estates increases in rates, already severe, with the effect of continuous disruption of estates and of economic and social consequences: legacy duty was abolished (1949): gifts *inter vivos* were effective in escaping estate duty only if made at least earlier than within five years of the date of decease of the donor (1946). Concurrently, and varied from time to time, purchase tax and the older indirect taxes took a heavy toll and were necessary in discouraging personal consumption. While the excess profits tax was terminated at the end of 1946, the profits tax (formerly N.D.C.) was increased and was regarded as an exchange for E.P.T.

Certain exemptions included partnerships and small traders, small businesses and professions. For 1947 the rate was 25 per cent. with non-distribution relief on undistributed profits of 15 per cent., in effect a 10 per cent. tax on profits ploughed back. The rates were changed in several subsequent Budgets. This tax on companies in addition to income tax was the subject of frequent adverse comment from chairmen of companies, having regard to the unfavourable effect on ploughed-back profits in face of the mounting cost of replacement of assets and of capital extensions.

The high level of taxation, particularly in the immediate post-war years, was required to meet the heavy expenditure of the Government; also in the endeavour to stem the increasing inflationary pressure while production was being regeared to peace-time requirements and the public were clamouring for goods of all kinds. Greatly concerned at the inflationary situation and the state of the gold and dollar reserves, the Chancellor of the Exchequer in 1948 made an appeal for restraint in wages, dividends, and personal consumption. A 'special contribution' was enacted for one year, and was practically a once-for-all capital levy, based on the surtax level of incomes as a rough index of the personal capital resources of those to be taxed. Strict foreign exchange control was continuous in order to protect the pool of gold and dollars of the Sterling Area, which meant the United Kingdom, the Commonwealth (excluding Canada), and some other countries. Yet, as some had feared, in the autumn of 1949, sterling was devalued from $4·03 = £1 (par) to $2·80 = £1 (par), after being $3·538 in the market. Although devaluation helped the export trade and discouraged imports, there were people who thought later that its working through the economy of the country stimulated a rising level of prices. Inflation seemed to be chronic. The perpetually rising cost of living was reflected in the intractable problem of the level of wages and salaries; this in turn reacted on prices, perhaps too easily raised in a sellers' market, in part to absorb the increased wage-cost. But there were considerable areas of remuneration—particularly for administrative work—where the level of salaries by no means kept pace with the cost of living. 'Marshall Aid'—initiated by the U.S.A. at the instance, and by the wisdom, of General Marshall—brought organized financial and technical help to the countries of Europe and elsewhere; it greatly assisted physical restoration and the resumption of economic activities to make good the ravages of war.

The burden of taxation—already briefly outlined—heavy and ubiquitous as it was, may perhaps be viewed more favourably in relation to concurrent circumstances from 1945 to 1949 and later. For one thing, the national income upon which ultimately taxation fell, had increased; and for another, the country had committed itself to wide reforms and extension of education and to the promotion of social services, notably health, national insurance, and children's allowances: these benefits were inevitably costly, and some of them cost more than was anticipated. Again there was the less welcome expenditure on defence, occasioned by unpropitious international affairs; and tremendous sums were required to meet both war-damage claims, as reconstruction progressed, and capital requirements when impetus was given to building houses. These internal affairs in the economy of a trading nation, however, could not be isolated: persistently the problem of the balance of payments—with its attendant export-import and gold and dollar reserves factors—has been written large in the history of the country since the war.

*   *   *

In the sphere of international politics, the period 1945-9 after the cessation of hostilities was crowded with difficulties. The success of the air-lift (1948) by the Western countries to Berlin —cut off from the West by military obstruction of road and rail transport—removed the potential peril of another war.

*   *   *

In January 1946 Lord Plender, G.B.E., F.C.A., who was the most distinguished figure in the accountancy profession, died at eighty-four years of age. Three times President of the English Institute and President of the International Congress 1933, he was held in honour in the profession throughout the world. In the same year E. Furnival Jones, President of the English Institute—its only President who was also a member of the Society—died while in office. He was a singularly witty after-dinner speaker with a whimsical sense of humour.

The Return from His Majesty's Forces

For the Society, the five years from 1945 to 1949 were a period of transition and of the rehabilitation of its organization. Attuned to circumstances much changed since 1939, its life was quickened and reinvigorated.

The Council was impressed by the urgency to afford definite help to members returning from their service to the country: in 1945 it sought the goodwill of colleges at Oxford and Cambridge and requested out-of-term facilities for the purpose of residential courses of about one week each. Thanks to the ready response of the Heads and Fellows, three courses were given— at New College and Balliol College, Oxford, and at Caius College, Cambridge (1945-6)—at which ex-service members were the guests of the Society. Experience gained at the pre-war courses was invaluable in organizing the programmes and arrangements. The men and the few women members present were welcomed by the President (Fred Woolley) and other members of the Council. An early opportunity was afforded at an open meeting for the members to make their views known: at the first course, these early proceedings gave an impression that many were somewhat anxious about the immediate future, and the President invited them to confer with him on their individual problems: actually their number proved to be small. The lectures and tuition were given by members of the Society and visitors, and were particularly directed to the changes which had taken place in the work of the profession during the war: these met the much-felt want of people who had been absent for so long. At the New College course in December 1945, the Bishop of Lichfield (the late Dr. Edward Woods, who was well known for his wide sympathies and broadcasts) accepted an invitation to spend a week-end at the college, and, at a service in the college chapel, gave an address, which was published in *Accountancy*. By invitation of the Warden (the late A. H. Smith, C.B.E.) the course was present at a recital of Christmas music given by the distinguished New College choir. Among the visitors to the Caius course in 1946 were the Bishop of Sheffield, who kindly addressed the members; and two Cambridge economists (now Professors), Mr. Austin Robinson and Mr. Richard Stone. The Head or a Fellow and the Dean of each college took considerable interest in the proceedings of the course and were present at the guest-night dinner, when the President of the Society took the chair. With help from the domestic bursars and college kitchens, the Society was able to offer hospitality as far as available and prescribed supplies of food and wine permitted. Immensely successful in their immediate purpose, the courses promoted morale and helpfulness as well as re-creating interest in resumed professional work and in the activities of the Society. Happily the early doubts about employment did not materialize and ex-service members were soon absorbed upon being demobilized.

Another immediate question concerned personnel of the profession in His Majesty's forces or serving temporarily in Government departments—particularly junior partners and senior staff whose early return firms were anxious to secure. The Liaison Committee, of which Mr. (Sir) Harold Barton, who had become President of the Institute, was chairman, made representations to the Ministry of Labour and the Board of Trade about the discharge from the forces, within the limits of policy determined by Parliament, of men normally engaged in the profession; but accelerated discharge was quite exceptional.

There was an equal responsibility towards articled clerks and by-law candidates to assist resumption of their training and studies interrupted by active service. The principle of reinstatement by former employers facilitated post-demobilization employment. Already the Council had defined, for ex-service candidates, permissible concessions in the regulations governing admission to the examinations (p. 231): the concessions included a reduction in the normal periods of prescribed professional service. The arrangements were buttressed by a scheme of training and maintenance grants under the Ministry of Labour, subject to express conditions of 'training' as distinct from 'employment' and to a limitation of period. Arising from the scheme, a system of 'trainee' agreements with employers was evolved, which applied to articled clerks: by-law candidates were eligible for educational grants but not for maintenance. These arrangements went through a gradual process of change in detail as circumstances altered: there were grafted on to

them for new candidates conditions necessitated by the obligation of national service, long continued after the war, and permissible deferment for the purposes of professional training.

Revision of By-laws and Examination Syllabus

In these matters Mr. Walter Holman and the members of the
Examination and Membership Committee worked with unfailing regularity and patience in considering over several years
the exceptionally large number of applications; each of them
needed individual attention. Before the war there had probably
been a rough balance between the numbers of Society articled
clerks and by-law candidates, with perhaps some slight pre-
ponderance of the latter; but with the expansion of the profession and the limitation on articled clerks in both the Institute
and the Society, the proportion of by-law candidates increased.
The special by-laws plus national service concessions became too
complicated; and indeed, designed under quite different conditions (1904), they called for complete revision, without changing fundamental principles. Accordingly, from May 1948 the
 pecial by-laws were based on six years' approved professional
service (instead of nine years) deemed to commence at 17½,
or at 16½ if a candidate had then qualified for exemption from
the preliminary examination: no concession was allowed for
national service. A revised examination syllabus (1951) omitted
statistics from the final, and other subjects were reorganized:
these changes and the acceptance for exemption from the preliminary of the General Certificate of Education, in specified
subjects at ordinary level or with fewer subjects if some were at
advanced level, brought the whole system up to date. The
G.C.E. could be taken at school or afterwards in one or several
subjects at ordinary or advanced level and took the place of the
former School Certificate, which had been limited to pupils in
public and secondary schools. The scheme for the G.C.E. was
based on reports of the Norwood Committee (1941) and of
the Secondary Schools Examination Council (1947) of which
Mr. R. Wynne Bankes, Secretary of the English Institute, was
a member. Division of the final examination of the Society into
two parts (optionally) was designed to meet the increasing
knowledge demanded.

A further revision of the syllabus was made and operated from November 1957. The changes in the syllabus were to effect proper balance between the various departments of current accountancy practice, and to give the right emphasis to company accounts under the 1948 Act, taxation and management accounting. In the final, taxation became the subject of a separate paper; economics was joined to financial knowledge; costing and management accounting were included together; and the legal papers were reduced from three to two.

Throughout, the basic character of experience required for admission to the Society remained unchanged. The by-law system, however, was greatly strengthened by a requirement of the formal registration of each by-law candidate (1953) as well as of articled clerks. Hitherto the practice had been to consider applications from by-law candidates for the intermediate and final examinations in the light of service which they had completed. The new arrangements implied that candidates had definitely embarked on a career upon taking up employment in the profession and had conformed with the conditions prescribed for preliminary education: the Council thus exercised some supervision over candidates during the time they were registered with the Society as such. Created in 1904, in the light of current circumstances in the profession, the special by-laws in detail lasted until 1948 and existed in principle up to 1957: the Council of 1904 built even better than it thought. The system had a definite influence on the progress of the Society, and, indeed, on the profession as a whole.

*   *   *

The Branches and District Societies quickly geared themselves to educational work in a variety of ways and found helpful recourse to the resumed panel of lecturers organized by head office: some arranged tuition facilities for examination candidates, for which the voluntary services of members locally and of visitors were enlisted. Mr. C. Evan-Jones became the Secretary of the London Students' Society, the committee of which had kept in touch throughout the war with students serving with the forces. Vigorous programmes were organized, and in particular pre-examination courses lasting one week were initiated—a residential course at Ashridge College, Herts., in the spring and a daily course at King's College, London, in the autumn. This useful extension of work on lines hitherto not contemplated was followed by some of the District Societies in the North in co-operation; the courses were given at Liverpool, Manchester, and Durham Universities, which offered welcome accommodation. In the two or three years after the war the President and the Secretary visited nearly all the District Societies: this was a mutually stimulating experience and was continued as a well-established tradition.

An indication of the extent of the work of admissions, professional education and examinations was given in the annual report for 1950. In that year 559 new articled clerks and 804 new by-law candidates were enrolled; 380 lectures had been organized by the District and Students' Societies; and 2,754 candidates sat for the examinations, of whom 1,163 were for the final (37 per cent. passed).

* * *

In December 1945 the Liverpool District Society (President, Mr. Bertram Nelson) celebrated its Fiftieth Anniversary. At the dinner Mr. Nelson received as guests the Lord Mayor (the Earl of Sefton), the Rt. Hon. Herbert Morrison (Lord President of the Council), the Viscount Leverhulme, the Bishop of Liverpool, and the Vice-Chancellor of the University. The proceedings were recorded for overseas broadcasting.

XVI. NATIONALIZATION: COMPANIES

THREE big questions of policy came before the profession in the 1945 to 1949 period, in which the Society actively participated: co-ordination, the audit of nationalized undertakings, and the Companies Act, 1948.

Co-ordination Dropped

The Joint Committee on Co-ordination pursued its deliberations: in consultation with legal advisers and parliamentary agents, the committee prepared a draft Public Accountants Bill. The Bill provided for a Public Accountants Council for (a) England and Wales, and (b) Scotland respectively, consisting of representatives of the principal ('qualifying') bodies and of nominees of the Privy Council, who it was intended should include a representative of practising accountants not members of the 'qualifying bodies'. The councils were to be vested with powers to issue licences to practise, to keep a roll of public accountants, to maintain the standard of examinations conducted by the 'qualifying bodies', and to act upon the disciplinary decisions of those bodies concerning the conduct of any of their members who were public accountants. There were other functions for promoting the general interests of the profession. It would have become an offence for a person to hold himself out as a public accountant if he had not a licence to practise. Among the conditions to be fulfilled by applicants, being members of a 'qualifying body' who had not served articles, was that, in addition to having passed the examinations of the 'qualifying body', they must have had at least thirty months' experience in a public accountant's office. Not a little difficulty was experienced in committee in reconciling divergent views on the length of this qualifying period. A clause safeguarded the rights of persons who, incidental to their main business, carried out classes of work which normally formed part of a public accountant's practice. The Bill set forth a definition of a 'public accountant' and statutory prescription of the several qualifications required of an applicant for a licence to practise as such, including conditions for persons not members of the 'qualifying bodies': suitable overseas bodies could be 'recognized' so that their members practising in the United Kingdom could obtain licences on the same footing as members of 'qualifying bodies'.

In 1946 the draft Bill was brought before special general meetings of the 'qualifying bodies', and was accepted by substantial majorities. The Society's meeting was held in the hall of the Royal Institute of British Architects: the President, Fred Woolley, was in the chair and Richard A. Witty presented the main features. Such critical comments as there were from members chiefly arose upon the essential requirement of thirty months' experience in a public accountant's office. It was a fair point to come from those who might be potentially affected: on the other hand, it could be argued that the condition in the majority of cases was sound in principle and was not too onerous for people who intended to devote themselves to public practice. Non-practising members were perhaps a little sensitive that the proposed statutory status was not applicable to themselves: any attempt to extend statutory status to other than public accountants was quite out of the question. The resolution passed at the general meetings left final details and procedure to the councils and the Co-ordination Committee. The Board of Trade was kept informed of progress made.

But in the course of further discussions serious misgivings arose as to whether a completely satisfactory definition of 'public accountant' in statutory language—which was fundamental—was practicable. Would the definition adequately protect public accountants in the exercise of their profession without attracting opposition from vested interests outside the profession, which might consider themselves prejudiced by the Bill—in particular, persons and entities conducting taxation business on behalf of others? And there were other difficulties: in fact there were many circles to be squared and the Bill bravely tried to square them. Early in 1950 it was decided that the proposals be dropped. There was some disappointment that the project could not be brought to a successful issue; and members of the Society were so informed at the annual general meeting that year. The decision was accepted. However, the discussions had not terminated in controversial deadlock, and the labours of the Co-ordination Committee in terms of mutual under-standing and knowledge were not wasted. By that time the Companies Act, 1948, was in operation and suggested another approach to the problem. Sir Harold Howitt had become chairman of the committee, which continued in being and later made a proposal to the Board of Trade (p. 262).

Perhaps a postscript may be added to the narration of these events. Long and careful consideration had been given to the co-ordination and licensing question. The outcome was that in the circumstances of 1950 it was questionable whether a com-prehensive statute to control the profession was attainable; or, if attainable, whether it would effectively secure the protection of the public and public practice. The doctrine of an *ad hoc* statute to regulate the profession had continuously been enter-tained by the Society; and even after the decision of 1950 some members of the Council had not lost their belief in an eventual structure of the profession on those lines. In some quarters the attitude was neutral or, after the thorough investigation made, there were more serious doubts about the desirability of legisla-tion. The strength of the 'qualifying bodies' left no room for doubt that they were quite capable of looking after themselves. But there remained the continuous complaint of practitioners in the smaller towns of unprofessional activities on the part of unqualified accountants and of other types of organization. Many of these members thought that unqualified and unpro-fessional practice could be eliminated only by legislation: nor could the formation of new bodies be otherwise prevented, although this might not matter very much.

The Nationalized Industries

The nationalization policy of the Labour Government of 1945 soon gave rise to questions in the profession about the audit of nationalized industries. Would a Government audit be imposed and, in any case, what changes would nationalization involve? Calling on the Secretary of the Society at the end of 1945, a member from south-west Wales gave an anxious account of the probable effect on his firm's practice of the transfer of a number of collieries to the proposed National Coal Board; others were similarly affected whether in regard to coal or the other industries earmarked. An Accountants' Joint Parliamentary Committee was formed and made representations to the Ministers responsible for coal, transport, electricity, civil aviation, gas, the new towns corporations, and steel (later denationalized in part). The committee endeavoured to secure statutory recognition of the principle that the nationalized industries should be subject to audit by independent qualified accountants. Some assurance was forthcoming, although perhaps hardly affording complete satisfaction, since the Government reserved the right to set up internal audit systems. There could be no objection to internal audit provided it did not go further than normal commercial practice; but information to the public could best be achieved by a completely independent audit and not merely by the check of an internal organization, however efficient.

Two special cases, distinct from the other nationalization Acts mentioned (p. 254), were the Bank of England Act, 1946, and the Cable and Wireless Act, 1946, in neither of which was any reference made to the appointment of auditors. Cable & Wireless Ltd., the Government-owned operating company, continued to be audited by professional auditors. But for the other nationalized industries and undertakings all the relevant Acts in the years 1946 to 1949 prescribed for in effect 'auditor (or auditors) to be appointed annually by the Minister', with the addition in respect of electricity, gas, iron and steel that the auditor must be a member of one or another of the English Institute, the Society, one of the (then) three bodies of Scottish Chartered Accountants, or the Association: by the Gas Act, and the Iron and Steel Act, members of the Irish Institute were similarly eligible. However, it turned out that professional auditors were appointed for each of the nationalized industries, whether or not accountancy qualifications were specifically indicated in the respective Acts. Some of the Acts stated that the accounts must conform with the best commercial standards. Under the New Towns Act, 1946, the Minister was required to prepare an account of sums issued from the Consolidated Fund to the corporations, or of sums paid by corporations to the Exchequer, and to transmit the account to the Comptroller and Auditor-General for his examination, together with a copy of the annual accounts of each corporation and the report of the auditor thereon. It is satisfactory on public and professional grounds that under the several Acts all the nationalized industries have professional audits by independent auditors, although more specific language in some of the statutes would have given greater assurance. The case for professional audits had to be submitted by the Accountants' Joint Parliamentary Committee with some vigour; but, unlike the attempts to secure professional audit of local authorities and education in the 1890's and 1900's (pp. 38–40), the representations met with a considerable measure of success.

Nationalization naturally meant concentration of audit work: some devolution was effected by local firms being appointed in the regions in addition to auditors of the undertaking as a whole. No compensation was payable to displaced auditors; fortunately professional work expanded in other directions. A passing phase was the setting up of panels of practising accountants by the Transport Commission, who were available on request to make investigations for the purpose of the acquisition of some three thousand of the smaller road haulage concerns. Sir Frederick Alban, C.B.E., President 1947–9, who had received the honour of knighthood in 1945, was appointed a member of the Electricity Arbitration Tribunal, of the Gas Arbitration Tribunal, and of the Iron and Steel Arbitration Tribunal: these tribunals dealt with questions or disputes arising from transfers of certain undertakings to the nationalized boards, mainly those the stocks of which were not regularly quoted on the Stock Exchange. He was also appointed by the Minister of Health as one of five members of a Departmental Committee set up to inquire into the problems of the Greater London water-supply.

The progress of the Welfare State was decisively marked by the coming into operation in July 1948 of the two great Acts passed in 1946 providing for universal national insurance, including State pensions, and the National Health Service. These measures had permanent social and financial implications, but their effect on the accountancy profession as such was general only, except in so far as several members received appointments as whole-time administrative officers in the National Health Service, and there was some loss of hospital audits. By the National Health Service Act, 1946, hospitals are audited by auditors appointed by the Minister. Both the hospitals section and the general practitioner section of the National Health Service are audited by an audit section of the Ministry, and services provided by local authorities under the Act are subject to district audit. The National Insurance Audit Department, which, under the previous insurance scheme, had audited 'approved societies', disappeared. Having been appointed first chairman of the Welsh Regional Hospital Board, Sir Frederick Alban carried the responsibilities of that important office for over eleven years. For many years Mr. E. Cassleton Elliott, a past President of the Society, was chairman of the Medical Distribution Committee of the Ministry of Health: he received the honour of C.B.E.

*   *   *

Each year the accountancy bodies received from parliamentary agents reports on private Bills, to be introduced into Parliament in the current session, which affected the interests of members of the profession—particularly the terms of audit clauses. Details of these Bills were discussed and largely settled in Private Bill Committees of both Houses, where interested parties were heard by counsel. The Joint Parliamentary Committee of the accountancy bodies exercised continuous vigilance after having given consideration to the parliamentary agents' reports. Existing circumstances and much past history suggested the possible extension of official activity under parliamentary powers, adverse to the interests of the profession. Even as late as 1956, in the Bills of two joint authorities, action was necessary on the old question of professional and district audit: this action was successful, and a decision was obtained in Parliament giving the authorities a choice between the two kinds of audit (instead of district audit only), as provided in the original form of the Bills. From 1919 to 1930 and earlier, these questions had been treated from the points of view of the interests of the municipal corporations or other authorities concerned and the interests of the accountancy bodies *inter se*—with co-operation between the Institute and the Society: questions, then the subject of continuous controversy, were eventually settled (pp. 184, 185). From 1945, however, the work of the Joint Parliamentary Committee was on behalf of the whole profession—a sign of a growing sense of common interests.

The Companies Act, 1948

The learned report of the Cohen Committee on Companies[1] was issued in 1945. Its significance was not only in its new outlook since the Companies Act, 1929, but in its demonstration of the will to think of the needs of the future, at a time when men's minds were preoccupied with immediately pressing problems. Its recommendations *inter alia* presaged legislative effect being given to what had already become the best practice in regard to the contents and the presentation of the accounts of companies. A Bill founded on the report became an Act in 1947: this was consolidated with other Acts in the Companies Act, 1948. Although parts of the 1947 Act came into force on 1 January 1948, it was the 1948 Act that became the comprehensive statute governing the affairs of companies. The terms of the previous Act (1929) on accounts were admittedly quite inadequate in 1948.

The Eighth Schedule of the 1948 Act prescribed in very great detail the essential contents, and the manner of presentation, of the profit and loss account (on which the 1929 Act was silent) and balance sheet: to elucidate the complications of a holding company group accounts (normally, a consolidated profit and loss account and balance sheet) were required. Generally the accounts must present 'a true and fair view'. An accounting point, namely, the setting forth of the remuneration, emoluments, and pensions of directors and of loans to officers of companies, was dealt with in the Act itself. A measure of flexibility was provided by exempting from some of the prescriptions in the schedule the accounts of banks, discount houses, and assurance companies: also by powers vested in the Board of Trade to grant certain relaxations in special cases and from time to time to make variations in the schedule, which experience might show to be desirable. The precise contents of the auditor's report on accounts were indicated in the Ninth Schedule. The Fourth Schedule called for more information in prospectuses

[1] Cmd. 6659, 1945.

and fixed responsibility therefor: the obligations became more definite. The auditor's report must cover profits and dividends paid during the five years previous to the prospectus (instead of three as hitherto) and deal with assets and liabilities, including those of subsidiaries, as at the date of the last completed accounts. Retirement of directors at seventy years of age was enjoined, unless a resolution, after due notice and disclosure of age, was adopted by shareholders: but this was not applicable to 'exempt private companies'. To enable alleged unsatisfactory conduct of a company to be investigated, two hundred shareholders or shareholders representing one-tenth of the issued capital could petition the Board of Trade to appoint inspectors; and the Board itself was empowered to initiate such investigations without petitions from shareholders. As far as legislation could do so, one of the purposes was to safeguard, and to give assurance to, the investing public without imposing excessive restraint on directors.

The keynote was greater publicity of the affairs of companies, both for information and as a salutary proceeding, as between directors on the one hand and shareholders and the public on the other. Even in the case of private companies, the Act provided that copies of the audited accounts must be sent to shareholders annually. A perusal of the published accounts of say half a dozen public companies over about ten years since the 1948 Act would indicate at once the more extensive information afforded: in fact some companies have gone further and, for example, have shown the amount of turnover and summarized comparative figures for a few years backwards. It need hardly be said that these improvements were welcomed in the City and in expert quarters elsewhere, as well as by private investors. The fuller and more precise information about companies which became available was invaluable to financial institutions, insurance companies, banks, the Stock Exchange, the financial press and information agencies, and in more academic circles.

In the nature of things, however, the less expert among shareholders could still find the published accounts of companies, with their technicalities and elaborate details, rather hard to digest: for them the statements of chairmen made at annual meetings, in many cases circulated by the companies, became increasingly helpful; and the comments of financial journalists were available in the specialized and general press. In his speech at the Society's annual meeting in 1949, the President addressed himself to this particular difficulty: 'Accountants stepping back to admire the products of their skill might well think on reflection that most of the people for whom the elaborate accounting service was being rendered did not understand what they were getting.' Tentatively he suggested that the possible publication, along with the detailed statutory accounts, of a simplified statement showing the same position, which could be readily understood, might be the next step in the evolutionary process of accounting. Commenting on this suggestion, *The Times* said it had no wish to reduce the force of the suggestion that the whole subject called for mature consideration. Yet two sets of accounts might tend to delay publication—then one of the consequences of new responsibilities under the Act. The note continued: 'A more fundamental danger, however, is that financial reporting for the layman might become a mere appendage of "public relations" with all that this implies, instead of the responsibility of the accountant. The dividing line between simplified accounting and selective propaganda could be very thin.' Yet as time has passed, a large number of companies have utilized various means to present information in simplified form, e.g. by pictorial representation. Certainly the emphasis on information for shareholders and the public generally arises from compliance with the Companies Act, 1948; hardly less from a marked change in the philosophy concerning companies, shareholders, employees, and the public, since these questions were discussed at the time of the 1929 Act. The form and contents of many companies' reports, which sometimes include coloured illustrations, would be startling to earlier generations of directors, secretaries, and auditors.

*   *   *

Important to the public and the profession alike were the provisions as to qualifications for appointment as auditor of a public or a 'non-exempt private company'. The point was discussed but Parliament did not extend these provisions to 'exempt private companies'. By section 161 (1) of the Companies Act, 1948:

A person shall not be qualified for appointment as auditor of a company unless either:

(a) he is a member of a body of accountants established in the United Kingdom and for the time being recognised for the purposes of this provision by the Board of Trade; or

(b) he is for the time being authorised by the Board of Trade to be so appointed either as having similar qualifications obtained outside the United Kingdom or as having obtained adequate knowledge and experience in the course of his employment by a member of a body of accountants recognised for the purposes of the foregoing paragraph or as having before the sixth day of August, nineteen hundred and forty-seven, practised in Great Britain as an accountant:

Provided that this subsection shall not apply in the case of a private company which at the time of the auditor's appointment is an exempt private company.

The bodies whose qualifications were formally recognized by the Board of Trade under the section were the English Institute, the Society, the Association, the (then existing) three bodies of Scottish Chartered Accountants, and the Irish Institute. A statutory obligation on a company to appoint an auditor had been in force since 1900: but forty-eight years elapsed before the qualifications of auditors of companies were defined by Statute.

The general benefits of the Act left little room for question: but is it not paradoxical that before very long some informed opinion rather wondered whether, particularly in the Eighth Schedule, a degree of simplification would be possible? The financial, business, and administrative operations, which were the subject-matter of the Act, were inevitably complicated; and the Act extended to no less than 462 sections with the addition of eighteen schedules, covering some 374 pages of the official publication *Public General Acts* (Companies Act, 1929: 385 sections, 12 schedules, 293 pages). It was a vital but formidable piece of legislation. As was to be expected, the operation of the Act threw up some problems, especially the creation of 'A' non-voting shares with voting rights reserved for existing shares and the procedure of 'take-over bids'. In a broad way the Act was significant in the economic circumstances of increasing divorce between the management and ownership of undertakings.

*   *   *

The new situation demanded much study on the part of auditors, upon whom the Act placed heavier responsibilities than hitherto. At the same time the Act strengthened the position of an auditor against removal from office without the shareholders being fully informed before passing the necessary resolution. A proposed change in the appointment of an auditor by the shareholders was subject to prescribed procedure; it included notice to the existing auditor and facilities for him, if he so desired, to make his views known to shareholders, in advance of a resolution at the annual meeting.

The President of the Board of Trade set up a Consultative Committee on Companies (Mr. Bertram Nelson was appointed on its formation) and an Accountancy Advisory Committee (to which Mr. E. Cassleton Elliott was similarly appointed). These committees were to advise the President upon the use of his powers under the Companies Act: the arrangement permitted company practice and new needs to be kept under review. In 1956 Mr. Bertram Nelson received the honour of C.B.E. in recognition of his services.

*   *   *

For an appreciable time the new Companies Act provided ample material for discussion at courses and meetings of the Society, and for articles in the professional journals. Under the auspices of the Society's Research Committee, Mr. F. Sewell Bray and Mr. H. Basil Sheasby prepared, with meticulous care and within limited time, *Company Accounts under the Companies Act 1947* (and *1948*)—a booklet setting out with full references a skeleton form of company accounts; over 10,000 copies were sold and the booklet went to several editions. Members of the profession were aided by counsel's opinion taken by the Institute: the opinion and the form of auditor's report drafted by counsel were published, and companies' accounts were discussed in issues of the Institute's series *Accounting Principles* The contents of the booklet *Company Accounts* first appeared in *Accountancy*: afterwards the editor published special articles on the subject. Increasingly the professional bodies aimed at affording assistance to members in their daily responsibilities.

*   *   *

While the more elaborate proposals for co-ordination had been dropped, the Companies Act defined a partial register. With that situation in mind, the Co-ordination Committee suggested to the President of the Board of Trade that the audit provisions and the rules for the qualifications of auditors should be extended to all companies, that is, including 'exempt private companies'. This it was thought would provide a *de facto* register of accountants, and would avoid the difficulties of a precise definition of public accountant. There could be very little public practice of accountancy, as generally understood, which did not comprise the audit of exempt private companies. The proposal offered considerable attractions, but was less simple than it seemed: on its initiation, provision would need to be made to include persons, not holding one of the prescribed qualifications, who were at the time engaged as auditors of exempt private companies. To make such provision might have involved revising the standard already fixed, which on general grounds it was undesirable to modify. The proposal has not been implemented.

*   *   *

Two important decisions about public companies were made by the Council of the London Stock Exchange in 1948 and 1950. A memorandum was prepared, after consultation with the English Institute and the Society, upon the contents of certificates of profits given by reporting auditors or accountants for prospectuses, offers for sale, and advertised statements. In the second case there was similar consultation, also with the Chartered Institute of Secretaries: the Stock Exchange Council suggested a revised specimen form of preliminary statement, more informative than that used since 1938, for adoption by companies whose securities were quoted, announcing profits and dividends to the Stock Exchange, the public, and the press. This useful form of announcement is common practice and is familiar to the investing public.

Solicitors' Accounts Rules

An aspect of the responsibility of solicitors for clients' moneys was before the Law Society about 1945 and was discussed with representatives of the accountancy profession. Afterwards, the Accountant's Certificate Rules, 1946, were issued by the Law Society, and a copy of a memorandum was sent to each practising member of the accountancy bodies. The examination of solicitors' accounts and the annual certificate required were set forth in the Rules; the Rules were made under section 1 of the Solicitors Act, 1941, and were brought into force in November 1946.

XVII. RESUMPTION OF SOCIAL
ACTIVITIES

Visits Abroad

THE slightly improved conditions of travel permitted more active relationships with other accountancy bodies and with the overseas Branches of the Society; also visits to Dublin and Belfast. In 1948 Sir Frederick Alban, President, Mr. Bertram Nelson, and the Secretary were the guests of the American Institute of Accountants at a convention in Chicago and were afterwards entertained by the Canadian Chartered Accountants and by the Society's members in Toronto and Montreal. They were fortunate in travelling to America with Gilbert Shepherd (immediate past President), Mr. (Sir) Thomas Robson, and Mr. R. Wynne Bankes (Secretary) representing the English Institute. At Chicago Sir Frederick presented a paper on 'Socialization in Great Britain and its effect on the accountancy profession' which created interest on both sides of the Atlantic: prints of this innocent thesis in a parcel excited some suspicion on the part of United States customs officers on the quay at New York, but the suspicions were soon dispelled and the visitors and papers allowed to proceed. The persistent fall in the value of money had raised a new problem of provision for the cost of the replacement of assets, for which depreciation on an historic cost basis was inadequate, and of how this additional charge should be treated in accounts. Lively discussions on this subject took place at the regular sessions at Chicago and were continued informally far into the night. The President of the American Institute entertained at a private dinner the principal delegates from other bodies, who discussed the prospects for an international congress on accounting, which it was agreed should be held in London in the 1950's.

Conversations in Canada assisted growing mutual understanding between Canadian Chartered Accountants and the Society. Entry to the profession in Canada, whether as to professional qualifications or to carry on practice, was governed by the provincial Acts and by-laws for the constitution and conduct of the bodies of chartered accountants in the respective provinces. The prospective developments in Canada impressed the Council of the Society with the opportunities in the profession in that great country. Acknowledgement was made of the facilities courteously accorded by the Canadian bodies under their by-laws to members of the Society who might seek careers in Canada.

*   *   *

Social activities were gradually resumed after the war on a limited scale. By unique coincidence in 1947 both the President of the Institute, Gilbert Shepherd, and the President of the Society, Sir Frederick Alban, were members of the profession practising in Cardiff. Their fellow members in South Wales and Monmouthshire marked the event by jointly giving a dinner in Cardiff in honour of the two Presidents, who were personal friends.

A long interval had elapsed since the Society had given a conference in the autumn and a longer one since this once biennial event had taken place in Birmingham. Enthusiastically the Birmingham District Society extended an invitation for a conference in that city to be held in 1949, during the presidency of A. Stuart Allen. The visitors were received by the Lord Mayor and Lady Mayoress, and by courtesy of the Vice-Chancellor the meetings were held in the university buildings at Edgbaston. A. Stuart Allen, who had exceptional experience in taxation matters, gave a paper on 'The democratic principle in income tax', and Mr. Richard Yeabsley, who was on the Council of the British Institute of Management, discussed 'What may management expect from the accountancy profession?' The Birmingham members were thanked cordially for the arrangements made, including the provision of hotel accommodation for visitors, which at that date was not free from difficulty.

*   *   *

Through its committees in Melbourne and Sydney, the Society had long-standing relations with the profession in Australia, although its Australian membership was small. At infrequent intervals the Council had received visits in London from members of the profession in Australia: perhaps some regret may be felt that opportunity did not seem to have occurred in the past for any representative of the Council to visit Australia officially. A special occasion, however, presented itself by the receipt of an invitation to the Society to participate in an Accountants' Congress to be held in Sydney in 1949. The invitation prompted the Council to nominate Mr. A. A. Garrett, the Secretary, to represent the Society and also to visit the profession in New Zealand and South Africa. Frank Way, President of the Institute of Chartered Accountants in Australia (Sydney), was the genial President of the Congress, and Mr. Clifford Andersen, General Registrar of the Commonwealth Institute of Accountants (which became the Australian Society of Accountants), was Secretary: the Secretary of the Executive Committee was Mr. S. J. Walton, General Registrar of the Institute of Chartered Accountants in Australia. The English Institute was represented by Gilbert Shepherd, past President, and Mr. R. Wynne Bankes, Secretary. Nothing could exceed the kindness and hospitality with which the visitors were welcomed both at the congress and at the other cities in Australia. Among the guests were the Chief Justice of Australia and the Governor of New South Wales. 'The future role of the Accountant' was the subject of an able paper by Gilbert Shepherd, from the point of view of the English Institute. He reviewed comprehensively the developing functions of the practising accountant (which had gradually been extended to accounting services to management) and of the industrial accountant in the context of 'the accountancy profession as a whole': 'the accountancy profession' was wider than the earlier subsisting concept of 'the profession of public accountant'. But, as he was convinced and the Institute's by-laws required (by way of articles of clerkship), it was the public accountant's office which provided the training ground to produce accountants having the breadth of knowledge and groundwork which would enable them to satisfy the calls on the profession as a whole and its varied responsibilities. Mr. F. Sewell Bray, F.C.A., F.S.A.A., London, who had received a personal invitation to the congress, broke new ground by his paper dealing with the influence of economic ideas on accounting, and adumbrating a structure of accounts leading to social accounting—a technique then being evolved by economists. A galaxy of papers were contributed by Australian accountants, reflecting problems which seemed common to the profession everywhere. The large attendance at the sessions, the contents of the papers, and the quality of the discussions demonstrated the vigour of the profession in Australia.

*   *   *

Through the kindness of the New Zealand Society of Accountants, the visitors were entertained in the principal cities, and—a rare opportunity—were enabled to see some of the scenery of that fascinating country and the hot springs in the North Island. There were many informal talks with leaders of the profession, particularly as to the status of public accountants and on the question of professional training. Membership of the New Zealand Society was subject to having passed specific examinations conducted by the University of New Zealand. The members consisted of public accountants and their assistants (F.P.A.N.Z.; A.P.A.N.Z.) and registered accountants (F.R.A.N.Z.; A.R.A.N.Z.): classification was mainly dependent on occupation. The New Zealand Society of Accountants Act, 1908, was then in force but has been repealed subsequently by a new Act. Among the younger members of the profession were those who, with scholarships from the two accountancy bodies in New Zealand, had previously spent two years with firms in London after some years' experience in their own country. Two of them—the first scholarship holders—had during their visit qualified as incorporated accountants. Their personal hospitality gave added pleasure during this memorable visit; and all the visitors received much courteous attention from the President (Mr. R. D. Brown), the Council and Secretary (Mr. James Tocker) of the New Zealand Society, from C. Douglas Morpeth, F.S.A.A., the doyen of the profession in that country, and Sir Will Appleton, who was also Mayor of Wellington.

*   *   *

The return journey via the Cape enabled Mr. Garrett to meet the three committees of the Society in South Africa. The South African Committees represented a large and important membership and, along with the South African Societies, were influential in professional policy, then being directed to drafting, in consultation with the Government, a comprehensive Bill to control the whole profession. Several occasions of hospitality permitted the pleasure of acknowledging on behalf of the Council of the Society the long and valued services of the South African Committees and the three honorary secretaries. Through the good offices of a member, General Smuts was kind enough to receive Mr. Garrett for a few minutes in his private room in the House of Assembly, Cape Town.

*　　　*　　　*

During short calls at Bombay and Colombo on the outward voyage, information was afforded by members of the early working of the Indian Act establishing the Institute of Chartered Accountants of India and of the Accountancy Board set up in Ceylon. The members kindly extended hospitality.

Retirement of Mr. A. A. Garrett from the Secretaryship

On 31 December 1949 Mr. Garrett, who had been elected an honorary member of the Society, retired from the position of Secretary after forty-one years in the Society's service: in May 1950 Mrs. Garrett and he were entertained at dinner in London, at which a large company assembled, and were presented with some handsome gifts and with many kind thoughts expressed by the President (A. Stuart Allen), Sir Thomas Keens, Mr. Edward Baldry, and Mervyn Bell (Dublin).

1950-1957

XVIII. COMMENCEMENT OF THE
REIGN OF QUEEN ELIZABETH II

Death of King George VI: Coronation of Queen Elizabeth II

THIS period opened with some anxiety in the country, occasioned by a distant but critical civil war in Korea in which forces from different countries under United Nations' direction took part to quell aggression. As a consequence of the Korean War, the economies of most countries, still in a state of convalescence, became subject to a severe bout of inflation; and at home an increase in taxation ensued for two years. Shortages of food, clothing, and household goods continued for a time, but with decreasing severity, until rationing was entirely removed in, however, a situation of rising prices. Yet economic or financial crises occurred and minor trade recessions set in about 1952 and again during 1956, with deleterious effects on employment. The activities of the United Nations and the North Atlantic Treaty Organization (N.A.T.O.) were continuous in international affairs as well as those of several other international organizations in Europe and elsewhere. Following the nationalization of the Suez Canal by Egypt, the Suez incident was a cause of considerable apprehension for a few months in 1956. Intensive activity in the building trade was directed to new houses, reconstructions, factories, and modern offices. Several 'new towns' were commenced and others already established were extended to relieve congestion in the big cities and to effect a better distribution of industry. Trades unions became a powerful force in the industrial and political life of the country. In the City the Stock Exchange Council developed publicity of the Stock Exchange and a gallery was provided where the public could view the Stock Exchange at work: it had previously been a closed institution. Sir John Braithwaite, the chairman, prominent in developing these ideas, was from time to time a welcome visitor to the Society and gave addresses on the finance of companies from the point of view of stock-brokers and their clients. As the area of investment and of investors spread, investors of all types favoured the merits of equities, which offered some hedge against inflation; gilt-edged securities suffered in consequence.

*   *   *

Londoners walking in the street on the morning of 6 February 1952 received a shock on reading the placards of the early editions of the evening newspapers: 'Death of the King'. His Majesty had passed away in his sleep. The Princess Elizabeth and the Duke of Edinburgh were on a visit to East Africa and returned immediately to London, where the Princess was proclaimed Queen as Elizabeth II. The heart of the Commonwealth warmed towards her and her consort and towards the grief-stricken gracious lady, now the Queen Mother. All her subjects realized the great responsibilities which had so suddenly fallen to Her Majesty, the young Queen. With the sadness of the nation was mingled thankfulness for the life of a monarch called to the Throne in unpropitious circumstances, imbued with a high sense of duty, yet often dogged by indifferent health: having surmounted the anxieties of war, George VI witnessed with unfailing royal judgement, and responded to the great social changes in the first years of peace. The members of the Society remembered that George VI, when Duke of York, had formally opened Incorporated Accountants' Hall. A Loyal Address of Condolence from the Society submitted to Her Majesty Queen Elizabeth II was followed in 1953 by a Dutiful Address of Congratulation on her Coronation. The Coronation at Westminster Abbey was witnessed not only by the distinguished congregation but by thousands of Her Majesty's subjects through the new medium of television. The President, Mr. C. Percy Barrowcliff, was commanded to be present in Westminster Abbey and some official seats in the Mall were allotted to members of Council: unfortunately on Coronation Day the weather was very bad.

*   *   *

In 1951 the Rt. Hon. Sir Winston Churchill, K.G., O.M.,

C.H., M.P., once again was called to lead a Conservative Administration. His eightieth birthday, 30 November 1954, was celebrated with heartfelt and widespread affection and befitting honour; and in April 1955 he laid down the office of Prime Minister but continued to be a member of the House of Commons. His courage in war, magnanimity in controversy, and his versatile genius gave him a great place among statesmen and in the world of letters and art.

*   *   *

The pace of scientific research in all fields brought great changes in industry, in transport, and in medicine. The prospect of nuclear energy became a practical possibility whilst oil increasingly replaced coal as a primary fuel for heating and power. 'Automation', electronics, and electrical power found ever-increasing applications. The prospects and interests offered by accountancy as a profession were enhanced by the possibilities —as well as the problems—presented by mechanical and electrically controlled accounting systems, by the application of electronics and the operation of large-scale computers. By contrast, yet significantly, even the small country shop acquired a mechanical or electrical till and an adding machine.

As permissible allowances of foreign exchange for holiday expenses were gradually increased, foreign travel became more general. The family motor-car, television sets, and new labour-saving appliances in the home—facilitated by developing but varying hire-purchase accommodation—indicated a greater degree of leisure time; and concurrently there was widespread interest in sport.

Government Accounts

An age avid for information was marked by a growing output of Government white papers, blue books, and other publications and by the published results of research sponsored by universities, institutions, and industry. A change in one white paper and the issue for the first time of three others may be noted.

The annual Financial Statement issued by the Chancellor of the Exchequer each April sets forth the 'Out-turn' for the previous year and the Budget proposals for the ensuing fiscal

year. In April 1949,[1] for the first time, the 1948-9 'Out-turn'
and the 1949-50 Budget estimate were set out side by side in
two separate accounts, headed 'Conventional Form' and 'Alternative Classification'. (In April 1948 the idea had been applied
to 'Out-turn' only.) The 'Alternative Classification' consisted
of (a) revenue items (receipts and payments), and, separately,
(b) loans and other non-revenue items (receipts and payments).
After being used for several years the 'Alternative Classification' was dropped, but the 'Conventional Form of Accounts'
survives, now headed '1959-60 Out-turn and 1960-1 Estimates
after 1960-1 Budget changes'.[2] The statement is divided into
two sections 'Above the line' and 'Below the line'. 'Above the
line' items are revenue from taxation, and from minor sources;
and expenditure on Consolidated Fund Services and Supply
Services, which conceivably may cover some items of a capital
character.[3] 'Below the line' receipts and payments cover items
of a non-revenue character: the payments are those which
Parliament has authorized may be met by borrowing;[3] and the
items (both sides) include loans to, and repayments by, local
authorities, nationalized industries, post office, and—whether
logically or not—payments for post-war credits and war
damage (excess profits tax refunds were formerly mentioned).
The Crick Committee on Government Accounts (1948 to
1950)[4] pointed out that the last three items were a discharge of
outstanding (if unrecorded) liabilities. That committee deprecated the use of the term 'capital' for the items set out 'below
the line'. (Actually the committee were discussing them on the
basis of the previous 'Alternative Classification'.) There was
considerable variety of opinion about classification and it was
quite impossible to make a satisfying division, particularly in
the time available before the Budget was introduced: the
Financial Statement was not strictly a public accounting document but a memorandum of material required promptly for
the Budget debates. The balance 'below the line' was the net
sum borrowed or met from the surplus ('above the line'). This
arrangement of the national accounts enabled some view to be
formed of inflationary or deflationary effects, according to the

[1, 2] *House of Commons Papers* 124, 1948-9; 157, 1959-60.
[3] Brittain, *The British Budgetary System*.   [4] Cmd. 7969, 1950.

degree in which the surplus 'above the line' covered the deficit 'below the line'.

The evidence before the Crick Committee (chairman, Mr. W. F. Crick, C.B.E., Midland Bank) was given by civil servants, individual members of the accountancy profession, the English Institute, the Society's Research Committee, economists, and representatives of industry and banking. The committee's report set out at length its view of fundamental differences in purpose and method between Government and commercial accounting: Government accounts in the main were directed to stewardship of moneys voted by Parliament, not to record profit or loss. The Committee's principal conclusion was that the main exchequer accounts and both estimates and appropriation accounts should remain on a cash basis. An income and expenditure basis would encounter insuperable practical difficulties in regard to capitalization and depreciation of fixed assets. For large-scale trading (e.g. Ministry of Food), the Committee viewed with approval the practice of having income and expenditure accounts, but recommended that a 'Trading Fund' be set up to finance such operations: for lesser trading activities trading accounts should be published. The report met with some professional criticism directed to the 'cash basis' and the limited approach towards 'income and expenditure'.

*   *   *

Work on the national income enabled the publication of the Statement of National Income and Expenditure to be made in 1941[1] (it was for the years 1938 and 1940) and subsequently annually. The contents, which cover the calendar, not the fiscal, year, have been continuously refined and expanded from year to year to be a guide for the purpose of economic and fiscal policy. A preliminary estimate is available immediately prior to the Budget. The first annual economic survey made its appearance in 1947[2]—an interesting publication although its contents or anticipations have not always escaped criticism. An annual Abstract of Statistics had been prepared by the Board of Trade for more than a century. The responsibility was transferred to the Central Statistical Office: an Abstract was published in 1947

[1] Cmd. 6261, 1941.   [2] Cmd. 7046, 1947.

(covering the years 1935 to 1946)[1] and afterwards annually. From 1946 a monthly digest was issued additionally.

Taxation of Business Profits: Retirement Pensions and Tax Relief

A prominent feature since the end of the war has been the large number of Government committees appointed to inquire into matters upon which the Society—either singly or jointly with others—tendered evidence. The preparation of the evidence fell upon members of the Council and the Research Committee. The interesting list of subjects reviewed is long and a few references only are possible.

A Committee on the Taxation of Business Profits sat under the chairmanship of Mr. (Sir) John Millard Tucker, Q.C., and reported in April 1951.[2] The inquiry was intended as a first stage in a general review of the system of taxation of profits and income, which was undertaken by the Royal Commission appointed in January 1951.

The second Millard Tucker Committee and its report (February 1954)[3] created more general interest, for it reviewed and made recommendations upon retirement provisions in relation to taxation and tax relief. Up to that time pension schemes whether independent or effected through insurance companies, for the benefit of *employees*, could be approved by the Board of Inland Revenue. In that case contributions by employers and employees were deductible—within limits—for income-tax purposes: pensions when drawn were taxable but attracted the earned allowance. Such facilities were not available to self-employed persons; and, especially in the case of professional people working on their own account, their absence produced much hardship, accentuated by high taxation, limited capacity for saving, and increase in cost of living. Again, the whole amount of ordinary annuities for life was subject to the full tax, although there were special 'annuities certain' which afforded some relief. As a result of the Millard Tucker Committee's second report, the Finance Act, 1956, gave tax relief to self-employed persons who, by contributions during working life, provided through appropriate schemes for eventual retirement, and their pensions were to be subject to earned allowance.

[1] No. 84, 1947.   [2] Cmd. 8189, 1951.   [3] Cmd. 9063, 1954.

Further, if a whole-life annuity were purchased, the annual capital element was not taxable. Much impetus was given to the provision of retirement pensions, whether for self-employed or employed persons, with a substantial increase in this class of business for assurance companies and in the formation of sound independent schemes. Provision for retirement must be classed as one of the major social phenomena of the post-war period; and it has had a marked effect upon the volume of investment business and as an element in the nation's savings. Professionally, pension schemes are mainly the concern of actuaries, but the introduction of pension schemes, with attendant finance required and taxation reliefs, has come within the experience of both practising and industrial accountants.

The Royal Commission on Taxation

Perhaps for accountants the most significant of the inquiries since the war was the Royal Commission on the Taxation of Profits and Income. The chairman was Lord Radcliffe (Lord of Appeal in Ordinary), and Mr. (Sir) William Carrington, F.C.A., was one of the members, who otherwise included representatives of the legal profession, the City, and trade unions and economists. Some public sessions of the commission were held at Incorporated Accountants' Hall.

In parenthesis, the Income Tax Act of 1952, consolidating legislation since the 1918 Act, was a helpful statute: reference by lawyers and accountants engaged in income-tax practice was thus much facilitated. The publication by the Board of Inland Revenue, annually from 1949, of the list of extra-statutory concessions was also a welcome step for the profession.

Lengthy, but presented with lucidity and the least possible amount of technicalities, the final report (1955) of the Royal Commission[1] was both impressive and readable. The terms of reference specifically mentioned the necessity to maintain the revenue, from profits and income; the commission conducted its deliberations subject also to the general premise that 'there would not be any marked increase or decrease in the purchasing power of money'—unfortunately one which did not subsequently materialize. The penetrating minds of the members of

[1] Cmd. 9474, 1955.

the commission analysed the various phases of taxation of income and profits: it was more concerned with evidence and circumstances than with impressions. The report stated expressly, 'even when everything possible has been done to remove inequities . . . it [the system] will retain defects: and they will be felt as serious defects by reason of the weight of tax'. Although the overburdened taxpayer reading the report, might not find a great deal of comfort for his *bêtes noires*, effective proposals —perhaps limited in extent—were made to remedy clear inequities and discrimination.

Steep graduation—and disincentive—occurred at the marginal point of £2,025 earned income by the coincidence of the limit of earned relief at that point and the commencement of surtax after £2,000.[1] No recommendation was made to vary the point of impact of surtax, except that for single persons the point should be dropped to £1,500, and for married people with children, additional allowances should be permitted. The marginal point for earned allowance (income tax) should be raised to £2,500, with allowance at half rate on the next £500. These suggestions—omitting the drop to £1,500—have since been implemented in somewhat more liberal detail.

Much consideration was given to the question of 'expenses' allowable in making assessments: the language of the report was singularly judicious in commenting on 'impressions' and evidence of possible abuse. Schedule D amounts were allowable only if 'wholly and exclusively for the purpose of the trade': the commission considered that the test 'for the purpose of earning profits' (judicially decided in 1906) should be disowned by statute. Dissecting the implications of the schedule E rule that expenses are deductible only if 'wholly, exclusively and necessarily' incurred in the performance of the duties of employment, the commission remarked 'There can have been no part of the income tax code which has been so regularly the subject of unfavourable notice' (by the courts), and that generally its administration was attended by widespread dissatisfaction. The conclusion reached was to propose the substitution of the words 'all expenses reasonably incurred for the appropriate performance of the duties of the office or employment'—a

[1] Second Report, Cmd. 9105, 1954.

reform which remains to be implemented. Legislation in 1948 had tightened procedure for schedule E in respect of all benefits to employees earning over £2,000 (including expenses and benefits in kind) and to directors (without the earnings limit). This discrimination against directors, unless controlling directors, the commission sought to remove, and to allow exemption, as well for directors as for employees, of the value of accommodation, if living on the premises were essential. But it was not proposed to repeal the 1948 procedure: the onus of showing that allowances for expenses covered items only within the rule under schedule E for deductible expenses was upon the recipient—unless 'dispensation' were given by the Inspector of Taxes. Some relief was recommended to cover the travelling expenses of people with more than one calling—for instance, a director of several companies, geographically separated, and the classical case of the Recorder of a provincial city. The solution offered was to be a selection by the taxpayer of the place of 'a main source of income', from which travel for other work would give rise to an allowable expense. Statutory effect to this proposal was advised in place of 'extra-statutory concessions' that had been recently operative. A point of detailed administration —the deduction of notional 'home saving' from travelling expenses—was considered to be a source of irritation and some ill will, by reason of the personal inquiries involved. And the commission recommended that the attempt to take 'home savings' into account should be abandoned.

Perhaps it may be said of some comments of the commission that the Board of Inland Revenue was doubtless concerned that the extension of concessions or relaxation of the standard of administration might lead to demands for further concessions, with the risk of continuous erosion of the base of direct taxation.

*   *   *

Of measures to frustrate tax avoidance, the commission took an empirical view—that, as in the past, gaps in the system should be stopped by new legislation as any undesirable practices presented themselves, rather than by countering tax avoidance by reference to a general principle declared by statute. But attention was drawn to the obscure wording of much anti-avoidance legislation, often drawn more widely than required; and the commission proposed expert review with the purpose of securing greater brevity and precision. Under the heading of 'tax evasion', four recommendations were made which could give little ground for criticism. People carrying on a trade, profession, or vocation should be under a legal obligation to keep simple business records; accounts, if submitted to support a return, should themselves rank as part of the return; the taxpayer should give a certificate as to the completeness of underlying records, takings and stock being particularly in mind; a wife should sign the joint return in respect of her own income.

For the (then) existing three-tier tax on companies (income tax, and profits tax on distributed and undistributed profits at two rates), the commission, while rejecting the suggestion of one special tax for companies, recommended the continuance of income tax, but profits tax to be at a flat rate. The suggestion of one special tax, however, was supported in a minority report and by good argument, on the grounds that company profits were of quite a different character from individual income.

The report comprised two chapters and a memorandum from the Board of Inland Revenue on the possibility of taxing capital gains. The majority found that although such taxation 'might discourage a small number of people who were enabled by obtaining capital gains to maintain a standard of living out of relation to their income, its general effect would be to tax a very much larger number of persons without the justification of any equitable design'. The yield of such a tax was extremely uncertain and its administration would call for additional staff of 500 in the Chief Inspector's office. The majority, therefore, did not recommend that capital gains should be subject to income tax or surtax or to a special flat rate tax. A minority of three contributed a full discussion in favour of bringing capital gains within the conception of income for income tax but not for surtax. They also dissociated themselves from many of the majority recommendations on the nature of reliefs. On the other hand, they favoured earned income allowance without upper income limit for schedule E, and for schedule D in the case of a profession or vocation subject to the schedule E expenses rule. They believed that their proposals, which generally extended the taxation base, would permit of a more moderate scale of progression in the schedule of rates of taxation.

In concluding their labours, the members of the commission referred to the ardent desire, with which they commenced the inquiry, to leave the structure and the conceptions of tax simpler than they found them. But they stated that these could never be simple and that income tax must reflect the intricacy and complication of the social and industrial structure of the country. The previous Codification Committee after nine years' work had submitted a report in 1936. In the final chapter of its report, the Royal Commission quoted—apparently with regretful approval—the opinion of the 1936 Committee: 'to expect from us a codification of the law of income tax which the layman could easily read and understand was a vain hope, which only the uninstructed could cherish'. However, the commission made three excellent proposals:

1. The possibility that some separate branch of the law might be codified.
2. Consolidation might be made regularly every ten years (1918 to 1952 had been too long); and continuity in the numbering of basic sections should be preserved.
3. Greater clarity and concision might be possible in drafting income-tax legislation.

Published Accounts of Companies

In 1953 *The Accountant* decided to make one or more awards annually to companies whose shares were quoted on a recognized Stock Exchange in respect of the form and contents of the published report and accounts: the factors included the adequacy of the information given and its presentation. A panel of judges was invited to make the annual recommendations: the panel consisted of representatives of the accountancy bodies and the Editor of *The Accountant* (then Mr. Derek du Pré) with Montagu Gedge, Q.C., as the first chairman. The presentation of the Award has been made each year by the Lord Mayor at the Mansion House, London.

XIX. A NEW PHASE IN THE SOCIETY

Administrative and Constitutional Changes: Restoration of the Hall

THE Council appointed as Secretary (from 1 January 1950) Mr. I. A. F. Craig, O.B.E., B.A., formerly an officer on Earl Mountbatten's Combined Staff in the Far East (S.E.A.C.), who was already Deputy Secretary; and as Deputy Secretary, Mr. C. A. Evan-Jones, M.B.E., who had been a Gordon Highlander and a Brigadier. Quickly they brought to the work of the Society fresh minds and new ideas; they established friendly relations with secretaries of other bodies at home and overseas and with institutions and Government departments with which the Society had connexions, as well as with the Branches and District Societies. With much insight they provided, through the Council, more information for members. The annual reports, syllabuses, and other Society literature became, as increasing paper supplies permitted, more interesting in content and artistic in appearance. The list of members was published in a new and improved form: the traditional dark-blue binding was retained. The annual conference of the District Society representatives with members of the Council had already established itself as an integral part of the Society's organization—and indeed in a long-term review of the articles it was proposed to provide that the conference become a part of the Society's constitution. Increasingly the conference developed into an organ by which the Council and head office were kept in touch with the feeling and views of the general body of members throughout the country. As an administrative procedure a meeting was held periodically at head office of the Secretary and Deputy Secretary with the Secretaries of District Societies. This new procedure effectively assisted the liaison with head office and the administration of day-to-day District Society business. In 1950, Mr. J. D. Nightingirl, A.S.A.A., became Assistant Secretary.

Stimulated by new features and by expanded contents, the circulation of *Accountancy* much increased under the continuing editorship of Leo T. Little, B.Sc. (Econ.), assisted by Miss

A. H. Page, M.A., who had been the Society's Librarian. A section was reserved for news of the Society's activities, but the greater part of the space was devoted to an editorial, articles, and notes on subjects of interest to the profession generally. The outside cover, of modern design on grey paper, bore the name and arms of the Society, and the caption

ACCOUNTANCY
Established 1889

Accounting : Management : Finance.

Increasing costs in printing and paper demanded considerable ingenuity in designing a format and layout which at once provided adequate space, permitted the use of easily read type, and avoided overcrowding. The subscription in 1957 was £1. 1s. per annum, a modest sum if it is recalled that when the *Incorporated Accountants' Journal*—the parent of *Accountancy*—became a monthly publication in 1895 the subscription was 7s. 6d. In 1957 the circulation had reached 14,000.

*   *   *

The much-damaged Hall had been patched and shored up early in 1946, yet the first floor was completely unusable. Meantime Sir Percy Thomas, P.R.I.B.A., prepared plans for restoration and for an additional wing on the west side. After much delay a licence, limited to restoration, was granted by the Ministry of Works, and work commenced in 1948. For this purpose the administration was moved to a disused warehouse in Milford Lane at the rear of the Hall: here for two years the business of the Society was conducted, amid unavoidable discomfort. The work of restoration by Trollope & Colls Ltd., directed by Sir Percy Thomas, was well done and was completed by April 1951. The strong room leading from the large hall was completely removed and a new office room (adjacent to the Secretary's room) substituted; one office on the ground floor was enlarged and another was much improved; and in the library shelves were fixed to the walls only: the previous book stacks, projecting from the south wall, were dispensed with, so that the library could be used as necessary for other purposes. The Hall was refurnished and gifts towards the more decorative items were generously made by the Irish Branch, the South

African Branches, and several individuals. The total cost exceeded £100,000, most of which was met from war damage claims. After completion of the work in the spring of 1951, the reopening was marked by an informal reception in May at which the immediate past President, A. Stuart Allen, and the new President, Mr. C. Percy Barrowcliff, welcomed the Lord Mayor and other guests. The Council and committees could once again meet in suitable and dignified rooms, the expanding administration was more efficiently accommodated, and the library service improved: but with the development of a Research Department, the welcome advent of an Appointments Officer (Mr. F. H. H. Finch), and expansion of other sections of work, some additional rooms in neighbouring offices had to be rented within a year or two of the date of reoccupation. Valued help had been given over several years by the Chartered Auctioneers' and Estate Agents' Institute and the Royal Institute of British Architects. Now the large hall became again the setting for general and other meetings of members. The Council was able to entertain at dinner from time to time distinguished guests in the Society's own home, among whom were the Lord High Chancellor (Viscount Kilmuir), the President of the Board of Trade (Mr. Peter Thorneycroft), Viscount Jowitt (a former Lord Chancellor), Earl Attlee, Lord Woolton, Lord Birkett (a former Lord Justice). A useful development was a dinner given by the London Students' Society; and more frequent and larger functions organized by the London District Society took place at other venues. During the chairmanship of Sir Richard Yeabsley the London members entertained Sir Raymond (Lord) Evershed, Master of the Rolls, the Hon. Mr. Justice Upjohn, and Lord Piercy.

*   *   *

Two important changes in the constitution of the Society, affecting its title and the members of Council, were approved by the members in 1954 and 1955. After legal advice, the title was abbreviated with much advantage to 'The Society of Incorporated Accountants' (omitting 'and Auditors')—a proposal that had long since been mooted but which for good reasons had not been recommended: the initial letters F.S.A.A. and A.S.A.A. remained unchanged. The memorandum of associa-

THE LIBRARY

THE LARGE HALL

tion was also brought up to date by extending the objects clauses to include research, education, and representations to the Government. For at least a quarter of a century the permissible number of members of Council was thirty, which, apart from two from Scotland and a proportion between London and the provinces, was not subject to any geographical distribution. The number was increased to thirty-eight—(1949) —again on the same principle. Some District Societies had suggested direct representation; this presented difficulties, but in practice Council members were drawn from different parts of the country. Elected in 1949, Miss Phyllis Ridgway, B.A., J. P., Hull, was the first and only woman member of the Council. A further revision (1955) brought to thirty-six (including one from Scotland) the number of Council members affected by periodical retirement; and all past Presidents who were willing continued to serve. These arrangements enabled further practising members and some members who held important appointments in industry to be elected.

*   *   *

A useful innovation was made by the preparation of *A booklet for the guidance of newly elected Incorporated Accountants*. It indicated the facilities available to enable members to take part in the life of the Society, and contained a report of a paper on the etiquette of the profession by Richard A. Witty, previously read at the courses for ex-service members. The practice was initiated of sending a copy of the booklet to each new member upon election.

The Stamp–Martin Chair of Accounting

After intensifying its work, Mr. Bertram Nelson in 1952 relinquished the chair of the Research Committee to Mr. F. Sewell Bray, who had earlier been appointed (part-time) Senior Nuffield Fellow in the Department of Applied Economics, Cambridge. In 1948 the Cambridge University Press had agreed to publish *Accounting Research* for the Research Committee, under the joint editorship of Mr. Sewell Bray and Leo T. Little, as a quarterly learned periodical. The scope of the periodical was to explore the common region on the borders of accounting and economics, and it attracted contributions as well as subscriptions from all over the world. A substantial project was undertaken jointly by representatives of the Research Committee, of the Institute of Municipal Treasurers, of the County Accountants' Association, and of the University College of the South-West on local government finances: a series of reports was published in *Accounting Research*. The findings of another effort directed to 'The effect of de-rating and re-rating on industrial costs' were similarly published.

In order to give a higher place to research as a function of the Society, the Council founded the Stamp–Martin Chair of Accounting at Incorporated Accountants' Hall (1952), to which Mr. Sewell Bray was elected as first Professor. It was the first chair of its kind sponsored by a body of accountants and followed a precedent of some professorships connected with professional and learned bodies. The title 'Stamp–Martin' commemorated the late Lord Stamp's challenge to the profession on the question of research in its own field and the unique service of the late Sir James Martin to the Society from 1885 to 1935. Mr. T. W. South, barrister-at-law, became secretary to the Research Committee. The establishment of the chair was marked by Professor Bray's inaugural lecture 'An accounting progression' to which the third Lord Stamp and representatives from the universities and the profession were invited. The Research Department established, Professor Bray surrounded himself with some keen minds and worked with great intensity: advanced discussions at seminars were opened by members and visitors, who included those who were, or became, Professors of Accounting at Cambridge, London, Bristol, Melbourne, and some American universities. Under the auspices of the Research Committee, some members in Leicester co-operated with the Federated Associations of Boot and Shoe Manufacturers and produced an extensive work on *Cost accounting in the footwear industry* which appeared in book form and found much acceptance in the boot and shoe industry. This work represented the combined experience of executives and practising and industrial accountants with first-hand knowledge of the subject. A series of *Practice Notes*, the work of people interested in research, and books written by Professor Bray himself, were published, the latter by the Oxford University Press: among them was a work on *The Measurement of Profit*, which went to a second impression, and another on *Farm Accounts* (with Dr. C. V. Dawe). The whole arrangement provided the Society with a small organization which was able to give consideration to sections of the current work of the profession whenever the Council was requested or desired to express an authoritative view. To extend interest in research the Council agreed to the establishment of research prizes and the acceptance, in relation to the chair, of members as formal research students; a few scholarships tenable at a university were made available to suitable people who were members or who, in special cases, had passed the Society's intermediate examination or on leaving school intended to qualify as incorporated accountants: the purpose was to enable them to pursue studies for a degree. Professor Bray supervised these activities and also gave a number of lectures in London and elsewhere and by invitation at some of the universities.

*   *   *

Quite independently of the Research Committee, a useful development was started in London and elsewhere on the initiative of individual members of the Society. Small groups of members interested in specialized subjects met periodically for informal discussions. Taxation and Management Accounting were among the topics selected. These proceedings demonstrated the effectiveness of free discussion among not more than thirty people in place of the necessary formalities of a lecture.

The Irish Branch

Formed in 1901, the Irish Branch of the Society, desirous of a special occasion to mark its jubilee, gave an invitation to a conference which was held in Dublin in 1951. The arrangements were ably organized by the Irish Council of the Society, of which Mervyn Bell was the President and Mr. John Love was Secretary. The Northern Ireland District Society gave its full co-operation, and Mr. Herbert Walkey, Dublin, and Robert Bell, Belfast, the two members from Ireland on the Society's Council, supported all the proceedings. The papers read reviewed the economic development of the Republic of

Ireland and the special features of companies in the Republic and Northern Ireland, which were subject to their own legislation respectively. The charm of Dublin, the official and other entertainment, and the success of the proceedings gave pleasure to visitors from Great Britain, and the conference was indicative of the status of the Society in Ireland. It happened that this was the last conference of the Society.

Education and the Examinations

During succeeding years it was found both convenient and suitable to hold short courses at Oxford and Cambridge; they were always well supported. Although there were many pleasant social events in the programmes, the emphasis was on consideration of professional topics: aspects of accounting relative to management were increasingly dealt with. At two of the courses the members had the opportunity of hearing addresses by past Presidents of the American Institute—Mr. J. W. Hope and Mr. Harold Stewart—and of meeting Mr. Arthur Christmas, a past President of the New Zealand Society. In 1953, when the course was devoted to taxation subjects, the number of members participating was such that accommodation at both King's College and Caius College was kindly afforded by the Fellows. On that occasion the course was addressed by Sir Eric St. John Bamford, chairman of the Board of Inland Revenue.

*   *   *

Without publicity, the organization of the examinations, particularly setting questions, marking scripts and standards, was continuously improved, and the work of the Board of Examiners, advisory to the Council, was extended. The value of prizes awarded by the Society was increased; and through gifts, the subject of trust funds of £500 each, the Council had at its disposal the Henry Morgan Memorial Prize (the capital a gift from his brother), the Arthur E. Piggott Prize (founded by the Manchester members), and the Irish Jubilee Prize (established by the Irish Branch). In 1956 some reorganization of all the prize awards was made, which henceforth took the form of specially bound books. In London the London District Society and the London Students' Society worked in harmonious cooperation, and, as convenient, joint meetings were arranged:

there were lectures particularly for the benefit of new students. The Students' Society revised its constitution: the composition of the committee was modified to ensure that there was always a proportion of students serving and some junior qualified members: a chairman of the committee was elected each year (a new feature) and a senior member was invited by the committee to be President.

Finances of the Society

An unexpected and welcome gift was made to the Society in 1953 by Colonel S. A. Medcalf, O.B.E., T.D., D.L., a friend of a member. The property known as Capel House, scheduled as an 'historic building', with sixty acres, situated near Enfield, Middlesex, was transferred by Colonel Medcalf to trustees with an endowment fund of £27,000 for upkeep and maintenance. Colonel Medcalf and his sister were to remain in occupation for life, and the purpose of the gift was to permit the house being used by the Society for educational work.

From the beginning of the Society, its finances had been carefully controlled by the Finance Committee of the Council, of which there had been only six chairmen since 1885, the last being Mr. E. Cassleton Elliott. The Society's expansion since the end of the Second World War, recorded in this and the preceding chapter, the considerable additional expense consequent upon the damage to the Hall, and the great increase in prices, placed considerable burden upon the finances of the Society. But that situation was met by the members, who, first in 1947, agreed to a 50 per cent. increase in the rate of subscriptions and again in 1956 to a further increase, which became necessary. In 1945 the Society's income was £26,000 and by 1956 it disposed of some £86,000 annually.

Some Government Inquiries

The Companies Act, 1948, inevitably presented problems and left some gaps for further exploration. To give assistance to members, the Council made recommendations upon the duties of auditors in regard to directors' emoluments under the Act, and took counsel's opinion: further, a useful booklet was published by the Society comprising lectures given by Mr. Bertram Nelson and Mr. P. J. Sykes, barrister-at-law, to the London members and students. The Cohen Committee had reported against shares of no par value, but a private member's Bill in 1952, although defeated, seemed to have elicited some sympathetic expression from the Government towards 'no par'. The question was exhaustively considered in 1954 by a committee under Montagu Gedge, Q.C., which recommended amendment[1] of the 1948 Act to permit, subject to qualifications, the issue of no par value shares. The matter has not subsequently progressed. The death of Montagu Gedge not long afterwards was greatly deplored.

A new feature was introduced into the regulation of trade and manufacturing by Parliament through the setting up of the Monopolies Commission and by the Monopolies and Restrictive Practices (Inquiry and Control) Act, 1948. Mr. Richard Yeabsley, F.C.A., F.S.A.A., was appointed a member of the commission: he was also Accountant Adviser to the Board of Trade. Later he received the honour of knighthood.

In response to an invitation from the Board of Inland Revenue, the Council submitted (1953) a memorandum upon the incidence of estate duty on family businesses. Section 55, Finance Act, 1940, was concerned with the valuation of shares and debentures of deceased persons in private companies: the section had given rise to continuous trouble and inequity. The memorandum recommended that the section should be applied only where it was proved that the formation or acquisition of control of a company had, as one of its main purposes, the avoidance of estate duty: proposals of similar effect were made by other professional and representative bodies. These submissions made an impression on the Board of Inland Revenue, and the Finance Act, 1954, offered some alleviation. The difficulty of realizing shares in private companies to meet estate duty became increasingly acute. To assist in mitigating this situation, the Estate Duties Investment Trust Ltd. was formed in March 1953. The company was managed by the Industrial and Commercial Finance Corporation Ltd. (sponsored by the banks), the business of which was to facilitate the financing of smaller undertakings. Other finance companies also offered similar facilities.

*   *   *

[1] Cmd. 9112, 1954.

A major and very satisfactory change was made in the use of cheques by the Cheques Act, 1957. The endorsement of 'order' cheques had long been a necessary but unrewarding burden, only too familiar to people engaged in business and administration, to say nothing of the vast amount of consequential work borne by the staffs of banks. In 1955 Mr. R. Graham Page, M.P., introduced a private member's Bill aimed at reforming the system. The Bill did not seem to safeguard sufficiently all the interests concerned and it did not receive a second reading: but the debate thereon drew the attention of Parliament to the situation. Subsequently a committee under Mr. A. A. Mocatta, Q.C., investigated the matter,[1] aided by memoranda and evidence from informed quarters, including the accountancy bodies. Mr. Graham Page's effort was rewarded by the passage of the Cheques Act, 1957—although it was rather different from the Mocatta draft Bill. The question was complicated by the common practice of receipt forms on the backs of cheques, to be signed by payees, a facility which many firms (including insurance companies), building societies, and local authorities used. The Mocatta Committee had pointed out that such receipts in simple form were no better evidence of payment than paid endorsed cheques; and the 1957 Act made paid unendorsed cheques evidence of receipt. The Act enabled bankers to pay unendorsed order cheques if credited to the accounts of the payees: it was permissible for signed receipts on the back of cheques (designated R cheques) to continue by arrangements between banks and customers—an arrangement, however, not encouraged by the banks. Commercial practice led to paid unendorsed cheques being treated as acknowledgements of payment; and frequently, unless otherwise requested by customers, the omission of the issue of formal receipts. As a precaution the banks required uncrossed order cheques presented over-the-counter for cash, and cheques negotiated by payees to others, to be formally endorsed, though it was believed the Act did not so require. Government warrants and foreign drafts continued to need endorsement. There was no question of the great advantages of the Act: but two problems were involved—the payment by a banker of an unendorsed

[1] Cmnd. 3, 1956.

cheque on which the name of the payee might vary slightly from the name of the customer; and the allocation of a paid cheque to the item, invoice, or statement of which it was a payment in discharge. These two questions were of concern to bankers, accountants, and auditors and required some adjustments in audit practice, which auditors prepared themselves to meet. Accuracy in drawing order cheques and crossing them 'a/c payee', 'not negotiable', were valuable safeguards.

*   *   *

During the final ten years of the Society, company law, superannuation, and taxation had been the subjects of official review and of much legislation; and in 1957 the committee under His Honour Judge Blagden issued its report on Bankruptcy and Deeds of Arrangement.[1] Except for a minor Act in 1926, the last legislation was as far back as 1914. The Society submitted a memorandum to the Blagden Committee and oral evidence was given on its behalf. The recommendations in the report would fortify the position of trustees under deeds of arrangement and reform the existing procedure relative to bankrupt persons obtaining discharge. So far amending legislation has not been introduced.

[1] Cmnd. 221, 1957.

XX. THE LAST YEARS OF THE SOCIETY

Sixth International Congress, London

IN 1952 was held the Sixth International Congress on Accounting, sponsored by the accountancy bodies in Great Britain and Ireland. Royal Festival Hall, London, on the south bank of the Thames opened in 1951, proved to be a convenient centre for the meetings and some of the functions. The President was Sir Harold Howitt, G.B.E., D.S.O., M.C., F.C.A., the Vice-President Mr. C. Percy Barrowcliff, F.S.A.A., and the Secretary Mr. Alan S. MacIver, M.C. (Secretary, English Institute), whose work of organization met with high appreciation. Some 2,500 people, including hosts, visitors, and ladies, participated, and represented over one hundred accountancy bodies from ten territories of the British Commonwealth and from twenty-three other countries: they were entertained in London, in Scotland, and in Ireland. There were opening services in Westminster Abbey (address by the Dean, the Very Rev. Alan C. Don, K.C.V.O., D.D.) and in Westminster Cathedral (R.C.).

In his presidential address of welcome Sir Harold Howitt presented four features which at that date faced accountants everywhere: they were reflected in the subjects discussed at the congress.

1. The problem in periodical accounting arising from changes in the value of money.
2. The State, through taxation, had become a major partner in enterprise; and without the trust imposed in the professional accountant, the State revenues could not be raised.
3. The difficulty of raising or retaining capital for development.
4. The accountant in public practice had to direct his thoughts primarily to the past and to the present: while the professional accountant in the commercial field, and indeed the practising accountant who helped him, thought even more of the future.

Offering his view that the twin purpose of final accounts always remained the same, namely to show whether and to what extent a surplus or deficit had accrued over a period of time, and the financial position, Sir Harold declared that a single form of accounts could not stand the stresses involved in attempting to satisfy the diversified requests to which they were subject from proprietors, temporary investors, wage-earners, creditors, economists, tax collectors, and even politicians.

It fell to Mr. C. Percy Barrowcliff, the President of the Society, to present to the congress a paper on 'Fluctuating price levels in relation to accounts'. He set forth details of current accountancy practice in Great Britain and marshalled, with careful documentation, the considerations which suggested some modifications. Mr. Barrowcliff believed that the measurement of profit called for depreciation of fixed assets based on current replacement cost and not on original or historical cost. More tentatively, the same type of principle could be applicable to inventories—at a time when the price level was more stabilized. But he was in favour of the existing convention of adherence to original costs in the balance sheet—a document of the stewardship of contributed capital, capital gains, and savings. Views, both critical and supporting—in varying degrees—were submitted in the discussion. Mr. W. H. Lawson, F.C.A., drew attention to the English Institute's recommendations: historical cost should continue to be the basis for annual accounts; any amount set aside in respect of changes in purchasing power should be by way of an appropriation of profits (not a charge in arriving at profits) and normally treated as a capital reserve; except in special circumstances fixed assets should not be written up. But it was desirable to experiment cautiously with new methods for dealing with the problem; this view seemed to be shared by other speakers, whatever position they took in the discussion. Meantime, the general practice continues to be on the method outlined by Mr. Lawson.

Descriptive papers on 'The Accountant in industry', 'The Accountant in practice', and 'The Accountant in public service' indicated on an international basis the great scope of the profession as a whole, as well as the divisions proper to its several functions: and there were warnings against over-specialization.

The papers by the United Kingdom delegates described trends and changing circumstances which later helped to bring about the major events of 1957. Dr. A. H. Marshall, F.S.A.A., F.I.M.T.A., dealing with 'the Accountant in public service' referred to the fact that in Government types of organization the profits criterion did not always exist; therefore accounting techniques and reports as applied to public administration or even to nationalized undertakings, in which the criterion may be service rather than profit, have special significance in promoting efficiency. In concluding the discussion on this broad subject, G. F. Saunders, F.C.A., gave a charming and human reminder to accountants everywhere of the gratitude owing 'to their wives for the patience with which they endure the all too frequent occasions of grass-widowhood'.

A unique experience for many of the visitors was their entertainment at the banquet given in Guildhall, graced by the presence of the Lord Mayor and other distinguished guests. The toast of 'the Accountancy Profession' was proposed in a brilliant speech by Lord Radcliffe: the reply for the guests, given by His Grace the Archbishop of Canterbury, was full of wisdom. More personal entertainment by members of the sponsoring bodies added to the friendly spirit of the congress. Using the excellent facilities at Incorporated Accountants' Hall, the members of the Society's Council gave several luncheons and dinners at which they were able to receive a large number of the visiting delegates and their ladies: there were brief speeches of cordial welcome and of response.

Commemorations in 1954 and 1955

Two notable events in Scotland afforded pleasure in the profession, particularly north of the Tweed and indeed in wider regions—the constitution of the Institute of Chartered Accountants of Scotland and the centenary of the Scottish Chartered Accountants. The three Scottish bodies—the Edinburgh Society founded in 1854 (the oldest body of organized accountants in the world), the Glasgow Institute in 1855, and the Aberdeen Society in 1867—had been linked by a General Examining Board (1892), responsible for the examinations, and by similar systems of apprenticeship; and there was a Joint Committee dating from the First World War, which considered other common problems, such as parliamentary and Government business. Actually 'the Scottish Chartered Accountants' formed a quite definite if unincorporated entity, fortified by professional seniority, repute, and Scottish cohesion. Yet each body (constituted by Royal Charter) subsisted independently, was centred on its own historic city, and had been served by a succession of devoted secretaries who were also partners in firms. These circumstances moved progressive minds to negotiations for merging the three bodies. Notwithstanding strongly held and independent traditions, they were brought to a successful issue: a merger was effected in 1951 by the Glasgow and Aberdeen bodies joining the Edinburgh Society to become by supplementary charter 'The Institute of Chartered Accountants of Scotland': thus continuity from the foundation date 1854 was preserved. Under the revised constitution a whole-time permanent Secretary (Mr. E. H. V. McDougall) and secretarial staff were appointed. And so the Institute of Chartered Accountants of Scotland bid its members, and invited its friends from all over the world, to the centenary celebrations held in Edinburgh in June 1954 under the presidency of Sir John Somerville, C.A., F.R.S.E. The President of the Society (Mr. Bertram Nelson), the Vice-President (Sir Richard Yeabsley), Mr. Festus Moffat, and the Secretary had the pleasure of being guests and of conveying the felicitations of the Society upon the auspicious occasion. A permanent record *A History of the Chartered Accountants of Scotland from the earliest times to 1954* was published. Graceful acknowledgement was made therein to the friendly co-operation between the five recognized bodies in the profession in the United Kingdom—a profession built up 'without subsidy or doles from any Government or other body for the education of its members'. It is perhaps not too fanciful to suggest that these events in Scotland contributed to the movement of thought elsewhere.

*   *   *

The seventy-fifth anniversary of the Institute of Chartered Accountants in England and Wales followed in 1955, when Mr. Donald V. House, London, was the President. The Institute was honoured by the presence of His Royal Highness the Duke of Edinburgh at the dinner in Guildhall, London. In proposing the toast of the Institute he remarked 'Taxmanship on the one hand, is the art of scoring off the Inland Revenue without actually cheating and on the other there is the brutal business of extracting Tax without actually using the thumbscrew!' Other speeches were by the Lord High Chancellor (Viscount Kilmuir) and the Lord Mayor. The Institute also entertained a large number of friends at an evening function in the Royal Festival Hall. Messages of congratulation were received from accountancy bodies throughout the world. It is meet to add to this brief note a reference to the successive Secretaries of the English Institute, whose personal relations with the Secretaries of the Society were continuously friendly and whose courteous accessibility always facilitated the consideration of mutual business. The Secretaries were W. G. Howgrave, 1880 to 1899; the Hon. George Colville, M.B.E., 1899 to 1935; Mr. R. Wynne Bankes, C.B.E., 1935 to 1949; and from 1950 onwards Mr. Alan S. MacIver, C.B.E., M.C.

*   *   *

Another celebration was the Golden Jubilee of the Association of Certified and Corporate Accountants, which took place in London in December 1954. The proceedings included a banquet at Guildhall—the President, Mr. W. Macfarlane Gray, was in the chair, and speeches were delivered by the Lord Mayor; the Rt. Hon. Hugh Gaitskell, M.P., who proposed the toast of the Association; and Lord Latham (past President). At the Jubilee meeting, the President of the Association extended the felicitations of the members to Mr. J. C. Latham, D.L., Director, during whose tenure of office as Secretary the Association had made vigorous progress and had obtained recognition by Parliament. Its history was recorded in the publication *Fifty Years*. The Secretary is Mr. F. Cameron Osbourn, M.B.E.

The Profession in the Commonwealth and U.S.A.

Overseas relations, which the Society established during its first twenty years, were the object of sustained interest and solicitude on the part of the Council. These valued contacts with bodies in the Commonwealth—in some cases through its own Branches and committees—and the U.S.A. enabled the Council to have continuous information of the great activity in the profession in the 1950's, concurrently with so much that was happening in the profession at home. Relationships were strengthened by increasing mutual visits and communication; also by the opportunities afforded at international congresses and through acceptance of invitations to representatives of the profession from overseas bodies.

*   *   *

The provincial bodies of chartered accountants in Canada—the earliest formed in Quebec, 1880—had specific relations with the Dominion Association (1902), which became the Canadian Institute of Chartered Accountants. Examinations for all the provincial bodies, research, and dominion affairs are now the responsibility of the Canadian Institute: its membership ran concurrently with membership of each provincial body, which, as provided by its own Act, retained its own constitution and prerogatives. In Quebec membership of the Quebec Institute was essential for practice and there were regulatory conditions in the other provinces. Whenever Presidents of the Society had the opportunity to visit Canada, the Canadian Chartered Accountants and the Society's Canadian Committee (Chairman, Colonel H. D. Lockhart Gordon, D.S.O., V.D., Toronto; Honorary Secretary, Mr. Alexander Archibald, Montreal) were happy to extend hospitality and to exchange views.

The Institute of Chartered Accountants in Australia was incorporated by Royal Charter in 1928 and is the only body of accountants outside Great Britain and Ireland so constituted. The Head Office and the General Registrar are in Sydney, and there are branches in each of the States of Australia. Admission to membership is subject to service with Chartered Accountants and passing that Institute's examinations; its Council has promoted progressive educational and research activities. The Institute is mainly concerned with public practice. About 70 per cent. of its members comprise Fellows and Associates in practice and Associates in the service of practising members. Members engaged in commerce or industry are registered on a 'separate list', which is set forth under its own heading in the published list of members.

The Commonwealth Institute—an amalgamation of State

institutes, of which the South Australian and Victorian dated from 1887—absorbed two other bodies and was reconstituted in 1952 as the 'Australian Society of Accountants' (incorporated in Canberra). The administration and the General Registrar are in Melbourne. It has a large membership consisting mainly of persons not trained in professional offices but which includes a number of chartered accountants. The Australian Society holds examinations throughout Australia and has actively interested itself in education and research. Among the members of the Institute and of the Society are those who are ministers in State Governments. In New South Wales and Queensland there are Public Accountants Registration Acts. A Companies Auditors Board in Victoria issues licences for auditors of companies, the qualifications for which include membership of either body.

Discussion about introducing a practical experience requirement for admission and a revision of the 1908 Act occupied the attention of the New Zealand Society of Accountants for a period, and culminated in the New Zealand Society of Accountants Act, 1958. The Act gives power for rules to be made for examinations, the classification of members as being public accountants or registered accountants, and the prescription of practical experience requirements for admission; also in respect of disciplinary procedure. Under the New Zealand Companies Act, 1955, an auditor of a company must be a member of the New Zealand Society except for a ministerial power to approve members of bodies constituted in the British Commonwealth outside New Zealand. Awards of scholarships to younger members, enabling them to obtain experience elsewhere, has been a successful feature of the profession in New Zealand. A member, Mr. W. A. Hadlee, Christchurch, was captain of the New Zealand cricket team which played against England in the Test matches in 1949.

The strongest of the Society's direct overseas connexions was to be found in South Africa. In the Union, simultaneously with training for the membership of one of the four South African Societies, articled clerks could qualify for the Incorporated Society: they were required to pass the examinations of the General Examining Board, South Africa, followed by the

Society's special final examination, conducted in South Africa by the three committees, but controlled by the Council in London. The last attempt at closer union in South Africa became lost in the events of 1940, but under Government inspiration the proposals were renewed: conferences between representatives of the bodies of accountants having activities in South Africa and with Government officials commenced in 1947 and resulted in a comprehensive measure—the Public Accountants and Auditors Act, 1951—being passed by the Union Parliament. To administer its affairs, the Act set up a Public Accountants Board consisting of civil servants, university professors, nominees of the four South African Societies, of the Incorporated Society's South African branches and some others. No person unless registered could practise as a public accountant and auditor or accept an appointment as auditor, if the audit were prescribed by law. A registered Accountant who was not a member could be admitted to a Provincial Society and become a Chartered Accountant (South Africa); if he was originally registered, the applicant must have had six years' experience in practice or in an accountant's office and pass the Board's Final examination.[1] For the future, articles (without premiums) and examinations were compulsory, and the arrangement exercised by the Incorporated Society (p. 297) was continued. Disciplinary powers vested in the Board were in addition to the retention by the accountancy bodies of their own disciplinary functions. An auditor of an undertaking, who must be a qualified person, became subject to a new and onerous obligation:

[An auditor] shall report to the person in charge of that undertaking any material irregularity of which he has cause to complain in his capacity as auditor, and shall, if that irregularity is not dealt with to his satisfaction or rectified within a period of one month after the date on which it was so reported, in writing inform the Board [the Public Accountants Board] thereof.

The Board was empowered in certain circumstances to refer the report to the Attorney-General. This provision caused considerable discussion in professional circles in South Africa and has not been free from questions arising. The Society nominated its representative on the Board, and other members

[1] G. E. Noyce, *The Accountancy Profession in South Africa*.

in their capacity as Chartered Accountants (South Africa) have held various offices in the administration of the scheme, which involved some geographical devolution. Extensive organization of professional education has been developed in conjunction with the several South African universities. The marked expansion of industry generally, and in mining on the Rand and in the Orange Free State, has been favourable to the growth of the profession, now placed on a statutory basis. A short history of the profession in South Africa was written by Mr. Gordon Noyce, F.S.A.A., C.A. (S.A.), Durban. In 1955 a South African Council of the Society was formed to co-ordinate the work of the three Branches, the administrative affairs of which were admirably served by the Honorary Secretaries, Mr. Hugh Hyslop, Cape Town, Mr. R. E. Grieveson, Johannesburg, and Mr. Alan Butcher, Durban. Mr. G. W. A. Chubb, A.S.A.A., C.A. (S.A.), Johannesburg, played cricket with distinction for South Africa in the 1951 Test matches in the Union.

Until 1954 the South African (Northern) Committee of the Society, Johannesburg, had been responsible for members in Commonwealth territories north of the Limpopo, where the principal body was the Rhodesia Society of Accountants. Increase in the Society's membership and economic progress prompted the formation in that year of a Central African Branch, Salisbury, covering the Federated Territories of Southern and Northern Rhodesia and Nyasaland, in which there were then 83 members.

*   *   *

Two years after India became independent, the legislature passed the Chartered Accountants Act, 1949, to regulate the profession of chartered accountant and to establish the Institute of Chartered Accountants of India. The Act prescribed the persons entitled to become members, set up a Council, protected the designation and conferred disciplinary and examining powers. The effect of the Act was virtually to close the profession in favour of the members of the Indian Institute.

*   *   *

Commencing in 1887 the American Institute of Accountants (formerly known as the American Association of Public Accountants) had absorbed (1936) the American Society of

Certified Public Accountants, and in 1957 changed its name to the American Institute of Certified Public Accountants. This was a more precise description, which its President said highlighted 'the importance of certification and emphasised the responsibility which the Institute assumes when it speaks or acts'. Legislation in each State prescribed the qualifications of certified public accountants and the practice of public accounting: but the influence of the American Institute, a national and voluntary body, had grown; and, at the International Congress in 1957, the Director of Research reported that all fifty-three States and other jurisdictions used the certified public accountants examinations prepared by the American Institute. Admission to the American Institute is open to certified public accountants who satisfy the Institute's requirements, including in particular an experience requirement. In 1957 the membership was about 30,000. Mr. John L. Carey, Executive Director, has undertaken considerable authorship; he is well known to many members of the profession in the United Kingdom.

The American Institute maintains an extensive Research Department and sponsors many publications, including *The Journal of Accountancy* and the *Accountants' Index* (1920) (a bibliography of accounting literature), to which supplements are issued at intervals. In recent years, three past Presidents (Mr. T. Coleman Andrews, Mr. Percival Brundage, amd Mr. Maurice H. Stans) have held high office in Departments of the American Government in Washington. Always hospitable to visitors, its Council regularly invites to the annual meeting and convention, held in the autumn in different cities, representatives of bodies in the United Kingdom and elsewhere—who have the most pleasant recollections of their participation in the proceedings and of their professional brethren in America.

*   *   *

Visits abroad by members of the profession became more frequent—which with other events reflected the world-wide character of accountancy. Presidents of the Society were guests of the profession in the Netherlands, and in 1952 Mr. C. Percy Barrowcliff, President, was invited to meetings of the Canadian Institute (President, Monsieur Emile Beauvais) in Montreal and Quebec, marking the fiftieth year since its foundation, and was the guest of the American Institute in New York. In 1954, in acceptance of invitations from the American Institute to its annual meeting, the President of the Scottish Institute (Sir John Somerville), the President of the English Institute (Mr. Donald House), and the President of the Society (Mr. Bertram Nelson) visited the U.S.A. accompanied by Mr. Alan S. MacIver (Secretary of the English Institute). Travelling together, the members of the party had the opportunity of many informal conversations on the future relations of their bodies. The subject had been opened in its initial stages before their departure and it was doubtless advanced at that juncture, especially by the friendly relations between the three Presidents and by the guidance of the Secretary. The visit was indeed fruitful both in the renewal of valued friendships with members of the American Institute and for the future of the profession at home.

Seventh International Congress, Amsterdam

The Seventh International Congress took place in Amsterdam in September 1957, organized by the bodies of accountants in the Netherlands, the President being Mr. J. Kraayenhof and the Secretary Mr. A. L. de Bruyne (Director of the Netherlands Institute of Accountants). There were present 1,700 accountants from forty countries and 104 accountancy bodies, and 1,200 ladies. The congress, which was honoured by Her Majesty the Queen of the Netherlands and by His Royal Highness Prince Bernhard, the Prince of the Netherlands, was a fine organization, helpful in discussions, and heart-warming to visitors. Her Majesty graciously received a representative party of delegates in the Royal Palace.

This congress was the last major event in which the Society was represented as a separate entity. The delegation of incorporated accountants was headed by Sir Richard Yeabsley, C.B.E., President, supported by the Vice-President; Sir Richard presented a paper on 'The verification of the existence of assets'. The discussion thereon disclosed the heavy responsibilities which fell upon auditors everywhere in this difficult branch of their work, and it showed that there were both a common point of view and some variation of opinion—particularly about stock-in-trade.

'Principles for the accountant's profession' covered a wide survey led by Sir Thomas Robson, M.B.E., F.C.A., past President of the English Institute, followed by respective contributions on the position and recent developments in the U.S.A., Sweden, the Netherlands, and Germany. Certainly among bodies in the United Kingdom and in many other countries practical experience is an invariable requirement for obtaining membership, while the broad conception of methods of training and studies continues to be an important subject of discussion and exploration.

Pervading the discussion was insistence everywhere on a high standard of qualification, integrity, independence, mutual respect, and professional discipline. Information was given of legislation which affected the status of the profession and the responsibilities of its members: these laws varied in form and directness from country to country. The discussion indicated some difference of emphasis in several countries on experience and education as elements in training for an accountancy qualification.

The Society, 1957

Among those in the Society who during the years after the war held high public office were Sir Thomas Keens, D.L. (President 1926-9, *obiit* 1953), chairman of the Bedfordshire County Council 1935 to 1952; Sir Arthur Middleton (member of the Council, *obiit* 1953), chairman of the London County Council in the Coronation Year; the Rt. Hon. Ernest Marples, M.P. (member of the Society), who became Her Majesty's Postmaster-General in 1957; Sir Frederick Alban, C.B.E. (President 1947 to 1949), chairman of the Welsh Regional Hospital Board.

And regretfully the obituary contains the names of many who gave their interest and affection to the Society: C. Hewetson Nelson, Liverpool, then senior past President; Fred Woolley, Southampton, President 1945 to 1947; A. Stuart Allen, London, President 1949 to 1951; J. Paterson Brodie, Stoke-on-Trent, Vice-President in office (*obiit* 1948); Sir Harry Hands, K.B.E., Cape Town, chairman, S. African (Western) Committee, 1921 to 1932; James Paterson, Greenock, Scottish member of Council, 1906 to 1953; Sir Adam Maitland, sometime M.P. for

Faversham; H. J. Burgess, C.C., London, sometime chairman of the Society's Benevolent Fund; Sir Roland Burrows, K.C., Examiner; William Strachan, London, sometime Assistant Secretary of the Society and Editor of the *Journal*; R. B. Hogg, M.C., sometime Secretary of the S. African (Northern) Committee; George S. Anderson, Hon. Secretary, Victorian Committee; James C. Fay, the Society's chief clerk 1909 to 1945 and Secretary, London Students' Society. And as this narrative closes, unhappily there must be added the names of Richard A. Witty, President 1942-5 (*obiit* 1959), Robert Bell, Belfast, (*obiit* 1959), Mervyn Bell, Dublin (*obiit* 1960), members of Council, and Leo T. Little (*obiit* 1960), Editor of *Accountancy*.

The Incorporated Accountants' Benevolent Fund was in its sixty-fifth year. Notwithstanding changes in general circumstances since the fund was founded, it continued with much advantage its beneficent work, which was additional to the facilities of the Welfare State. Both financial and personal help were extended with much comfort to some forty or fifty people a year—some, members affected by illness or fortuitous circumstances, but mainly widows, often anxious about the care and education of their families. The income of the fund from voluntary subscriptions and dividends was about £4,500. Mr. Percy Toothill, the chairman, and the other trustees had devoted themselves to this rewarding work for many years; and they were assisted by Mr. Ian Craig, Hon. Secretary, and Mrs. Irene Duncalf, Assistant Hon. Secretary.

Mrs. Duncalf, of long service with the Society, was also head of the secretariat staff, until she went to the Institute after Integration. The longest record of service on the staff of 1956 was held by Miss Joan Derry, who concluded her useful work and retired at the end of that year after being thirty-six years with the Society.

*   *   *

By 1957 the Society had Branches in Scotland and Ireland, seven Branches in the Commonwealth, and twenty-three District Societies (two in India). The final published list of members (March 1957) recorded a membership of 11,335. The topographical section comprised 1,403 cities and towns throughout the world where incorporated accountants were to be found and, arranged alphabetically, commenced with Aba (Nigeria) and ended with Zürich. There were about 9,000 articled clerks and by-law candidates.

Discharging onerous and responsible duties at a critical time in the history of the Society, Sir Richard Yeabsley, C.B.E.—the only President to be a member of the Society and of the English Institute—and Mr. Edward Baldry held the offices of President and Vice-President with distinction until Integration with the Institutes of Chartered Accountants in November 1957.

SIR RICHARD YEABSLEY, C.B.E.
President 1956 and 1957

EDWARD BALDRY, O.B.E.
Vice-President 1956 and 1957

E. CASSLETON ELLIOTT, C.B.E.
Senior Past President (President 1932–1935)

1956 AND 1957

XXI. THE BACKGROUND TO INTEGRATION

Chartered Accountants: Incorporated Accountants

AN almost forgotten event was the scheme of 1897 for the absorption of the Society's members by the English Institute, which proved abortive, (p. 19). From that date until the 1950's no serious attempt was made to revive its basic purpose. No doubt over the years many members of the Society thought in a general way that an arrangement with the Institute would be favourable, and the question had been talked about in personal conversations. But whatever hopes or desires any individual members may have entertained, or if such ideas ever crossed the minds of Council members, there was nothing to suggest that they would be acceptable to the Institute. The proposals for legislation in 1911, 1930, and 1946 provided that each body should retain its own constitution, examinations, and separate membership (pp. 71, 168, 251). The Council had been concerned to develop the policy and strength of the Society as an independent entity while working in harmony with the other recognized bodies of accountants. When the co-ordination proposals were dropped at the end of 1949, the position of the 'qualifying bodies' remained as it was except for the recognition given under the Companies Act, 1948 (p. 260). It seemed then to those in the Society in close touch with the situation that, whatever changes might or might not happen, there was little prospect of any arrangement with the Institute, as far as could be seen into the future. However, circumstances both inside and outside the profession began to exert significant, if unobtrusive, influence. The period was marked by a great expansion in the work of the profession as a whole. Practising firms experienced difficulty in finding and retaining adequate qualified staff and in having sufficient choice in selecting junior partners;

and, as a rule, little capital could be found by incoming partners to acquire a share of goodwill. Whole-time appointments in industry and commerce at home and overseas for chartered and incorporated accountants claimed an increasing proportion of younger members, who, generally speaking, intended to follow careers to which such openings led. Notwithstanding that accountancy occupied a high place in the list of callings chosen by boys and girls leaving school, a lot of competition arose amongst a variety of occupations to attract the (then) comparatively low number of those of School Certificate (later G.C.E.) standard. The low birth-rate of the war years was beginning to tell and there were increasing opportunities to go to the university, in insurance, banking, and business, as well as in technology, engineering, and science. The appointment of 'careers masters' and 'careers mistresses' at schools, a variety of advisory services, publications of the Ministry of Labour, and demand for their services eased the careers problems of young people of good education and above the average in intelligence. The Appointments Departments of the accountancy bodies and booklets issued by them were specifically helpful to both applicants and firms.

In the English Institute (and the Irish Institute), time-honoured regulations permitted each practising member to receive two articled clerks; the articles were required to be served in England and Wales (or Ireland). These facilities had become inadequate. The number of apprentices for Scottish C.A.'s was unlimited, except outside Scotland. (A consequence was that in Scotland Society candidates were few and membership small.) Practising Fellows of the Society could take three articled clerks and practising Associates two, at home or overseas. Further, in the social and economic circumstances of the times, the payment of premiums to principals on the signing of articles of clerkship was falling away, and salaries were being paid to articled clerks: the level of these salaries naturally took into account time required for study and examinations to comply with the relevant regulations. (The English Institute stated that currently on only 14 per cent. of articles registered were premiums paid.) Firms employed and continued to engage, in addition to articled clerks, young men and women of good educational standard, who were encouraged to become registered by-law students of the Society with a view to qualifying as incorporated accountants. This procedure spread, and considerable proportions of staffs of firms of chartered accountants qualified as members of the Society. It seemed to some members of the Institute to be an anomaly that these men and women were trained with chartered accountants to become incorporated accountants and owed allegiance to a body—admittedly a body of standing—other than that to which the partners belonged. It was perhaps a matter of sentiment rather than of substance—except for eligibility to become partners—but was not devoid of logic. This pointed to widening the permitted quota of articled clerks in the Institute, a development which it could be claimed would have ample justification on grounds of public policy, as offering additional opportunities to young people to become chartered accountants. However, the eventual policy of Integration was promoted on much wider and higher grounds.

The effects of the situation in regard to staffs were felt favourably in the Society, which examined each year a large number of articled clerks (articled to members) and by-law candidates. There can be no doubt that the high standard of the Society's examinations and requirements and the system of registration of by-law candidates contributed to this satisfactory position. The proportion of Society examination candidates in the special classes, not trained in the offices of practising accountants, became gradually less, and represented a small percentage.

*   *   *

It was axiomatic that a firm could practise as chartered accountants only if all the partners were chartered accountants: the same consideration applied to firms of incorporated accountants. Cumulatively over time, two factors were of material effect. For some years the English Institute's by-laws had permitted a person of upwards of thirty-five years of age and having ten years service as clerk to chartered accountants, by special vote of the Council, to be exempted from the preliminary examination and to serve three years' articles; in the course of the articles he had to pass the intermediate and final examinations: this arrangement depended upon there being a vacancy for an articled clerk within the quota of two per partner. One purpose was doubtless to enable senior assistants to become chartered accountants with a view to partnership. It was quite likely that many in this category had first qualified as incorporated accountants after by-law service, and they had again to submit themselves to the rigours of study and of the Institute's examinations. In the Society article 13 gave the Council power, by special vote, to elect to membership a person who, engaged in the profession, had passed examinations of another body approved by the Council. This article in practice was mainly applied to a chartered accountant in partnership with incorporated accountants: the applicant undertook that the firm would practise as incorporated accountants, and that the number of his articled clerks—chartered and incorporated— would not together exceed the number permitted by the Society's regulations. A number of chartered accountants were elected to the Society in this way. The two factors, amongst others, caused noticeable cross-fertilization. Thus there were:

Firms in which all partners were chartered accountants only.

Firms of chartered accountants, in which a partner or partners might also be members of the Society (or of another body).

Firms in which all partners were incorporated accountants only.

Firms of incorporated accountants in which a partner or partners might also be chartered accountants (or members of another body).

Firms which could use only the description 'accountants', since some partners were 'chartered' only and some 'incorporated' only.

Obviously there was much variety in the composition and descriptions of firms.

Subsequent to the establishment of the nationalized industries overtures were made to the Society to extend the operation of its by-laws—which the Council had declined to do for over a quarter of a century—to cover accountancy assistants in these large undertakings. Not surprisingly the attitude of the Council was hesitant and indeterminate. On the one hand such a policy would have ended any idea of integration with the Chartered Institutes (then barely in the seminal stage), and, on the other, it might have had long-term repercussions which could not be precisely foreseen—a possibility of which the Institute's Council was mindful.

Preliminary Conversations: Fundamental Principles

Broadly, the structure of the profession was awkward and un-satisfactory and called for some partial rationalization at any rate; and the foregoing outline indicates that in detail its pattern was complicated and in parts paradoxical. Already there was a degree of integration at the level of firms and of staffs and in industry, but corporate integration was lacking. The Council of the Institute, representing the largest number of qualified accountants, felt responsibility to take some initiative and to ex-plore prospects. That was the approach when by good fortune conversations were started between some leading members of the English Institute and of the Society, with a feeling of com-plete goodwill. Accepting the broad objective, the negotiators had to consider the practical possibility of integrating the Society's members into the English, Scottish, and Irish Institutes, with acceptability to the general bodies of members. The con-versations were helped by three of the respective Presidents and the Secretary of the English Institute travelling together to the U.S.A. in 1954. Sufficient progress was made to enable the Councils to appoint negotiating committees. The Scottish In-stitute and the Irish Institute joined in the negotiations.

The negotiations became subject to the following funda-mental principles:

On the part of the three Institutes:

(a) That for members of the Society, for the purpose of Integration, experience in a practising accountant's office at home (excluding overseas) must be an essential condition of membership as chartered accountants. Articled service or by-law service performed with 'public accountants' in England and Wales was agreed to be accepted by the English Institute; with chartered or incorporated accountants in the United Kingdom by the Scottish Institute; or with 'public accountants' in Ireland by the Irish Institute.

(b) That in any case chartered accountants in practice should in future each have the right to accept four articled clerks, with facility to obtain permission to take more, subject to giving satisfaction that the training available in the firm was adequate for the purpose. This arrangement would go forward irrespective of the successful accomplishment of Integration. (In Scotland the number of apprentices was already unlimited.)

On the part of the Society:

(a) That every member must, upon application, be eligible for membership of one or another of the three Institutes.

(b) That all articled clerks and by-law candidates accepted by the Society up to an appointed day must be able to complete their qualification.

The great difficulty in reconciling these principles was the position of those members of the Society who qualified by service in Government or local government accountancy and of others who qualified by service under articles or otherwise overseas. An early suggestion was that they become incorporated accountant members of the English Institute. After negotiations extending over two to three years, agreement between the Councils was reached by favourable majorities: at the same time the Council of the Society was somewhat uneasy about certain features, which it had not been found possible to eliminate (they are discussed later in this chapter). Three separate but similar schemes of Integration were prepared and put into legal form—applicable respectively to the English, Scottish, and Irish Chartered Institutes on the one hand and the Society on the other.

Schemes as agreed by Councils

It may be convenient to indicate the main elements of the scheme relative to the English Institute.

Members of the Society who (i) were engaged in practice as 'public accountants' in England and Wales, or (ii) had qualified after articled or by-law service with a 'public accountant' practising in England and Wales, in accordance with the constitution of the Society, were eligible for admission as members of the English Institute with the right to describe themselves as chartered accountants. The definition of 'public accountant' was given by reference to a person who was a member of a body of accountants in the United Kingdom, membership of which was formally recognized by the Board of Trade as a qualification for appointment as auditor of public companies under the Companies Act, 1948, and whose main occupation consisted of practice as an accountant.

Fellows of the Society who had practised as public accountants for five years could become Fellows of the Institute, F.C.A., and Fellows or Associates qualified to become Associates, A.C.A., could become Fellows F.C.A. after completing five years in practice. All admitted under (i) and (ii) would cease to use the designation 'Incorporated Accountant', F.S.A.A., or A.S.A.A. Fellows of the Society not-in-practice eligible under (ii) to become A.C.A. (but not qualified by practice to become F.C.A.) could optionally continue to use the description 'Incorporated Accountant', F.S.A.A.: these were mainly members of the Society who had been elected Fellows from Associates by reason of holding exceptional positions which were regarded for the purpose of the Society's articles as 'equivalent to practice'.

All other members of the Society not qualified under (i) or (ii) became eligible for admission as 'incorporated accountant members of the Institute': they would continue to use the designation and the initial letters F.S.A.A., A.S.A.A., and would have all the rights of members of the Institute generally, except that as such they were not entitled to receive articled clerks for training to become chartered or incorporated accountants. But the scheme contained provisions under which an incorporated accountant member of the Institute of Chartered Accountants in England and Wales could, after satisfying the experience requirements specified for this purpose, become a chartered accountant, provided he had passed the Society's final examination (not being the special or modified final in South Africa) or the Institute's final examination. The Society's facilities for candidates engaged in Government or municipal accountancy and for articled clerks overseas were to be withdrawn: the Society's 'by-law' system would cease.

After Integration, as before, admission to the three Institutes would be by service under articles or apprenticeship in England and Wales, Scotland, and Ireland only and passing the prescribed examinations. The extension of the permitted quota of articled clerks per member to four with permission to apply for more (English and Irish Institutes) was an essential part of the scheme.

The arrangements relative to the Scottish Institute and the Irish Institute were similar to the English Institute's scheme, *mutatis mutandis* geographically with some differences of detail, including the omission of incorporated accountant membership: the English Institute would absorb all those members of the Society affected. There being only one class of members in the Scottish Institute, the provisions for Fellowship (p. 311) did not apply.

For *all* members of the Society, Integration would be effected by each making individual application in accordance with the schemes, which in one way or another covered the whole membership.

Society candidates, of whom there were about 9,000, had to be fitted into the proposed Integration arrangements for members. Articled clerks could have their articles transferred on their principals becoming chartered accountants: by-law candidates of less than five years' service with practising firms were required to enter into articles to complete qualifying service or to continue without articles and qualify as incorporated accountant members of the Institute: if five years' by-law service had been served, candidates could complete without articles and become chartered accountants. The transfer to, or execution of, chartered articles was made possible by the extension of the quota. Articled clerks (a comparatively small number) and by-law candidates serving with municipal treasurer members, a few candidates in Government service, and articled clerks serving with practising incorporated accountants overseas could complete existing arrangements and become incorporated accountant members of the English Institute. The scheme indicated those among all the candidates who must take the final examination of one of the Institutes, but provided for the continuation of the Society's examinations for a transitional period. This avoided hardship which a change of syllabus would entail for candidates whose studies had already been planned; also it enabled those who would become incorporated accountant members to take their examinations, including the special final in South Africa and Rhodesia.

*   *   *

Some administrative details must be noted. After the acceptance of Integration the Society would be put into liquidation and its net assets would be transferred to the English Institute, which would make financial adjustments with the Scottish and Irish Institutes. Ten members of the Society would be nominated as additional members of the English Institute's Council (initially only) and similarly four for the Irish Institute's Council: no such provision was made in Scotland.[1] A major administrative point was that the English Institute undertook to offer suitable appointments to the Society's officers and staff or to pay compensation. In order to co-ordinate future policy a Joint Standing Committee of the three Institutes would be set up after Integration.

*   *   *

By the end of 1956 the time had come to put members of all the bodies in possession of full information. A copy of the three schemes was printed: a memorandum prepared by each body gave blessing to the proposals and discussed the issues from the point of view of its own members. These documents were posted to members just before the New Year, 1957. The Society was about to enter the most exciting year of its history. The drafting of the schemes and of the memoranda had placed an enormous burden of work and responsibility on the negotiating committees and the secretariats, whose researches enabled vital information to be given to the members. Until the issue of the documents the negotiations had been kept strictly private; otherwise premature and half-informed rumour and discussion might have occurred, with unfavourable consequences.

[1] A former member of the Society, however, was appointed to the Council of the Scottish Institute.

XXII. INTEGRATION ACCOMPLISHED

Memoranda Issued to Members

THE four memoranda covered a certain amount of common ground. Following a suitable introduction, the Institute's memorandum gave a descriptive analysis of the Society's membership and presented the case for admitting as chartered accountants members of the Society who had trained as by-law candidates with practising firms in England and Wales and the reasons for the new class of incorporated accountant members of the Institute. Enlarging on the broader effects of the scheme, the memorandum pointed to the removal of considerable existing confusion in the minds of the public about the implications of various accountancy qualifications (an aspect which incorporated accountants undoubtedly felt), referred to the resulting increase in the authority of the Institute and represented that Integration would lead to an advancement of accountancy standards. With engaging candour, the memorandum did not burke the prejudicial effect—in the absence of Integration—of the proposed extended system of Institute articled clerks on the by-law facilities of the Society; nor the likelihood in those circumstances of the Society having to broaden its base of recruitment: that would have been a retrograde step affecting the profession as a whole. Behind the language of the memorandum were undoubtedly sympathetic feelings and friendly respect on the part of members of the Institute's Council towards the Society and particularly for the (hypothetical) situation with which it would be faced. The adoption of the scheme would eliminate those difficulties, remove restrictions on the description of mixed firms, and facilitate partnership and possible amalgamation arrangements, and should stimulate the activities of enlarged District and Students' Societies, particularly in the smaller areas: and notably it would increase training facilities for people to qualify as chartered accountants, thus taking the place of the Society's by-law arrangements. But if details were material, it was on the broad and firm ground of the future of the profession and of its public recognition and responsibilities that the scheme was recommended to its members by the Institute's Council.

The memoranda of the Scottish and Irish Institutes respectively set forth all the issues of policy with suitable inflexion to meet the particular circumstances in so far as they were slightly different from those in England and Wales.

★   ★   ★

The members of the Society were given the details of the three schemes and the memorandum comprised a discussion of the issues from the Society's point of view headed 'The Scheme considered'. The following statistics were furnished (they had been included in substance in the English Institute's memorandum):

1. Approximate estimates of the Society's membership as at 30 June 1956, as under Integration it would be distributed among the three Institutes.

2. A statement of recent final examination candidates and an analysis of membership.

	English Institute	Scottish Institute	Irish Institute	Total
Incorporated accountants who are already chartered accountants .	589	33	17	639
Eligible for admission as chartered accountants	7,794	93	354	8,241
Eligible for admission as incorporated accountants:				
(a) in the United Kingdom and the Republic of Ireland . .	1,140	..	..	1,140
(b) overseas	925	..	..	925
	10,448	126	371	10,945
Membership of the Institutes as at 30 June 1956	19,112	5,947	986	26,045
	29,560	6,073	1,357	36,990
Deduct: incorporated accountants already chartered accountants (as above)	589	33	17	639
Integrated membership . . .	28,971	6,040	1,340	36,351

The activities of the Society and the Institutes have for many years past coincided to a notable extent and there are similar examination standards and methods of training. Of the candidates who passed the

Society's Final examinations in 1955, 232 (44 per cent) were trained in the offices of Chartered Accountants and another 50 (10 per cent) were trained in firms in which there was at least one Chartered Accountant partner. A recent analysis of the Society membership shows that of the 3,113 members in practice as principals in the United Kingdom and the Republic of Ireland, 974 (31 per cent) are themselves also Chartered Accountants or are in partnership with Chartered Accountants. Of the 2,048 members employed by practising accountants in these countries, 1,586 (77 per cent) are employed by firms in which there is at least one Chartered Accountant partner. There are many firms in the United Kingdom and the Republic of Ireland in which there are Chartered and Incorporated Accountant partners.

These analyses illustrate some of the general influences at work in the profession indicated in the early part of this section.

With discretion and vigour the Council made quite plain to the members what from the Society's point of view were the most disputable elements in the proposals: it concluded with an unequivocal presentation of the advantages of Integration to the Society as a whole, and of its favourable impact on the future of the profession and in advancing the public interest. The following extracts are quoted:

First, there were the 925 members who were trained overseas and who for the most part would become incorporated accountant members of the Institute, and likewise the group of 1,140 members in the service of public and local authorities: to their work and contribution to the life of the Society the Council paid warm tribute, and to the cordial relations of the Society with the Institute of Municipal Treasurers and Accountants.

Whilst all members of the Society may become members of one of the Institutes, it is a matter of concern to the Council that the Institutes have not been able to agree that all the Society's members should be admitted as Chartered Accountants. . . . The council has made the strongest representations in the matter, but it is and always has been a fundamental principle of all three Institutes that service in a practising accountant's office at home must be an essential condition of membership. After prolonged negotiation it became clear that the Institutes could not abandon this principle in the integration scheme and that wider proposals would not be acceptable to their members. It must be recognized that in negotiations involving so many persons and principles of such importance, it is not reasonable to expect that any one participating organisation will secure acceptance of all its suggestions. The Institutes have all made considerable concessions in order that the scheme now formulated might command and deserve the widest possible acceptance.

Attention was then called to the particular rights and privileges which incorporated accountant members of the Institute would enjoy as set out in the actual scheme (p. 311).

Secondly, in regard to members who were industrial accountants, some of whom, Fellows, would become A.C.A. or optionally incorporated accountant members, F.S.A.A., the note was:

The Council feels that the interests [of these members] will not be prejudiced. On the contrary they should be enhanced. . . . A fusion of the 'industrial' members of the Institutes and of the Society must be expected to lead to a fuller recognition of the status and value of the work upon which they are engaged and to an accelerated study of the principles and techniques upon which it is based.

And finally:

After anxious deliberation and on the footing that all members of the Society will be eligible to become members of one or other of the Institutes, the Council is of the opinion that the scheme is desirable in the interests both of the public and the accountancy profession.

The Society and the Institutes have worked together . . . in pursuit of the same principal objectives [and] the integration of the Society with the Institutes is a natural evolution. . . .

The multiplicity of accountancy bodies has caused, and is still causing, confusion in the minds of the public. It can only be in the public interest and to the benefit of the standing of the profession in public esteem that a high proportion of all practising accountants should practise under the same title and be subject to common standards of etiquette and discipline. For the same reasons, the scheme should also assist the accountancy profession in its recruitment problem, where it is in competition with other professions and with industry.

*   *   *

On 12 February 1957 a special article appeared in *The Times*, headed 'Accountants seek unity: the proposed merger and its consequences'. This was a broad and independent survey of past events and of the existing situation. While not opposing, the article commented and offered criticisms on the proposed Integration, and adumbrated possibilities for the future of other accountancy bodies.

Commenting on the proposals, *The Economist*[1] said:

It appears the Institute has set the pace, notably on qualifications. One reason why it favours integration seems to be a fear that the Society would broaden the base of its recruitment to accept service in industry as a qualification. Fierce discussions about these proposals are likely to occur in the profession—and should be welcomed there, though members of both organisations must avoid being stiff-necked or up-stage. The new proposals, if they go through, will establish one body, demanding high standards of training and of qualification, with a massive—and even a dominant—voice in the profession. Yet in the past the friendly rivalry between the Institute and the Society has been good for both and for the profession as a whole, and the experience of other giant authoritative institutions suggests that without care voices, especially those from the lower ranks, can be muffled. That and an unthinking devotion to tradition should be avoided. This integration cannot avoid having an effect on the standing of other accountancy institutions, especially the Association of Certified and Corporate Accountants, and it should not be forgotten that these bodies have their value in training men who are not able to take up articles.

Procedure

The procedure for each body was to be that, as convenient, delegated council members and the Secretary should visit District Societies so that there could be preliminary discussion at local level; thus, when the time came to reach a decision, members would have been adequately prepared and informed. The whole question was too important and indeed complicated to be left solely to the chances of large general meetings at which sentiment—perhaps even prejudice—rather than reason might prevail. The Society had also to think of its members overseas —particularly of the largest aggregation in South Africa. It happened that at the time of the issue of the memoranda Mr. Edward Baldry, Vice-President, was in Cape Town and he had the opportunity of informal conversations with the Cape Town Committee. Later, Mr. Bertram Nelson, immediate past

[1] 22 December 1956.

President, who had been intimately concerned in all the negotiations, paid a visit to South and East Africa for the special purpose of explaining the situation and the difficulties the Council had about the class of incorporated accountant members of the English Institute into which the Society's South African members would mainly fall. Inevitably they were restive and concerned at the feature which particularly affected them; but if Mr. Nelson's visit could not completely assuage their feelings, it manifested the deep concern of the Council and that the South African members were not being neglected—nor indeed were any of the members overseas. Mr. Nelson was able to give assurance of the English Institute's interest in members and in bodies in the Commonwealth through its special Overseas Relations Committee.

Arrangements were made for holding in succession general meetings of the English, Scottish, and Irish Institutes and the Society—in that order—each meeting after the first being dependent upon acceptance of the scheme by the previous meeting *and* by favourable postal votes. The several constitutions required in the case of the English Institute a favourable vote of two-thirds of those voting at the meeting and by post, of the Scottish Institute two-thirds, of the Irish Institute a simple majority, and of the Society three-quarters of those voting.

Meetings of the English, Scottish, and Irish Institutes

The special meeting of the English Institute's members was held on 19 February 1957 at the Royal Festival Hall, London, at which some 2,250 members were present. The President, Mr. A. S. H. Dicker, M.B.E., Norwich, was in the chair: he made a general statement and moved the formal enabling resolution: he then called on the Vice-President, Mr. W. H. Lawson, C.B.E., whom Mr. Dicker described as the chief architect of the scheme, to address the members. In a lucid speech Mr. Lawson opened by referring to the unsatisfactory structure of the profession and to the initiative taken by the Institute to see if improvement were possible. He gave an outline of the three Chartered Institutes and of the Society, covered by the schemes, of the Association of Certified and Corporate Accountants—a body recognized by Parliament and under the Companies Act,

1948, which accepted training both in accountants' offices and in industry; and of the two bodies which offered specialist qualifications, the Institute of Municipal Treasurers and Accountants and the Institute of Cost and Works Accountants. It was material that the whole of the members of the Chartered Institutes and a great majority of the Society had obtained their experience in the offices of practising accountants.

Fortified by the discussions and criticisms at local meetings, Mr. Lawson, in the main context of the proposed Integration as a measure of rationalization of the profession, dealt with some suggestions made for the revision of the scheme: these he believed to be quite impracticable and unacceptable to the Society. In particular, of the possible extension of the quota of articled clerks without Integration and its effect on the Society, Mr. Lawson felicitously said: 'We cannot concern ourselves only with our own domestic affairs and disregard the interests of the profession as a whole.' In conclusion he urged: 'The scheme is of vital importance to us all, whether it is regarded as complete in itself or as the first important step towards integration of the whole profession . . . [the Council] must seek the long-term good of the Institute and of the profession as a whole.'

Inevitably, with one exception, the opening speeches of the discussion were given by the critics—some were courteous and conservative, distinctly inclined to the *status quo*; one or two were forthright in asking what were the advantages to members of the Institute; others were somewhat sententious: the exception was a speech by a member—an M.P.—who testified from his experience in Parliament to the confusion of thought as to who was qualified to be an auditor and who qualified to be a company accountant. At that stage in the proceedings an onlooker could hardly fail to think that things were going badly. Then a member gave a piquant and effective speech: although a little critical of the absence of informed minority views from the Council, he said, amid applause: 'We cannot at this stage contemplate rejecting out of hand the work of the Council over two or three years . . . I cannot stand here and hear nothing but opposition. . . . I do ask you, gentlemen, to behave sensibly this afternoon. We cannot possibly go on in the way we have been going.' A change came over the meeting. A member of the

Council spoke and asked emphatically, 'Do you believe this is a step . . . to getting this great profession of ours put in order [and that] it is in the public interest?' A series of speeches strongly supporting Integration followed, both from the converted and the convinced, some with warm feelings towards incorporated accountants. In a brief reply the Vice-President undertook that a full report of the speeches would be sent to all members of the Institute, and dealt with one or two salient points raised in the discussion. The resolution was put by the President and carried by a majority of 80 per cent. A postal vote followed in the course of a week or two, and disclosed a majority in favour of 70·2 per cent., which exceeded the essential minimum of 66⅔ per cent. (details p. 325). The first hurdle had been taken successfully.

*   *   *

The meetings of the Scottish and Irish Institutes were held shortly afterwards. The outcome was not a foregone conclusion as there were conservative strains in the membership of each of the bodies which found expression in some critical observations: but here again those came from minorities. Both personal and postal votes yielded the necessary majorities for acceptance.

The Society's Meeting

In a dramatic atmosphere about 1,200 incorporated accountants assembled at the Royal Festival Hall, London, on 19 June 1957, to discuss and vote upon the schemes. The Council was aware of the critical attitude of members engaged in central and local government accountancy and of overseas members, and that opposition among them had been organized. Sir Richard Yeabsley, C.B.E., President, was in the chair: he delivered with assurance his speech in proposing the formal resolution; deployed with skill the incontrovertible facts in the general situation and indicated how they affected members of the Society taken as a whole. 'The advantages of the schemes', he said, 'are quite apparent' (they had been fully extended in the document previously issued). Then he discussed sympathetically the position of those who would become incorporated accountant members of the English Institute: they would not be disenfranchised, and under six headings he presented the privileges which they would enjoy. The Society took pride in its members who qualified in municipal accountancy and in the part played by the Society in the development of the profession overseas, where the disappearance of the Society would create some problems. There were, however, a few facts which bore on this troublesome aspect of the scheme. Most of those who qualified in municipal accountancy also belonged to the Institute of Municipal Treasurers, membership of which was now a principal qualification for senior municipal appointments. Moreover, of a total recruitment of 3,772 Society candidates in the last three years, 61 only were in local government service. Of the Society's members abroad, the majority of them were also members of overseas bodies, often Commonwealth Institutes of Chartered Accountants; and membership of these bodies was frequently a prerequisite to practice. They were able, if they so desired, to practise as partners of firms of chartered accountants in the United Kingdom. Yet, he emphasized, the Council had desired that all members of the Society should have an immediate and universal right to the designation 'Chartered Accountant', had made representations in the strongest terms and pressed them to the uttermost limits: but all three Institutes were quite adamant, first having regard to the essential principles upon which their membership was based (p. 309), and secondly that any schemes based on wider principles would have stood no prospect of commanding the requisite support. Then, continued Sir Richard:

The choice before us is not between integration and the Society with its articled clerks and bye-law candidates as it now exists and functions; but between integration and the Society denuded of one of its main supplies of new blood, namely by-law candidates in Chartered Accountants' offices, who would doubtless become Chartered articled clerks. The *status quo* is out of the question and integration has been offered on the terms now before you. . . . The council decided that these integration proposals are in the best interests of the Society as a whole and of the profession in general . . . I ask, can rejection of the schemes possibly benefit any single member of the Society? Any suggestions to-day of possible alternative schemes or amendments to the schemes before you would be quite profitless and to no purpose, because in my considered view they would constitute an outright rejection of the schemes. Therefore we should consider the schemes as they are and vote upon them and them alone. In this context let us recall those immortal words of Congreve—

> Defer not till to-morrow to be wise
> To-morrow's sun to thee may never rise.

The fate of the proposals and the future of the Society and its members now rests in your hands. On the record of this meeting and the result of the poll future generations will pronounce on the manner in which we to-day discharged our heavy responsibility. Let us quit ourselves like men and may we be blest with a right judgment in all things.

The President then moved a formal resolution that the schemes as submitted be approved and the resolution was seconded by the Vice-President.

★   ★   ★

As happened at the Institute's meeting, the opening speeches in the discussion were from the critics. Three speeches were delivered by members who apparently represented the organized opposition: the essential facts, as they saw them, were the element of discrimination against a minority group of members, and the diminishing value of the designation 'Incorporated Accountant': their views had found some support in comments in *The Times* and in the *Manchester Guardian* which were quoted. But on entering the region of broad policy, they went rather far in claiming that the scheme was one which 'does nothing to properly regulate the profession, which will create confusion in the mind of the public, which will debase the title of Incorporated Accountant and which will inflict a fundamental injustice on a minority of the members'. The opponents sought amendment, but it seemed were prepared to accept rejection. A private member from South Africa put what he believed to be the critical views of overseas members. At this stage a member of the Council, opposed to the scheme, spoke with strong disfavour on the disappearance of 'by-law' facilities and rejected as entirely defeatist the view presented of the future of the Society if the schemes were rejected. It was now the turn of members in practice—one of whom said he started with a table and two chairs—who understood the vicissitudes, the opportunities, and the fascination of practice:

they indeed knew something at the level of practice of the confusion in the public mind about accountancy qualifications and
there was no doubt about their welcome to the scheme. Point-
ing out that a mixed firm could only call themselves 'accountants', a member added humorously, 'the same as the man along
the street who will do your income tax return for half a crown,
insure your wife and sell you a couple of tickets for the panto-
mine'. A sagacious speech was contributed by a woman member
in practice (also a member of the Institute), who, while recognizing the difficulties, thought the schemes not unreasonable 'in
trying to find terms that are going to suit our present membership judged on the figures we have been given. . . . If you do
not accept this scheme you may find you are doing something,
and be forced to do something, which you would not willingly
do this afternoon.' At the call of Sir Richard Yeabsley, Richard
A. Witty, past President, London, who had been intimately
concerned with the work and policy of the Society from the
days of Sir James Martin, gave a winding-up speech, and ended
by saying, 'Let us make the 19th June 1957 a real landmark in
the history of our great profession.' Amid these speeches the
principal critic, seconded by the member from South Africa,
proposed an amendment in the form of an addition to the
resolution for approval: 'subject to the schemes being amended
to provide equal rights to all existing members of the Society
and candidates'. The President again stated that the amendment
would amount to outright rejection and appealed to the pro-
poser and seconder to reconsider their action and to withdraw
the amendment. However, they adhered tenaciously to their
course and the President had no option but to put the amendment, which was lost by 136 votes in favour, 938 against. The
formal resolution for approval was then put to the meeting
and carried by a majority of about 90 per cent. The meeting
ended with loud applause and the President exhorted members
to be sure of voting in the postal ballot. Sir Richard Yeabsley
received many congratulations upon the decision and upon his
handling of a difficult meeting which never got out of hand.

The postal vote followed. Eighty-nine per cent. of the members voted, and the majority in favour amongst those voting was
86·8 per cent. It seems a fair deduction to make from the figures

that some among the critics of the scheme in the Society generously voted in favour, or abstained, in the general interests of the Society.

Favourable Votes of All Four Bodies

The figures for the several votes of the four bodies were as follows:

	Majority required by constitutions %	Votes at meetings			Postal votes		
		In favour	Against	Majority in favour %	In favour	Against	Majority in favour %
Institute of Chartered Accountants in England and Wales	66⅔	1,097	278	80	10,242	4,340	70·2
Institute of Chartered Accountants of Scotland	66⅔	163	25	86·7	1,822	323	84·9
Institute of Chartered Accountants in Ireland	51	48	17	73·8	456	93	83·1
Society of Incorporated Accountants	75	972	111	89·8	8,747	1,327	86·8

In the case of the English Institute some 76 per cent. of all members voted; and in the Society 89 per cent.

XXIII. THE SOCIETY: ITS FINAL
RESPONSIBILITIES

Liquidation: Appointments to the Three Institutes' Councils

THE remaining months of 1957 were a period of intense administrative activity. The Privy Council approved alterations to the regulations of the English and Scottish Institutes; and the Northern Ireland Privy Council and the Government of the Republic of Ireland to those of the Irish Institute.

The Society, in addition to carrying on its current business and commitments, including its examinations, had to prepare for the liquidation meeting. In the immediate future considerable organization was required to enable each member of the Society to make a formal application for membership of one of the Institutes: similarly all articled clerks and by-law candidates had to be informed of the revised facilities available to them—a necessarily complicated business, which was in the hands of Mr. C. A. Evan-Jones, Deputy Secretary. Mr. Stanley I. Wallis, Nottingham, and Mr. James A. Allen, London (who succeeded his late partner Arthur Hughes), had been auditors of the Society for many years, and prospective liquidation gave them a particular responsibility for the financial affairs of the Society, as at the point of winding-up.

There was much urgent work for the Society's solicitors, who had advised and assisted the Council so effectively from the inception of the Society in 1885.

* * *

In the autumn there was the International Congress at Amsterdam (p. 301), and several of the District Societies held dinners. The members of the Manchester District Society—the senior among the District Societies—entertained the President

A. A. GARRETT, M.B.E., M.A.
Secretary 1919–1949

I. A. F. CRAIG, O.B.E., B.A.
Secretary 1950–1957

and other guests; the chairman was Mr. Thomas Hodgson and the Secretary Mr. C. Yates Lloyd. The final dinner of the Irish Branch took place in Dublin on 28 September 1957, President Mr. W. Keith, Belfast, when Sir Richard Yeabsley made warm acknowledgement of those who had rendered valuable service in Ireland, particularly Mr. A. H. Walkey, Mr. Robert Bell, and Mr. Mervyn Bell, members of the Council, Mr. John Love, Secretary, and Mr. Robert Neely, formerly Secretary in Belfast. The London members earlier in the year had invited to dinner the Rt. Hon. Ernest Marples, M.P., Postmaster-General (as he then was) and a member of the Society, when Mr. W. J. Crafter was chairman; they met again at a concluding luncheon on 20 November and entertained Sir Richard Yeabsley; the chairman was Mr. A. C. Simmonds. These functions had both a valedictory and forward-looking character. Members were moved by feelings of affection towards the Society, which a member once aptly said had become 'a community of friendship'; and perhaps those who were members of Council and those who were officers of Branches and District Societies bestowed 'the passing tribute of a sigh.'

★   ★   ★

The list of members of March 1957 disclosed the following summary:

Fellows			
In practice	.	.	1,838
Not in practice	.	.	367
			2,205
Associates			
In practice	.	.	1,867
Not in practice	.	.	7,263 9,130
			11,335

Of the foregoing number, about 100 were women members; there were also five honorary members. At that time there were twenty-one members who had passed the final examination in the last century, of whom twelve were still in active practice: the eldest amongst them was Mr. S. T. Coulson, F.S.A.A., West Hartlepool, then ninety years of age, who passed the final in 1899. Another of the twenty-one passed as early as 1893. The senior member in South Africa was Hon. W. J. O'Brien,

THE COUNCIL, 23 OCTOBER 1957

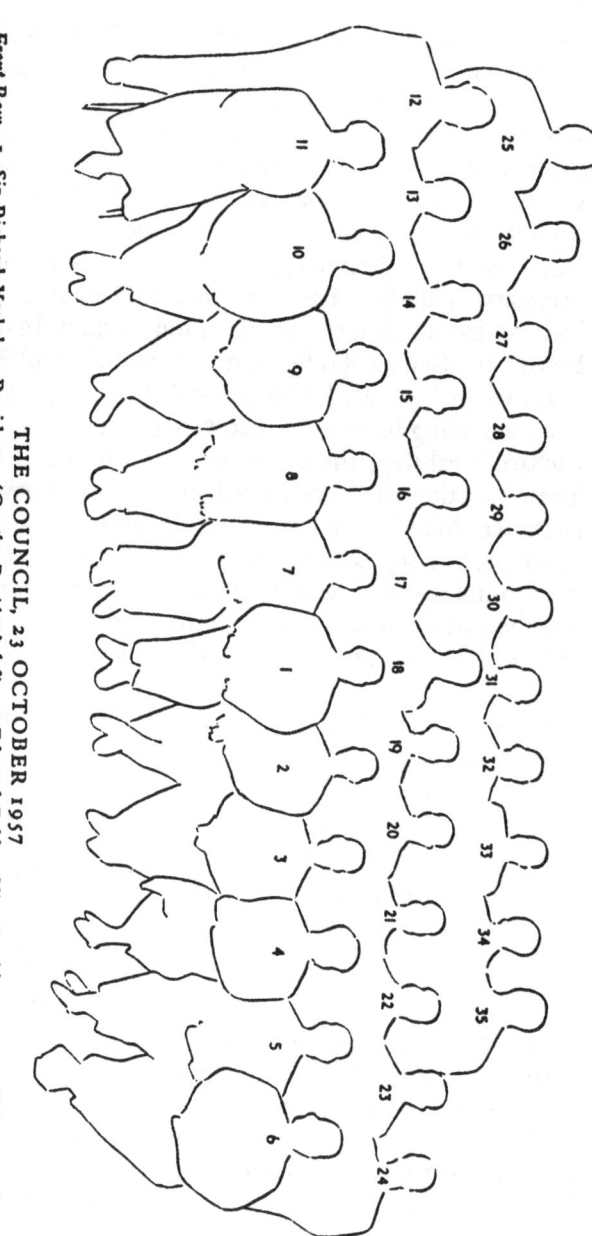

Front Row. 1. Sir Richard Yeabsley, President. (*On the President's left*) 2. Edward Baldry, Vice-President; 3. R. Wilson Bartlett, Past President; 4. Miss Phyllis Ridgway; 5. P. G. S. Ritchie; 6. Joseph Stephenson. (*On the President's right*) 7. E. Cassleton Elliott, Past President; 8. Richard A. Witty, Past President; 9. C. Percy Barrowcliff, Past President; 10. Hugh O. Johnson; 11. Mrs. Irene Duncalf (Secretariat).

Second Row. 12. J. W. Richardson; 13. C. Yates Lloyd; 14. Henry Brown; 15. Festus Moffat; 16. P. D. Pascho; 17. W. G. A. Russell; 18. C. V. Best; 19. R. E. Starkie; 20. F. V. Arnold; 21. E. J. Waldron; 22. J. S. Heaton; 23. W. R. Booth; 24. H. L. Layton.

Third Row. 25. C. Evan-Jones, Deputy Secretary; 26. I. A. F. Craig, Secretary; 27. Mervyn Bell; 28. F. E. Price; 29. A. Blackburn; 30. C. H. Sutton; 31. W. F. Edwards; 32. J. A. Jackson; 33. R. C. L. Thomas; 34. Bertram Nelson, Past President; 35. S. L. Pleasance.

THE COUNCIL, 23 OCTOBER 1957

Sir Richard Yeabsley, C.B.E., President

O.B.E., D.Phil., Pietermaritzburg (1895), sometime member of the South African Senate (*obiit* 1959).

*   *   *

On 1 November 1957 an extraordinary general meeting of the Society was held at Incorporated Accountants' Hall for the purpose of putting the Society into liquidation. There was a large attendance, necessitating an overflow into the library: the speeches were relayed by loudspeakers. By this time most of the critics, having made their views known, took the good part and withdrew from active opposition: nevertheless, there was one speech again expressing the attitude of a small hard core of members still not reconciled. However, the formal resolutions received 225 votes in favour and there were 42 votes against them. Mr. James A. Allen, F.S.A.A., and Mr. I. A. F. Craig, O.B.E., were appointed joint-liquidators.

Members' thoughts were now directed to the future, and the President announced the names of those who would become members of the Council of the English Institute and of the Council of the Irish Institute (see Appendix VII). Subsequently one who had been a member of the Society was elected to the Council of the Scottish Institute. In a final speech Sir Richard Yeabsley reviewed briefly the accomplishments of the Society over its seventy-two years of history—not least that it was probable that some 14,000 people had been members who, but for the Society, might not have joined the profession. Bringing the past of the Society into relationship with the immediate present, Sir Richard said: 'It has been through the courage and wisdom of our leaders that we have recognised our duties and discharged them so well and we, the present generation, have by their example and precept achieved such a high standard in the profession that integration was the natural outcome.' He concluded with warm feelings of the regard of all the members towards the past Presidents, the members of the Council, the officers of the Branches and District Societies, and to the secretariat and staff, 'who by their zeal, kindliness and devotion to duty have served us so well'. And retrospectively he referred to the two previous Secretaries, Sir James Martin and Mr. A. A. Garrett; and presently to Mr. Ian Craig, the Secretary, who had worked so indefatigably in regard to Integration and to whom Sir Richard expressed the great appreciation of all the members. In conclusion Mr. Cassleton Elliott made what was the last public speech in the Society, in which he invited the members to adopt a resolution of thanks to Sir Richard Yeabsley. Mr. Elliott warmly commended Sir Richard's keen and energetic work during the past eighteen months and the ability with which he had conducted all the proceedings leading to Integration. The resolution was carried by loud applause; 1957 had redeemed 1897.

By agreement between all the four bodies, there was an immediate declaration that 2 November 1957 was the effective date for the coming into force of the schemes of Integration.

The final meeting of the Council of the Society was held on Thursday, 16 January 1958. Afterwards Mr. E. Cassleton Elliott, C.B.E., senior past President, and Mrs. Elliott kindly entertained to luncheon at Whitehall Court, London, the members of the Council and their wives. To commemorate Sir Richard's presidency of the Society, the last in its history, a presentation of a pair of silver candelabra was made to him and Lady Yeabsley on behalf of the Council members, with many good wishes. An additional pleasure was that in the Queen's Birthday Honours List, 1958, it was announced that Mr. Edward Baldry, lately Vice-President of the Society of Incorporated Accountants, received the honour of O.B.E.

Secretary, Deputy Secretary, and Staff: 'Accountancy'

The Secretary, Deputy Secretary, and staff of the Society were gradually merged into the administration of the English Institute, of which Mr. Ian Craig, O.B.E., and Mr. C. A. Evan-Jones, M.B.E., were appointed Assistant Secretaries. *Accountancy*, with Leo T. Little (*obiit* 1960) continuing as Editor, became the journal of the Institute of Chartered Accountants in England and Wales and appeared for the first time in that form in January 1958. The Councils of the three Institutes lost no time in proceeding to implement the schemes. The English Institute expressed the hope that the process of admitting members of the Society to membership of the Institute would be completed in three large groups at the Council meetings in January, February, and March 1958; and this hope was substantially fulfilled. This was a noteworthy achievement facilitated by the unremitting labour of the secretariats and staffs. The District and Students' Societies were merged and some former members of the Society elected to committees. The London Students' Society was terminated by a dinner at Incorporated Accountants' Hall at which Mr. J. A. Jackson, the President, was in the chair. The students were welcomed by Sir Harold Gillett, the President of the Chartered Accountants Students' Society at a meeting in Guildhall, at which the Lord Mayor was present in state. There remained to be dealt with the Incorporated Accountants' Benevolent Fund amounting to over £30,000, a matter which involved some difficult legal problems. The welcome on the part of the chartered accountants, whether at Council or District Society level, to their new fellow members contributed to a happy commencement of the régime henceforth comprising the three Institutes of Chartered Accountants.

Members Integrated

In its annual report for 1958 the Council of the English Institute recorded the following information as to the progress of Integration:

Admitted to membership of:

The Institute of Chartered Accountants in England and Wales .	10,048
The Institute of Chartered Accountants of Scotland . . .	128
The Institute of Chartered Accountants in Ireland . . .	364
Members of the Society admitted to the three Institutes . .	10,540
Members of the Society who were already members of one of the Institutes	669
Applications deferred or still under consideration . . .	22
Known to have died, or to have decided not to seek admission, or by whom no response had been made	316
Society membership on 2 November 1957	11,547

Incorporated Accountants' Hall sold

After consideration, the Council of the English Institute came to the conclusion with much regret that Incorporated Accountants' Hall could not be used advantageously in the changed circumstances of administration and by reason of the projected policy of the Institute as to future accommodation. Accordingly, Incorporated Accountants' Hall was sold in 1959 and realized £168,000.

The Society's work fulfilled

Events in the profession in the course of some three-quarters of a century succeeded one another with increasing momentum, and yet the wheels of its history moved comparatively slowly, sometimes with difficulty. By the 1950's changes—clearly permanent changes—asserted themselves both in the profession itself and externally. Probably the major factor was the approximation in standards among the three Chartered Institutes and the Society: although there were differences in their constitutions and requirements for admission, actually their ways of doing things were not very different. Externally the financial, economic, and social circumstances of the country caused a great expansion in the profession and at the same time had a marked effect on the conditions of recruitment for the profession. The professional bodies and firms increasingly desired to provide more opportunities for capable young men and women attracted to accountancy. Ideas arose for improving the organization of the profession and simplifying its structure. Happily, the principal heads of the three Institutes and the Society felt that opportunity was knocking at the door, and they did not fail to respond; indeed, as far as human thought could contemplate, it was unlikely that the opportunity would recur. But they were not starry-eyed; they faced realities and rightly assessed the impalpable forces that move the minds of men organized in professional bodies, in which influence and prestige, reverence for the past, as well as hopes for the future are to be found: complete unanimity was hardly to be expected and they sought the greatest measure of probable common agreement. Not eschewing ideals, and maintaining the best in the traditions of the profession, the Councils of the four bodies found practical means to achieve a vague if long-desired purpose to which they believed the general bodies of members would give assent. This belief proved to be well founded and Integration was accomplished, with the assurance of its future benefit to the accountancy profession and to the public which it served. The Society's work was fulfilled.

APPENDIXES
I–IX

APPENDIX I

Presidents of the Society

1886–1887	JOSEPH SHAW GREEN	Warrington
1887–1890	REGINALD EMBLETON EMSON	London
1890–1894	EBENEZER CARR	London
1894–1898	FREDERIC WALMSLEY	Manchester
1898–1901	ANDREW WALLACE BARR	London
1901–1904	CHARLES HENRY WILSON (SIR CHARLES WILSON)	Leeds
1904–1907	WILLIAM GEORGE RAYNER	London
1907–1910	HARRY LLOYD PRICE	Manchester
1910–1913	ARTHUR EDWARD GREEN	London
1913–1916	CHARLES HEWETSON NELSON	Liverpool
1916–1919	ARTHUR EDWIN WOODINGTON	London
1919–1922	WILLIAM CLARIDGE	Bradford
1922–1923	SIR JAMES MARTIN, M.B.E.	London
1923–1926	GEORGE STANHOPE PITT	London
1926–1929	THOMAS KEENS (SIR THOMAS KEENS, D.L.)	London and Luton
1929–1932	HENRY MORGAN	London
1932–1935	EDWARD CASSLETON ELLIOTT, C.B.E.	London

1935 *50th Anniversary of the Foundation of the Society*

	SIR JAMES MARTIN, M.B.E., *President*	London
	CHARLES HEWETSON NELSON, *Vice-President*	Liverpool
1935–1937	RICHARD WILSON BARTLETT, D.L.	Newport (Mon.)
1937–1939	WALTER HOLMAN	London
1939–1942	PERCY TOOTHILL	Sheffield
1942–1945	RICHARD ALFRED WITTY	London
1945–1947	FRED WOOLLEY	Southampton

1947–1949	SIR FREDERICK JOHN ALBAN, C.B.E., LL.D.	Cardiff and Newport (Mon.)
1949–1951	ALBERT STUART ALLEN	London
1951–1954	CHARLES PERCY BARROWCLIFF	Middlesbrough
1954–1956	BERTRAM NELSON, C.B.E.	Liverpool and London
1956–1957	SIR RICHARD ERNEST YEABSLEY, C.B.E., *President*	London
	EDWARD BALDRY, O.B.E., *Vice-President*	London

The decorations indicated were not necessarily held during office

Secretaries

1886–1919	SIR JAMES MARTIN, M.B.E.
1919–1949	ALEXANDER ADNETT GARRETT, M.B.E., M.A.
1950–1957	IAN ARCHIBALD FORBES CRAIG, O.B.E., B.A.

APPENDIX II

Membership of the Principal Accountancy Bodies

	Formed	1885[3]	1888[3]	1902[1]	1911[1]	1930[2]	1937[1]	1952[1]	1957[3]
Institute of Chartered Accountants of Scotland[4]	1854	332	377	785	1,280	2,940	4,153	5,349	6,187
Institute of Chartered Accountants in England and Wales	1880	1,371	1,576	2,942	4,391	9,047	12,568	16,856	20,124
Society of Incorporated Accountants	1885	396	400	1,763	2,442	5,225	7,216	9,518	11,335
Institute of Chartered Accountants in Ireland	1888	..	44	60	100	261	404	860	1,044
Association of Certified and Corporate Accountants	1905	..	..	..	1,897	2,900	5,985	8,314	10,103
TOTAL		2,099	2,397	5,550	10,110	20,373	30,326	40,897	48,793
Institute of Municipal Treasurers and Accountants (Royal Charter 1959)	1885	68	85	247	455	642	1,022	2,169	2,804
Institute of Cost and Works Accountants	1919	..	..	..	..	796	1,131	3,912	5,758

[1] *Accountancy*, June 1953: 'Accountancy in Five Reigns' (commencement of the reigns of Edward VII, George V, George VI, Elizabeth II).

[2] Report of Departmental Committee on Registration, 1930.

[3] Information from the respective Secretaries or taken from *The Accountant*.

[4] Until 1951 there were three bodies of Chartered Accountants in Scotland (Edinburgh, Glasgow, and Aberdeen), which were then amalgamated.

APPENDIX III

*Speech of Sir James Martin, March 1920, on the Occasion
of the Presentation of his Portrait (by Solomon J. Solomon,
R.A.), subsequent to his relinquishing the Secretaryship of
the Society in April 1919*

THE English language seems poor in expression for such an occasion
as this—but it is more probable that my command of it fails. To
thank you all does not meet the occasion, to say no words of mine
can express my thanks seems commonplace. You each and all have
my deep and abiding gratitude for all your affectionate regard for
me. . . . My long connexion with the Society has extended over
35 years, during nearly 33 years of which I filled the position of
Secretary. I am one of the original members of the Society, a band
of pioneers now dwindled down to not more than 50 or 60 out of
the present-day roll of about 3,000. Upon incorporation, in the year
1885, I was made a member of the Council; a few months afterwards
I was requested by my colleagues to assume the Secretaryship and
I stipulated that I should not be called upon to relinquish my profession. . . .

There are three or four outstanding features that I can refer to with
some pride. The first is the right we secured to the use of the designation 'Incorporated Accountant'. This was confirmed in the Chancery
Division of the High Court of Justice in 1907. The learned Judge
decided that the conduct of the Society, in its training and examination of students and its rules and regulations as to membership, made
the designation a valuable one, and it was an indication to the public
indicating reliability and integrity.

The next decision of importance in regard to our professional
position was in the Houses of Parliament in 1914, when it was held
that the standard of audit of public local authorities was that of our
friends the Institute of Chartered Accountants and of the Society of
Incorporated Accountants and Auditors. Then came the war, and
disruption of our well-ordered lives. To enable proper control to be
exercised over the vast expenditure of the Navy, Army, Air Force,
and Ministry of Munitions, the assistance of our profession was
sought, and after some time, during which our younger men went

freely to the colours, it was declared by the Government that the accountancy profession was of national importance.

I had held the fort during the war, and as the armistice drew near I realized that my work should be brought to a conclusion, and I resigned in January 1919, but not before I had carried through on behalf of the members the necessary alterations to our constitution to enable women to be admitted as members. During the whole period of my Secretaryship, the Society's interests in India and our self-governing Dominions had been well looked after with the help of some of the ablest resident accountants. The result is that our diploma is recognized wherever the English language is spoken. . . .

To you, my friends and colleagues, I am no small debtor. No disagreeable incident has ever marred our association for more than a generation. You have conferred upon me every honour in your power and have showered generous gifts upon me and mine. Fortunately, today there is no sadness of farewell. To you, Mr. Woodington, to the President, the past Presidents, to Mr. Vinall as Honorary Secretary,[1] and to each and all the subscribers I tender my most grateful acknowledgements. Mr. Solomon's work will remain as lasting evidence of all your kindness to me, and will be cherished and valued long after the subject of the picture has passed away.

[1] Of the Testimonial Committee.

APPENDIX IV

Incorporated Accountants' Hall

A FORTUNATE event in architectural achievement was attributable to the decision of William Waldorf Astor—afterwards the first Viscount Astor—to erect a building for his home and private offices on Victoria Embankment, London: the building was completed in 1895 and was called Astor House. After Viscount Astor's death, it passed in 1922 to the Sun Life Assurance Company of Canada, from whom it was bought by the Society of Incorporated Accountants in 1928. The total cost to the Society, including some necessary restoration and furnishing, was some £110,000. At that time F. Loughborough Pearson, F.R.I.B.A., son of the original architect, was retained by the Society. Henceforth, until its sale in 1959, the building was known as Incorporated Accountants' Hall.

The (former) Hall is situated on a loop road (Temple Place) forming part of the Embankment in the City of Westminster, immediately on the borders of the City of London. Lying between Electra House on the west and the Middle Temple Garden on the east—in which the attractive Queen Elizabeth Building has been erected comparatively recently—it presents a pleasing appearance, seen either on approach from the west in Temple Place or from the south pavement of the Embankment looking north: at its rear are the historic Essex steps. Although relatively small, the building is not overshadowed by the mass of Electra House and stands out well in its setting.

As a matter of history, there seems ground for thinking that at one time the site was occupied by a small dock. However, in 1865, the Victoria Embankment was constructed and a print in the *Illustrated London News* of 4 February of that year shows the site during the progress of the works. When the first Lord Astor acquired the site in 1892, it was occupied by a warehouse of Gwynne's, the pump engineers, which he demolished.

For the erection of his house, Lord Astor commissioned John Loughborough Pearson, R.A., a distinguished architect of that period, among whose works are Truro Cathedral and restorations in Westminster Abbey. Apparently not severely restricted as to cost, Loughborough Pearson used the opportunity to exercise his creative talent in giving effect to Lord Astor's requirements. In consequence, and with the restoration work of 1950 by Sir Percy Thomas, P.P.R.I.B.A., the building is unique both in character and in the quality of material and standard of workmanship, although no doubt more elaborate than current fashion.

Constructed of Portland stone, its exterior (see frontispiece) presents a Tudor motif, modified at the entrance by a more expansive style. The main features are the artistic wrought-iron railings and gate, the splendid oriel windows, tall chimneys and gable roof, surmounted by an unusual gilded weather-vane (by J. Starkie Gardner): this is in the form of a ship intended to represent the vessel in which Columbus discovered America. On the west side the approach from the street is by a stone forecourt, flanked by a charming lawn. Suspended from a bracket on the front of the building was a wrought-iron coloured shield of the Society's Arms: this shield is preserved in the London Museum.

A distinct and warm Italian feeling informs the style of the interior. There are a lower-ground, ground and first floors. The small entrance lobby in stone contained two carved inscriptions, commemorating the opening of the Hall by H.R.H. the Duke of York (King George VI) and the members of the Society who fell in the Wars. The door at the south end of the lobby leads to the Library—occupying the whole south front, panelled in oak and fitted with wall shelves: a private office is at one end, and at the other a door leads to the administrative offices at the rear and east of the ground floor, and to the side stairs in a turret. The spacious lower-ground floor comprises store room, telephone room and hall-keepers' quarters.

A visitor stepping from the entrance lobby through the door to the Staircase Hall would be impressed with its dignity and varied features. The floor is paved in a pattern formed from many coloured stones, the wide staircase and gallery balustrade are in mahogany, whilst the substantial walls are covered with oak panelling. Inscribed panels recorded the acquisition of the Hall and the Society's Fiftieth Anniversary in 1935; between them was hung the portrait in oils of Sir James Martin by Solomon J. Solomon, R.A. In the gallery ebony columns support a roof of stained glass. Literature is extensively represented by a number of carved figures and by a frieze carved with scenes from Shakespeare's plays.

The large Hall on the south side opens from a gallery door, the inside of which is covered by nine panels in silver gilt by Sir George Frampton, R.A., depicting the heroines in the *Idylls of the King*. The roof is a hammer-beamed type in dark mahogany, and the pleasing cedar wood panelling (slightly chipped by bomb blast) is covered by a geometrical rectangular pattern. On top of the panelling is a frieze consisting of carved heads of fifty-four figures in history, literature, and art. At the east end is a stained glass window of a Swiss scene 'Sunrise' and at the west end the corresponding window is of 'Sunset': the glass is by Clayton & Bell, who also executed the west window in King's College, Cambridge. On a part of the wall adjacent to the south-east oriel window, the names of the Presidents of the Society were exhibited: the panel was presented by Mr. R. Wilson Bartlett, D.L., President 1935 to 1937. The Hall, 71 feet by 28 feet, accommodates some 200 people for a meeting.

The east gallery room was Lord Astor's Library, fitted with glass bookcases and panelled in satin wood, and was used for committee meetings of the Society. On the west side the Secretary's room was a reconstruction, in place of the original President's room: the original room, in *sabicu* (a rare wood) and surmounted by a gilt domed ceiling, was destroyed by enemy action in July 1944. The remaining room was contrived at the 1950 restoration, in place of the Astor strong-room, and was the office of the secretarial staff.

The members entertained much affection for Incorporated Accountants' Hall, which was at least one reason for the decision to restore the building—after it had suffered about sixty per cent. damage in the War—instead of the Council seeking an alternative plan or other accommodation. In the course of restoration, some interior rearrangement effected considerable improvement. A scheme to add a wing had been prepared but was suspended. In the changed circumstances after Integration, it was decided with regret that it was not practicable to retain the Hall and its disposal was concluded.

The Hall had been the scene of general and other meetings of the Society and of many distinguished functions, of which the former Council and members retain happy memories.

APPENDIX V

International Congresses on Accounting

1904	First Congress, St. Louis
1926	Second Congress, Amsterdam
1929	Third Congress, New York
1933	Fourth Congress, London
1938	Fifth Congress, Berlin
1952	Sixth Congress, London
1957	Seventh Congress, Amsterdam

Conferences of the Society

1898	Birmingham	1923	Cardiff
1899	Manchester	1924	Leeds and Bradford
1900	Leeds	1925	London
1901	Glasgow		(*40th Anniversary Dinner*)
1903	Liverpool	1927	Manchester
1905	Sheffield	1930	Sheffield
1906	London	1935	London
	(*21st Anniversary*)		(*50th Anniversary*)
1908	Cardiff	1937	Belfast
1911	Dublin	1939	Nottingham
1913	Liverpool	1949	Birmingham
1921	Liverpool	1951	Dublin
1922	London		

Short Courses given by the Society

Between 1934 and 1938, 1945 and 1957, fifteen short residential courses for members were arranged by the Society and were held at Gonville and Caius College and King's College, Cambridge, New College and Balliol College, Oxford, by kind permission of the Head and Fellows of each College. In 1950 a course was also given at Ashridge College, Herts.

Similar courses for students for revision of studies were organized from time to time after 1945 by District and Students' Societies, including courses at King's College, London, Ashridge College, Herts., Durham, Liverpool, and Manchester Universities.

APPENDIX VI

Branches and District Societies with dates of formation

BRANCHES

Australia, Victorian Committee, 1886.
South Africa, Western Branch, Cape Town, 1894.
Scotland (founded as The Scottish Institute of Accountants 1880), 1899.
Ireland, 1901.
South Africa, Northern Branch, Johannesburg, 1902.
Australia, New South Wales Committee, 1903.
Canada, 1905.
South Africa, Eastern Branch, Durban, 1928.
Central Africa, Salisbury (Southern Rhodesia), 1954.

DISTRICT SOCIETIES

Manchester, 1886
Sheffield, 1887
Birmingham, 1892
South Wales and Mon., 1894
Yorkshire, 1894
Liverpool, 1895
North of England, 1896
West of England, 1903
North Lancs., 1909
South of England, 1909
Bradford, 1910
Nottingham, Derby, and Lincoln, 1910

Northern Ireland, 1913
North Staffordshire, 1925
Swansea and S. West Wales, 1926
East Anglia, 1929
Hull, 1929
Leicestershire and Northants., 1929
London, 1930
Bombay, 1931
Bengal, 1933
Devon and Cornwall, 1934
Sussex, 1950

STUDENTS' SOCIETIES

London, 1890
Glasgow, 1907
Cardiff, 1914
Newport (Mon.), 1921

Dublin, 1926
Waterford, 1949
Cork, 1952

Students' Sections were attached to most of the other District Societies.

APPENDIX VII

Council of the Society

JULY 1957

President
[2] SIR RICHARD YEABSLEY, C.B.E., London

Vice-President
[2, 6] EDWARD BALDRY, London

[2, 7] JOHN AINSWORTH, M.B.E., M.COM.	Liverpool
[1] SIR FREDERICK JOHN ALBAN, C.B.E., LL.D., J.P.	Cardiff
[1] ALBERT STUART ALLEN (obiit Aug. 1957)	London
FREDERICK VERNON ARNOLD	Brighton
[1, 2] CHARLES PERCY BARROWCLIFF	Middlesbrough
[1] RICHARD WILSON BARTLETT, D.L., J.P.	Newport (Mon.)
[5] MERVYN BELL	Dublin
[5] ROBERT BELL	Belfast
CHARLES VICTOR BEST	London
ALBERT BLACKBURN	Newport (Mon.)
WILLIAM ROBERT BOOTH	London
FRANK SEWELL BRAY	London
ANDREW BRODIE	Stoke-on-Trent
HENRY BROWN, O.B.E.	Rochester
WILLIAM FREDERICK EDWARDS	London
[1] EDWARD CASSLETON ELLIOTT, C.B.E.	London
[2] LEONARD CECIL HAWKINS	London
[2] JAMES STANLEY HEATON	Keighley
WILLIAM HENRY HIGGINBOTHAM	Sheffield
[3] JAMES ALFRED JACKSON	London
[2] HUGH OLIVER JOHNSON	Bath
[2] HAROLD LESLIE LAYTON, M.S.M.	London
CHARLES YATES LLOYD	Manchester
[4] FESTUS MOFFAT, O.B.E., J.P.	Falkirk
[1, 2] BERTRAM NELSON, C.B.E., J.P.	Liverpool

Percival Dorton Pascho	Plymouth
Spencer Laurence Pleasance	London
² Frank Edward Price	Newport (Mon.)
Frederick Arthur Prior (*obiit* Aug. 1957)	Nottingham
John William Richardson	Sheffield
Phyllis Elizabeth Marie Ridgway, b.a., j.p.	Hull
Peter Grant Scott Ritchie	Glasgow
William George Ainge Russell	Birmingham
Robert Edward Starkie	Leeds
Joseph Stephenson, o.b.e.	London
Cecil Harry Sutton	Norwich
Robert Clifford Lloyd Thomas, m.c., t.d., d.l.	Newport (Mon.)
¹ Percy Toothill	Sheffield
Ernest John Waldron	Southampton
Arthur Herbert Walkey	Dublin
¹ Richard Alfred Witty	London

¹ Past Presidents.
² Appointed to Council of English Institute at Integration.
³ Appointed to Council of English Institute 1959.
⁴ Appointed to Council of Scottish Institute.
⁵ Appointed to Council of Irish Institute together with John Love, Dublin, and Robert John Neely, Belfast.
⁶ O.B.E. 1958.
⁷ C.B.E. 1960.

Secretary: Ian Archibald Forbes Craig, o.b.e., b.a.

Deputy Secretary: Cecil Artimus Evan-Jones, m.b.e.

Auditors: Stanley I. Wallis, f.s.a.a., Nottingham.
James A. Allen, f.s.a.a., London.

———

Editor of 'Accountancy': Leo Thomas Little, b.sc. (Econ.).

Stamp-Martin Professor of Accounting: Frank Sewell Bray, f.s.a.a., f.c.a.

APPENDIX VIII

Companies 1885–1957

	PUBLIC COMPANIES		PRIVATE COMPANIES		ALL COMPANIES HAVING A SHARE CAPITAL	
	Number (nearest hundred)	Paid-up capital (nearest £million)	Number (nearest hundred)	Paid-up capital (nearest £million)	Number (nearest hundred)	Paid-up capital (nearest £million)
		£m.		£m.		£m.
ENGLAND SCOTLAND, AND IRELAND						
Society founded 1885						
30 April 1886 . . .	..	..	..	..	9,500	530
The Companies Act, 1900						
30 April 1900 . . .	..	..	..	..	29,700	1,623
30 April 1902 . . .	..	..	..	..	33,300	1,805
30 April 1905 . . .	..	..	..	..	39,600	1,954
The Companies Act, 1907						
The Companies (Consolidation) Act, 1908						
(First provision for Private Companies)						
31 December 1908 . .	..	..	19,200	not available		
30 April 1909 . . .	..	..	..	..	46,500	2,163
31 December 1910 . .	..	..	28,600	not available		
30 April 1911 . . .	..	..	..	..	53,700	2,222

First World War, 1914–18						
31 December 1913	..	..	49,800	not available	..	..
30 April 1914	..	..	..	..	64,700	2,532
31 December 1919	..	..	58,100	not available	73,300	3,083
ENGLAND AND SCOTLAND						
The Companies Act, 1929						
31 December 1930	16,300	3,894	95,600	1,591	111,900	5,485
Second World War, 1939–45						
31 December 1938	14,400	4,097	143,200	1,894	157,600	5,991
31 December 1946	13,200	4,078	200,700	1,923	213,900	6,001
The Companies Act, 1948						
31 December 1949	12,100	3,854	231,400	2,094	243,500	5,948
The last year of the Society, 1957						
31 December 1957	11,000	4,537	304,300	2,607	315,300	7,144

The foregoing figures have been abstracted from the Annual Reports of the Board of Trade on Companies. The significance of the years selected is indicated by the sub-headings.

APPENDIX IX

Net Receipt of Inland Revenue Duties
to the nearest £million and exclusive of Excise Duties

	Income Tax		Supertax Surtax	Special contribution	M.L., E.P.D., C.P.T., N.D.C., E.P.T., E.P.L., Profits Tax (as and when each was in force)	Death duties	Other I.R. duties inclusive of stamp duties	Total
	Standard or normal rate in £	Net receipt						
		£m.	£m.	£m.	£m.	£m.	£m.	£m.
1885–6. First year of the Society	8d.	15	..	..	..	8	7	30
1899–1900. End of the nineteenth century. (1894 Harcourt Death Duties imposed)	8d.	19	..	..	..	18	11	48
1902–3. South African War	1/3	38	..	..	..	18	11	67
1903–4. After the South African War	11d.	31	..	..	..	17	10	58
1910–11. After the Lloyd George Budget, 1909 (receipts abnormal due to delay in passing Finance Bill for 1909–10)	1/2	60	3	..	..	26	15	104
1913–14. Before the First World War	1/2	44	3	..	..	27	14	88

1918–19. Last year of the First World War	6/-	35	258	..	284	31	16	624
1920–1. After the First World War	6/-	56	340	..	219	47	29	691
1931–2. The Great Depression	5/-	77	288	..	2	65	18	450
1938–9. Before the Second World War	5/6	63	336	..	23	77	22	521
1944–5. Last year of the Second World War	10/-	74	1,310	..	508	111	19	2,022
1949–50. Five years after the Second World War (1944 Education Act) (1946 National Insurance Act) (1946 National Health Service Act)	9/-	115	1,437	19 (1948/9 80)	296	189	52	2,108
1957–8. Last year of the Society	8/6	159	2,222	nominal	257	172	64	2,874

M.L.   Munitions Levy, 1915 and 1916.
E.P.D.   Excess Profits Duty, 1915 to 1926.
C.P.T.   Corporation Profits Tax, 1920 to 1924.
N.D.C.   National Defence Contribution 1937 to 1946
E.P.T.   Excess Profits Tax (alternative to N.D.C.). 1939 to 1946.
E.P.L.   Excess Profits Levy, 1952 and 1953.
Profits Tax (continuation of N.D.C.). 1946–7 and continued.

	Inland Revenue (supra)		Customs and Excise Duties		Total
	£m.		£m.		£m.
1885–6	30	40%	45	60%	75
1913–14	88	54%	75	46%	163
1938–9	521	58%	376	42%	897
1957–8	2,874	56%	2,250	44%	5,124

The foregoing figures have been abstracted from the Annual Reports of the Commissioners of Inland Revenue.

INDEX